# MARLENE SOROSKY'S

# Cooking for Holidays and Celebrations

# MARLENE SOROSKY'S

# Cooking for Holidays and Celebrations

HPBooks

This book is a completely revised and updated
edition of *Marlene Sorosky's Year 'Round Holiday Cookbook.*

HPBooks
Published by The Berkley Publishing Group
200 Madison Avenue
New York, NY 10016

Copyright © 1994 by Marlene Sorosky

Book design by Irving Perkins Associates
Cover and interior photographs © 1994 by Cormier Photography

Special thanks for props to Kim Darley, Pier 1; Tom Vignapiano, Crate and Barrel; Anne Hakes,
Williams-Sonoma; and Laurel Ramie, The Broadway, all in San Diego; and Annie Algar, Pottery
Shack, Laguna Beach.

Photo and Prop Styling by David Pogul. Assistant stylists: Jeff DeLeo and Alba Serta-Slavin.

First edition: November 1994

Published simultaneously in Canada.

NOTICE: The information printed in this book is true and complete
to the best of our knowledge. All recommendations
are made without any guarantees on the part of the author
or the publisher. The author and publisher disclaim
all liability in connection with the use of this information.

Library of Congress Cataloging-in-Publication Data
Sorosky, Marlene.
[Year-round holiday cookbook]
Marlene Sorosky's cooking for holidays and celebrations / by
Marlene Sorosky. — 1st HPBooks ed.
p.     cm.
Originally published: Marlene Sorosky's year-round holiday
cookbook. 1st ed. New York : Harper & Row. © 1982.
Includes index.
ISBN 1-55788-195-2
1. Entertaining.   2. Holiday cookery.   I. Title.   II. Title:
Cooking for holidays and celebrations.
TX731.S663   1994
641.5'68 — dc20                          94-4219
CIP

Printed in the United States of America

10 9 8 7 6 5 4 3 2 1

This book is printed on acid-free paper.
♾

# DEDICATION

To the memory of two very dear friends, Danny Kaye and Linda Kreisberg, whose love of good times and good food have greatly enhanced my life.

# ACKNOWLEDGMENTS

A very special thank-you to the following people, whose contributions greatly enhanced my book:

To Rita Calvert, one of the most creative and dedicated people I have ever worked with, for helping me revise the recipes.

To Linda Annarino, who so generously shared her creative writing talents.

To Ann Bernstein, for assisting me in my home and school cooking classes, and for helping with wine selections.

To Randy Fuhrman, who shared his creativity and expertise with such enthusiasm.

To Angela Wilson, Maddie Katz, Carol Halperin, Danny Fendel, and their families, for devotedly testing and tasting recipes.

# CONTENTS

# INTRODUCTION

The pleasures of life pass all too quickly, and the best way to capture time's passage is with holidays and celebrations. In our hectic, on-the-run lives, the weeks turn into months so fast that we tend to live from occasion to occasion, from holiday to holiday, with much anticipation. Cooking for these events is especially meaningful because each one becomes a cherished memory to hold on to forever.

If I had my way, I would have the merriment of holidays never end. I'd stretch the moments around the dinner table into many hours. But in order truly to enjoy celebrations as a host, it is necessary to take shortcuts to reduce the workload. And unless you're one of those people who likes to live on the edge, it helps to plan ahead. By choosing dishes you can pre-prepare and refrigerate or freeze, by the judicious use of packaged mixes, and by following a time plan, you'll find you can relax, have fun, and really be a carefree host.

I add my stamp by entertaining in a more casual, carefree manner, often with a theme. Days seem to be getting shorter and no matter how fast I work, there are never enough hours. Time has become so precious that more than ever I value the opportunity to get together with family and friends. My philosophy of life and entertaining hasn't changed through the years. I continue to derive great pleasure from opening my home and giving to others.

Though I never employ a shortcut that compromises flavor, I simplify recipes as much as possible. I use the microwave oven and food processor and continually look for alternative techniques to cut back time-consuming steps. My definition of an easy recipe is one that dirties only one or two bowls or pots and pans. I believe it's this philosophy that makes the cooking classes I teach so successful.

Because it takes little extra time and creativity to turn an ordinary dish into an applause winner, I try to make each dish look exceptional. When a dip with raw vegetables can become a vegetable garden by turning an ear of corn into a scarecrow and adding seed packets (page 110), everyone will smile and it will be long remembered. And isn't that what entertaining is all about?

Recipes in this book have been made lighter. Many have been altered from original versions to fit our new way of eating. Every effort was made to retain the recipes' tastes, but reduce the fat and cholesterol. Savory dishes have less cream, and butter is often replaced with olive oil. Dairy products such as milk, sour cream, and cream cheese are often offered with regular, low-fat, or nonfat options. Choose whichever best fits your needs, and be assured the results will be excellent or the alternative would not be offered. Some recipes, those that have been so popular they have become almost a tradition, haven't been changed at all. And others have been replaced with newer, livelier, more contemporary dishes.

I hope that the inspiration and instruction from this book will help you entertain your family and loved ones with events you'll remember fondly for years to come — and that you'll have fun while doing it.

# MARLENE SOROSKY'S

# Cooking for Holidays and Celebrations

# HERALD THE NEW YEAR

## New Year's Eve Midnight Supper

---

### MENU

*Blini Cups with Caviar*
*Mediterranean Tuna Paté*
*Ham Biscuits with Honey Mustard*
*Cassis Champagne with Raspberry Cubes*

*Chicken Breast Coq au Vin*
*Cooked noodles (if desired)*
*Orange-Glazed Carrots*
*Marbled Spinach-Cheese Gratin*

*Vanilla Mousse with Caramel Rum Sauce*

### WINE RECOMMENDATION:
*A young, light, fresh and fruity red wine such as a gamay or gamay Beaujolais*

---

New Year's Eve is a celebration with built-in excitement — a time for well-wishing, toasts, resolutions, and good cheer. A New Year's Eve supper is a combination of two parties in one: a cocktail party and a dinner party. It's a good idea to serve more hors d'oeuvres than usual to help tease your guests' appetites and prolong the dinner hour for a late midnight supper.

This menu is an exceptionally flexible one. Designed to serve eight to ten, it can be expanded for any number. The Chicken Breast Coq au Vin is easy to multiply and is equally as impressive served at a sit-down dinner or on a buffet. I serve it with the spinach casserole and glazed carrots, either with or without noodles. If you wish to serve noodles, you can cook them ahead, toss them with olive oil, and reheat them in the microwave oven.

At the end of the hectic holiday season, it is especially helpful to entertain with foods you've prepared ahead. Each of the dishes in this menu can be made at least two days in advance, and the Blini Cups, Ham Biscuits, and Marbled Spinach-Cheese Gratin can be frozen. If you wish to make a dessert that can be frozen before the whirl of holiday festivities begins, the Frozen Chocolate Almond Torte (page 54) is a great choice.

Decorate your table with a variety of time pieces — clocks, watches, hour glasses, etc. — and lots of confetti. Bring out the horns, hats, and bubbling champagne. Lift your glasses to good friends, happy times, and a thriving New Year.

# Blini Cups with Caviar

*Some of the clamor at your party may be over this luxurious version of Russian pancakes. Instead of cooking the batter on a griddle, it is poured into miniature muffin cups, baked, and topped with a swirl of caviar.*

**BLINI CUPS:**
1 pint regular or low-fat small-curd cottage cheese
½ teaspoon sugar
3 tablespoons butter or margarine, melted
3 eggs
1 tablespoon sour cream
½ cup buttermilk biscuit mix

**TOPPINGS:**
1 cup (½ pint) regular or low-fat sour cream
4 to 6 ounces black, red, or golden caviar
½ cup finely chopped onion (optional)

**Make blini cups:** Preheat oven to 350F (175C). Spray 1½-inch miniature muffin cups with non-stick cooking spray. In a food processor with the metal blade or in a bowl with electric mixer, process or mix cottage cheese, sugar, butter, eggs, and sour cream until blended. Add biscuit mix and pulse or mix just until blended. Pour batter into cups, filling three-fourths full. Bake 35 to 40 minutes or until tops are golden. Remove from oven, run around edges with the tip of a sharp knife, and remove from pans.

Place sour cream, caviar, and onion, if using, in small bowls. Let guests top warm blini as desired with toppings.

*Makes about 36 appetizers.*

**Make-Ahead Tips** Baked blini may be refrigerated up to 2 days or frozen up to 1 month. Before serving, preheat oven to 350F (175C). Place cups on baking sheets and bake 10 minutes or until hot.

# Mediterranean Tuna Pâté

*This smooth and creamy spread is reminiscent of an Italian tonnato sauce, a tuna sauce flavored with lemon and capers usually served with veal. It's made in a flash in a food processor or blender.*

2 garlic cloves, peeled
2 (6-oz.) cans tuna, packed in water and drained (Albacore preferred)
3 tablespoons capers, rinsed and drained
1 teaspoon juice from capers
1 (8-oz.) package regular or light cream cheese
2 tablespoons lemon juice
1 tablespoon olive oil
Capers and chopped green onion tops for garnishing
Crackers, bread rounds, or cucumber slices for serving

In a food processor with the metal blade or a blender, process garlic until minced. Add tuna, capers, caper juice, cream cheese, lemon juice, and olive oil. Process until smooth. Spoon into a crock or serving bowl.

Before serving, garnish top with a ring of capers and green onions. Serve with crackers, bread rounds, or cucumber slices.

*Makes 2 cups.*

**Make-Ahead Tip** Pâté may be covered and refrigerated up to 1 week.

Watch your favorite team and enjoy the *New Year's Day Souper Bowl:* Mushroom Barley Soup (page 8), Tomato & Scallop Chowder (page 9), Rosemary-Infused Olive Oil (page 12), Nonfat Herbed Cheese Spread (page 12), Onion Poppy-Seed Bread (page 10), and Beer Rye Bread (page 11).

# Ham Biscuits with Honey Mustard

*Instead of sandwiching bite-size biscuits with ham, in these tender biscuits the meat is incorporated right into the batter. A thumbprint in the top of each biscuit is filled with a golden dollop of honey mustard.*

**HAM BISCUITS:**
8 ounces smoked ham or Canadian bacon
½ cup coarsely chopped green onions (about 4)
1¼ cups all-purpose flour
2½ teaspoons baking powder
Dash salt
6 tablespoons vegetable shortening, butter, or margarine
⅓ cup regular, low-fat, or nonfat milk
¼ cup grated Parmesan cheese

**HONEY MUSTARD:**
2 tablespoons Dijon mustard
3 tablespoons regular, low-fat, or nonfat mayonnaise
1 tablespoon plus 1 teaspoon honey

**Make biscuits:** Preheat oven to 375F (190C). Grease 2 baking sheets or spray with nonstick cooking spray. In a food processor with the metal blade, pulse ham and green onion until minced. Remove to a bowl. Add flour, baking powder, and salt to processor. Pulse to combine. Add shortening or butter and pulse until the mixture resembles coarse meal. Add milk and pulse until dough holds together. Add Parmesan cheese and minced ham mixture. Pulse to incorporate.

Roll pastry into 1-inch balls. Place on baking sheets. Press an indentation in center of each with your thumb. Bake 10 minutes. Repress center. Bake 5 to 7 more minutes or until golden.

Meanwhile, make honey mustard by stirring together Dijon mustard, mayonnaise, and honey.

Remove biscuits from oven and fill indentations with a dollop of mustard. Return to oven and bake 3 to 5 minutes or until mustard is set.

*Makes about 42 biscuits.*

**Make-Ahead Tips** Biscuits may be refrigerated up to 2 days or frozen. Freeze in a single layer. When frozen, pack into an airtight container. Reheat in a preheated 375F (190C) oven 5 to 10 minutes or until heated through.

# Cassis Champagne with Raspberry Cubes

*It's not necessary to purchase an expensive champagne when you flavor it with black-currant liqueur. The raspberry ice cubes look like ruby jewels floating in this festive punch.*

1 to 2 (10-oz.) packages frozen raspberries in syrup, defrosted
½ to 1 cup water
½ cup crème de cassis, chilled
2 (750-ml.) bottles champagne, chilled

**Make ice cubes:** Strain syrup from raspberries to remove seeds; reserve syrup. Place berries and syrup in a bowl and stir in ½ cup water per package of berries. With a spoon, divide raspberries among ice-cube containers. Fill with raspberry liquid. Freeze until firm. Pop out of trays and freeze in plastic bags until ready to use.

To make in champagne glasses, spoon approximately 1 tablespoon crème de cassis in bottom of each glass and fill with champagne. Place 1 raspberry ice cube in each glass. To make in punch bowl, combine champagne and cassis in bowl. Add raspberry cubes.

*Makes 8 servings.*

Prepare *Valentine Day's Dinner* featuring: Salmon Wellingtons (page 16), Broccoli Bouquets (page 17), and Poached Pears in Raspberry Sauce (page 18).

# Chicken Breast Coq au Vin

*This easy, reduced-fat version of French chicken stew is made with boneless, skinless chicken breasts, mushrooms, and baby onions, which simmer in a balsamic vinegar, Madeira, and red wine sauce. It makes a wonderful party dish because it reheats splendidly and stays moist and flavorful on a buffet.*

10 to 12 boneless, skinless chicken breast halves (3 to 4 pounds)
Salt and pepper
1 to 2 tablespoons olive oil
1 pound medium-size mushrooms (about 32), stems trimmed
1 (16-oz.) bag frozen whole small onions, thawed and drained on paper towels
2 tablespoons sugar
4 large garlic cloves, minced
½ cup balsamic vinegar
1½ cups beef broth
¼ cup Madeira wine
¼ cup dry red wine
1 teaspoon dried leaf tarragon or 1 tablespoon fresh chopped tarragon
1 teaspoon dried leaf thyme or 1 tablespoon fresh chopped thyme
1 tablespoon plus 1 teaspoon tomato paste
1 (¾-oz.) package brown gravy mix
1 to 2 tablespoons cornstarch dissolved in 1 to 2 tablespoons water
1 pound flat wide egg noodles, cooked for serving (optional)
Fresh tarragon, thyme, or parsley sprigs for garnish

Preheat oven to 350F (175C). Sprinkle chicken with salt and pepper. In a wide, heavy saucepan or Dutch oven, heat 1 tablespoon olive oil over medium-high heat until hot. Sauté chicken in 2 batches, turning with tongs until brown on both sides. Remove to a platter. Sauté mushrooms in same saucepan, adding more oil if needed, until lightly browned. Remove to chicken with a slotted spoon. Add onions to saucepan. Sprinkle with sugar and sauté over medium heat, stirring until glazed and lightly browned. Stir in garlic, vinegar, broth, Madeira and red wine, herbs, tomato paste, and brown gravy mix. Bring to a boil, stirring constantly, scraping up any brown bits that stick to the bottom of the pan. Stir in chicken and mushrooms.

Cover and bake 45 minutes, stirring after 30 minutes. Remove chicken from pan. Stir in cornstarch mixture. Cook over medium-high heat, stirring, until sauce comes to a boil and thickens. Season with salt and pepper. If desired, serve over noodles. Garnish with fresh herbs.

*Makes 8 servings.*

**Make-Ahead Tip** Coq au Vin may be refrigerated up to 2 days. Reheat on top of stove or in a preheated 350F (175C) oven 20 to 30 minutes or until heated through.

---

# Orange-Glazed Carrots

*Orange marmalade and Grand Marnier highlight the natural sweetness of carrots. If you purchase the carrots trimmed and peeled, the majority of the work is done for you.*

2 tablespoons butter or margarine
¼ cup chicken broth
¼ teaspoon salt or to taste
2 pounds baby carrots, trimmed and peeled
1 cup orange marmalade
Pepper
2 tablespoons Grand Marnier (optional)
2 tablespoons snipped chives or green onion tops for garnish

In a 12-inch sauté pan or saucepan over medium heat, bring butter or margarine, broth, and ¼ teaspoon salt to a boil. Add carrots and cook covered over medium-low heat, stirring occasionally, until carrots are barely tender when pierced with the tip of a sharp knife, about 10 to 15 minutes.

Uncover and stir in the marmalade. Cook over low heat, stirring constantly, until liquid has reduced to a glaze. Season with pepper and additional salt, if needed. Stir in Grand Marnier, if using. Garnish with chives or green onion tops.

*Makes 8 servings.*

**Make-Ahead Tip** Carrots may be refrigerated overnight. Before serving, return carrots to saucepan or microwave-safe bowl. Reheat, stirring occasionally, until heated through.

## Marbled Spinach-Cheese Gratin

*I've gleefully watched many professed nonspinach eaters devour this casserole. It's chock-full of spinach and swirled throughout with a creamy cheese sauce. It's a terrific dish to make ahead to take to a friend's house, then bake when you get there.*

**CHEESE SAUCE:**
3 garlic cloves, peeled
2 (8-oz.) packages regular or light cream cheese
½ cup whole or low-fat milk
1 whole egg
2 egg whites
1 cup shredded Swiss or mozzarella cheese
¾ cup Parmesan cheese
1 tablespoon Dijon mustard

**SPINACH LAYER:**
2 leeks, white part only, coarsely chopped
2 medium-size onions, coarsely chopped
2 tablespoons olive oil
3 (10-oz.) bags fresh stemmed and washed spinach
2 teaspoons dried or 2 tablespoons fresh chopped basil
½ teaspoon salt or to taste
Pepper to taste
1 teaspoon Tabasco sauce
2 tablespoons all-purpose flour
¼ cup Parmesan cheese for topping

Preheat oven to 350F (175C). Generously grease a 13″ × 9″ baking dish. To make cheese sauce: In a food processor with the metal blade, mince garlic. Add cream cheese, milk, whole egg, and egg whites and process until blended. Add Swiss or mozzarella cheese, Parmesan cheese, and Dijon mustard and pulse until mixed. Remove from food processor. Measure 1 cup and return to processor.

To make spinach layer: Place leeks, onions, and olive oil in a very large microwave-safe bowl. Microwave, uncovered, on HIGH (100 percent) 10 to 14 minutes until soft, stirring once. Add contents of 1 bag of spinach, cover, and microwave on HIGH (100 percent) 3 minutes. Stir and microwave 3 to 5 more minutes until cooked through. Remove to processor with reserved 1 cup cheese sauce. Add basil, salt, pepper, Tabasco sauce, and flour. Add remaining 2 bags spinach to microwave-safe bowl, cover, and microwave 6 to 9 minutes or until cooked through. Add to processor and process until combined, but still slightly chunky.

Spread half the spinach mixture on the bottom of the prepared dish. Top with spoonfuls of cheese sauce. Spread lightly. Spread remaining spinach over the top. With a knife, gently swirl the sauce and top spinach layer together. Bake 35 minutes or until lightly browned and set.

Sprinkle top of casserole with ¼ cup Parmesan cheese. Bake another 10 to 15 minutes or until top is golden. Cut into squares to serve.

*Makes 16 servings.*

**Make-Ahead Tip** The baked casserole may be cooled, covered, and refrigerated up to 2 days or frozen up to 1 month. If frozen, defrost in refrigerator overnight. Bring to room temperature before reheating in a preheated 350F (175C) oven 10 to 15 minutes.

# Vanilla Mousse with Caramel Rum Sauce

*For a pretty presentation, use a fluted mold for this cool and creamy mousselike pudding. Cut it into wedges and drizzle with a delectable fat-free caramel sauce.*

**MOUSSE:**
3 envelopes unflavored gelatin
1 cup plus 2 tablespoons sugar
½ teaspoon salt (optional)
4 cups regular or low-fat (2 percent) milk
2 tablespoons vanilla extract
2 cups whipping cream
2 cups low-fat sour cream

**CARAMEL RUM SAUCE:**
¾ cup granulated sugar
1½ cups packed light brown sugar
1 cup nonfat plain yogurt
Dash of salt
5 tablespoons rum

**Make mousse:** In a medium-size saucepan, stir together gelatin, sugar, and salt. Slowly stir in milk. Cook over medium heat, stirring, until gelatin is dissolved and mixture begins to bubble around edges. Do not boil. Remove from heat. Pour into a bowl and stir in vanilla. Place bowl in a larger bowl filled with ice water. Stir frequently until mixture cools thoroughly and begins to thicken.

In a large bowl, beat whipping cream and sour cream until soft peaks form. Fold into cooled gelatin mixture. Lightly spray a 10- to 12-cup mold with nonstick cooking spray. Pour in mousse. Cover with plastic wrap and refrigerate until set, at least 3 hours.

**Make caramel rum sauce:** In a 12-cup (3-qt.) microwave-safe bowl, stir white and brown sugars, yogurt, and salt together until thoroughly moistened. Microwave, uncovered, on HIGH (100 percent) 10 to 14 minutes without stirring, until caramel colored, bubbly, and thickened. The sauce will continue to thicken as it cools. Remove from microwave oven and stir in rum. Makes 2 cups sauce.

Several hours before serving, run a small knife around edge of mold, dip in warm water and unmold onto platter. Refrigerate. Before serving, reheat sauce until warm (not hot or it will melt the mousse). Drizzle a little sauce around top and base of mousse and pass remaining sauce.

*Makes 10 to 12 servings.*

**Make-Ahead Tips** Mousse may be refrigerated up to 4 days.

Sauce may be refrigerated in a wide-mouth container up to 1 month.

# New Year's Day Souper Bowl

---

**M E N U**

*Country Minestrone*
*Mushroom Barley Soup*
*Tomato & Scallop Chowder*

*Onion Poppy-Seed Bread*
*Beer Rye Bread*

*Nonfat Herbed Cheese Spread*
*Rosemary-Infused Olive Oil*

*Coffee Toffee Trifle*

B E V E R A G E   R E C O M M E N D A T I O N :
*Bloody Marys or Beer*

---

New Year's Day has become synonymous with bowl games, so why not invite friends in for your own Souper Bowl buffet? You won't need to be in the kitchen missing out on the fun, because all of these soups can be frozen before the hectic holiday season begins. They can be reheated and served right from the pots on the stove. Don't worry if you don't have enough soup bowls. Coffee mugs make great stand-ins.

Drape baskets with colorful napkins to hold an assortment of delicious homemade breads. Onion Poppy-Seed and Beer Rye loaves are comparable to the best bakery varieties, yet they are extremely easy to make. If kneading by hand isn't your idea of therapy, each recipe includes directions for mixing and kneading in either the food processor or with the dough hook of an electric mixer. Be patient as the dough rises, even if it takes longer than stated. For best results, choose a warm, draft-free spot, such as inside a gas oven with the pilot light on or in an electric oven warmed at 200F (95C) for one minute and then turned off. Or, a fast, fail-safe way is to place a large shallow pan or roaster on the counter. Fill it half-full with boiling water. Place a baking sheet with the bowl of dough or shaped bread over the pan. Replenish the water as it cools. For a crisp crust, fill a small spray bottle with water and mist the bread at the beginning and once again during baking. To reheat, place loaf on a baking sheet and bake at 400F (205C) 10 to 15 minutes or until crisp.

For a hassle-free dessert, bring out a pretty bowl of Coffee Toffee Trifle, ready and waiting in the refrigerator.

The soups in this menu serve six to eight people. If you serve all three, you'll have enough for about twenty guests.

# Country Minestrone

*No matter what you add to or subtract from this soup, it always comes out superb.*
*Try serving it like the Italians do: Place a slice of Italian or sourdough bread in each*
*soup bowl, sprinkle it with Parmesan cheese and ladle the soup over the bread.*

3 tablespoons olive oil
1 large onion, coarsely chopped
1 stalk celery, coarsely chopped
2 large carrots, peeled and chopped
4 large garlic cloves, minced
¼ cup chopped parsley
2 zucchini, diced
½ small head green cabbage, chopped (about
  12 oz.)
1 (16-oz.) can whole tomatoes, undrained and
  chopped
¾ cup chopped fresh spinach
4 cups beef broth
1 potato, peeled and diced
½ cup elbow macaroni
Salt and pepper to taste
½ to 1 cup freshly grated Parmesan cheese
Additional freshly grated Parmesan cheese for
  serving (optional)

Heat olive oil in soup pot over medium heat until hot. Add onion, celery, carrots, garlic, and parsley and sauté 10 minutes, stirring occasionally until soft, but not brown. Add zucchini, cabbage, tomatoes with their juice, and spinach. Cover and simmer 10 minutes. Add broth, potato, and macaroni. Simmer, uncovered, 20 minutes or until potatoes and cabbage are tender. Season with salt and pepper.

Before serving, stir in Parmesan cheese to taste. Cook, stirring, until cheese melts. If desired, pass additional cheese.

*Makes 8 servings.*

**Make-Ahead Tip**   Soup may be refrigerated up to 4 days or frozen. Add Parmesan cheese and reheat before serving.

---

# Mushroom Barley Soup

*Thick, rich, creamy, and brimming with the pungency of dried mushrooms, here's an*
*old-fashioned soup to warm you in front of a crackling fire.*

¾ ounce dried mushrooms
2 tablespoons olive oil
1 large leek, white part only, chopped (about
  ¾ cup)
2 stalks celery, chopped (about 1 cup)
1 onion, chopped
4 cups chicken broth
⅓ cup pearl barley
¼ cup chopped parsley
1 bay leaf
½ teaspoon dried leaf thyme
½ teaspoon salt or to taste
Freshly ground pepper to taste
1 potato, peeled and diced (about 1½ cups)
½ cup whipping cream or half-and-half

**Soak** mushrooms in hot water to cover 30 minutes. Drain and squeeze dry. Cut off tough stems and chop mushrooms into small pieces. Set aside.

Meanwhile, in a medium-size soup pot over medium heat, heat olive oil until hot. Add leek, celery, and onion; sauté over medium-low heat, stirring occasionally, until soft but not brown, about 20 minutes. Add chicken broth and barley. Bring to a boil. Stir in parsley, bay leaf, thyme, salt, and pepper. Cover and simmer 1 hour, stirring occasionally. Add diced potato and dried mushrooms. Cover and simmer 30 minutes longer. Remove bay leaf. Stir in cream or half-and-half and adjust seasonings.

*Makes 6 servings.*

**Make-Ahead Tip**   Soup may be refrigerated up to 2 days or frozen. Reheat before serving.

# Tomato & Scallop Chowder

*From the south of France comes this smoky vegetable chowder usually made with fish fillets. But I much prefer it with delicately flavored scallops. To ensure they don't overcook, add them just before serving.*

6 slices regular or turkey bacon, diced
1 large onion, sliced (about 1 cup)
1 small green bell pepper, sliced into thin strips (about 1 cup)
2 carrots, thinly sliced (about 1 cup)
1 tablespoon chopped parsley
1 (1-lb. 12-oz.) can tomatoes, undrained and chopped
1 (7½-oz.) bottle clam juice
½ teaspoon salt or to taste
1 bay leaf
2 teaspoons bottled steak sauce
1 teaspoon dried leaf thyme
1½ cups chicken broth
2 medium-size potatoes, peeled and diced (about 2½ cups)
Freshly ground pepper
1 pound bay scallops or sea scallops, cut into bite-size pieces

In a medium-size soup pot over medium-high heat, sauté bacon until almost crisp. Add onion, bell pepper, carrots, and parsley. Sauté over low heat about 10 minutes, stirring occasionally. Add tomatoes with their juice, clam juice, salt, bay leaf, steak sauce, thyme, and chicken broth. Bring to a boil. Reduce heat and simmer, covered, 30 minutes. Add potatoes, cover, and simmer 30 minutes longer, or until potatoes are tender. Remove bay leaf. Season to taste with salt and pepper.

Before serving, stir in scallops. Cook 2 to 3 minutes or until scallops are cooked through. Do not overcook or scallops will become tough.

*Makes 6 to 8 servings.*

**Make-Ahead Tip**   Chowder may be refrigerated up to 2 days or frozen. Add scallops and cook until soup is hot and scallops are cooked through.

# Onion Poppy-Seed Bread

*If you're going to bake bread, make a loaf that's better than anything you can buy.*
*This one is shaped in a ring and swirled throughout with onions and poppy seeds.*

**DOUGH:**
1 package active dry yeast
¼ cup warm water (100–115F, 40–45C)
½ cup (1 stick) butter or margarine, melted
1 cup regular, low-fat, or nonfat milk
4 to 4½ cups all-purpose flour
¼ cup sugar
2 teaspoons salt
1 large egg

**ONION POPPY-SEED FILLING:**
1 medium-size onion, chopped (1 cup)
4 tablespoons (½ stick) butter or margarine, melted
3 tablespoons poppy seeds
¼ teaspoon salt

**TOPPING:**
1 egg, lightly beaten
1 tablespoon poppy seeds
1 tablespoon chopped onion

**Make dough:** In a large mixer bowl, dissolve yeast in warm water; let stand until foamy, 5 to 10 minutes. In a small saucepan over medium heat, heat butter and milk until lukewarm and butter melts. Add to yeast mixture. Stir in 2 cups of the flour, sugar, salt, and egg. Beat at medium speed 2 minutes, scraping down sides occasionally. Add 2 cups flour. Mix until blended. Dough should be moderately stiff. If too soft, add a little more flour. Knead on floured board or with dough hook until smooth and elastic, adding more flour as needed, 8 to 10 minutes. Shape dough into a ball, place in a greased bowl, and turn to grease all surfaces. Cover with buttered plastic wrap and a damp towel and let rise in a warm place (see page 7) until double in bulk, about 1 hour.

**Meanwhile, make Onion Poppy-Seed Filling:** In a small bowl, stir together onion, butter, poppy seeds, and salt. Set aside.

Punch dough down. On lightly floured board, roll dough into a 15″ × 10″ rectangle. Cut dough in half lengthwise, forming two 15″ × 5″ rectangles. Spread half of filling on each strip, leaving a ½-inch border all around. Fold in half lengthwise to cover filling. Pinch seams to seal. Twist into a long rope. Twist the ends of both ropes together to form a large ring. Lightly grease a baking sheet or spray with nonstick cooking spray. Place ring on greased baking sheet. Cover with a damp towel and let rise in a warm place until double in bulk, 45 minutes to 1 hour.

Preheat oven to 350F (175C). Brush loaf with lightly beaten egg. Sprinkle with poppy seeds and onion. Bake 40 minutes or until golden brown and bread sounds hollow when tapped on bottom with fingers. Cool on wire rack.

*Makes 1 loaf.*

**Make-Ahead Tip** Bread may be frozen. Do not refrigerate. To reheat, see page 7.

# Beer Rye Bread

*This dense, crusty, chestnut-brown loaf, enlivened with beer, molasses, orange peel, and caraway seeds, makes a perfect partner for main-dish soups.*

2 packages active dry yeast
¼ cup warm water (100–115F, 40–45C)
2 cups beer
¼ cup (½ stick) butter or margarine
⅓ cup molasses
½ cup wheat germ
1 tablespoon grated orange peel
3 tablespoons caraway seeds
2 teaspoons salt
2 cups rye flour
4 to 5 cups all-purpose flour
Cornmeal
1 egg mixed with 1 tablespoon water for glaze

Dissolve yeast in warm water in a small bowl; let stand until foamy, 5 to 10 minutes. In a small saucepan, heat beer, butter or margarine, and molasses until lukewarm. Pour mixture into a large bowl. Add wheat germ, orange peel, 1 tablespoon of the caraway seeds, salt, and yeast mixture. Blend well. Beat in rye flour and enough all-purpose flour to make a moderately stiff dough. Knead on floured board or with dough hook until smooth and elastic, about 10 minutes, adding more flour as needed.

Shape dough into a ball and place in a greased bowl, turning to coat all surfaces. Cover with buttered plastic wrap and a damp towel and let rise in a warm place (see page 7) until double in bulk, about 1½ to 2 hours.

Punch dough down and knead lightly. Cover and let rest 10 minutes. Divide dough in half and shape into 2 round loaves. Lightly grease a baking sheet or spray with nonstick cooking spray and lightly sprinkle it with cornmeal. Place loaves on baking sheet, cover with a damp towel, and let rise until double in bulk, about 1 hour. Brush with egg glaze. Preheat oven to 350F (175C). Bake loaves 25 minutes. Remove from oven, brush again with glaze, and sprinkle with remaining 2 tablespoons caraway seeds. Bake 15 to 20 minutes longer or until loaves sound hollow when tapped on bottom. Remove from pan to racks and cool.

*Makes 2 loaves.*

**Make-Ahead Tip**  Loaves may be frozen. Do not refrigerate.

# Nonfat Herbed Cheese Spread

*Here's a terrific alternative to butter that is sure to please even the most finicky palate.*

½ cup plain nonfat yogurt
½ cup skim-milk ricotta cheese
½ garlic clove, minced
2 teaspoons finely chopped fresh herbs, such as a
    mixture of basil, thyme, tarragon, or oregano
Salt and pepper to taste

Place a funnel or strainer over a small bowl. Line it with a double thickness of cheesecloth or a paper coffee filter. Spoon in yogurt and cover with plastic wrap. Place in a cool place up to 4 hours or refrigerate overnight. Discard liquid in bowl.

Place thickened yogurt in a small bowl. Stir in ricotta, garlic, herbs, salt, and pepper. Cover and refrigerate until chilled.

*Makes 1 cup spread.*

**Make-Ahead Tip**   The spread may be covered and refrigerated up to 1 week. Stir before using. Serve chilled.

---

# Rosemary-Infused Olive Oil

*It is considered very chic to dip bread into olive oil rather than spread it with butter.*
*Herb-infused oils are costly to buy and it's so easy to make them at home.*

½ cup olive oil
2 teaspoons fresh rosemary sprigs

In a small saucepan, heat oil and rosemary until hot, but not smoking. Cool and pour into a jar. Cover and let stand overnight.

To serve, pour oil into a cruet or small pitcher. Pass oil so guests can pour a small amount onto their plates and dip their bread into it.

*Makes ½ cup.*

**Make-Ahead Tip**   Rosemary oil may be stored in a dark place for several months.

---

# Coffee Toffee Trifle

*This is not really a trifle. A traditional trifle is cake doused with liqueur and layered*
*with custard and fruit. In this version, crushed English toffee or Heath Bars replace*
*the fruit. I guarantee no one will complain.*

1 large (5⅛-oz.) package vanilla instant pudding
3 cups evaporated whole or skimmed milk
6 cups (1½-inch pieces) angel food cake (about
    1 lb.)
½ cup Kahlua
¾ cup whipping cream
¾ cup light sour cream
1 tablespoon plus 1 teaspoon instant coffee or
    instant espresso
¼ cup sugar
1 teaspoon vanilla extract
½ pound English toffee or Heath Bars, broken into
    1-inch pieces and coarsely crushed

Prepare pudding as package directs, substituting evaporated milk for the milk. Sprinkle cake with Kahlua and let stand 5 minutes. Mix pudding and cake together; set aside. Stir whipping cream, sour cream, and coffee together in a bowl. Let stand 1 minute. Beat until mixture begins to thicken. Add sugar and vanilla. Continue beating until mixture forms soft peaks.

In an attractive 2-quart (8-cup) serving bowl, layer half the cake mixture, half the coffee-flavored whipped cream, and half the English toffee. Repeat with remaining cake mixture and whipped cream. Sprinkle remaining English toffee over the top. Cover with plastic wrap and refrigerate 1 to 2 hours for the flavors to blend.

*Makes 8 to 10 servings.*

**Make-Ahead Tip**   Trifle may be refrigerated overnight.

# WINTER WHIMSY

## Valentine's Day Dinner

---

**M E N U**

*Seasoned Nuts*

*Roasted Red Pepper & Carrot Soup*
*Curry Toast Hearts*

*Salmon Wellingtons*
*Broccoli Bouquets*

*Poached Pears in Raspberry Sauce*

W I N E   R E C O M M E N D A T I O N :
*A fresh, fruity, aromatic white wine such as Johannesburg Riesling*

---

Hearts, flowers, and a touch of pink are the theme for this amorous candlelight dinner. The menu is designed for eight, but can be multiplied for more, or divided for one loving couple. Tie pink ribbons on long-stemmed roses and place one on each woman's napkin.

Even the food conveys romance. Curry Toasts cut into hearts float atop flaming red pepper and carrot soup and pimiento ribbons tie up broccoli bouquets. Pink salmon fillets are wrapped in flaky pastry and decorated with pastry cutouts. Beautiful poached pears in a crimson raspberry sauce make a beautiful edible Valentine. You might wish to serve a cookie with the pears; consider English Currant Tarts (page 146) and Jam Logs & Thumbprints (page 146).

# Seasoned Nuts

*Vary the nuts, as well as the seasoning, according to your whim.*

1 (12-oz.) can mixed nuts (2 cups)
¼ cup (½ stick) unsalted butter or margarine, melted
2 tablespoons vegetable oil
2 teaspoons barbecue seasoning mix

**P**reheat oven to 350F (175C). Rub nuts in a dish towel to remove excess skins. Spread nuts in one layer in a baking dish or jellyroll pan. Lightly drizzle with butter and oil. Roast 15 to 20 minutes, shaking the pan several times to coat the nuts evenly. Place barbecue seasoning in a plastic bag. Add nuts and shake to coat. Empty into a bowl, shaking bag to remove all seasoning.

*Makes 2 cups nuts.*

**Variations**

GARLIC-SEASONED NUTS: Substitute ¾ teaspoon garlic powder and 2 teaspoons coarse salt for the barbecue seasoning.

CURRIED NUTS: Substitute 1 teaspoon curry powder for the barbecue seasoning.

**Make-Ahead Tip** Nuts may be stored airtight or frozen for several months.

# Roasted Red Pepper & Carrot Soup

*It's difficult to discern the subtle flavors of this velvety potage. Carrots add sweetness and the peppers impart a slightly smoky taste.*

2 tablespoons olive oil
2 leeks, white part only, coarsely chopped
1 medium-size potato, peeled and chopped (about 1½ cups)
6 cups chicken broth
⅓ cup imported dry vermouth or dry white wine
2 cups peeled baby carrots (about 12 oz.) or peeled sliced carrots
3 (7-oz.) jars roasted red bell peppers, drained
1 tablespoon sugar
¼ to ½ cup whipping cream (optional)
Salt and pepper to taste
Curry Toast Hearts (see below)

In a large saucepan or Dutch oven over medium-high heat, heat olive oil. Add leeks and potato and sauté until leeks are softened, about 10 minutes.

Add broth, vermouth or wine, and carrots. Bring to a boil, reduce heat, cover, and simmer 15 to 20 minutes or until carrots are very tender. Stir in bell peppers and sugar. Puree in batches in a blender for smoothest texture.

If desired, stir in cream to taste. Cook over medium heat, stirring occasionally, until hot. Season with salt and pepper. Ladle into soup bowls and top each serving with 3 or 4 Curry Toast Hearts.

*Makes 8 servings.*

**Make-Ahead Tip**   Soup may be refrigerated up to 2 days or frozen up to 1 month. Thaw overnight in the refrigerator. Add cream and reheat before serving.

# Curry Toast Hearts

*Serve these with soup or salad or as an hors d'oeuvre for an anniversary or adult birthday, or vary the shape to fit the occasion.*

6 slices good-quality white, egg, or wheat bread
3 tablespoons butter or margarine
1 garlic clove, minced
½ teaspoon curry powder

Using a heart-shaped cookie cutter, cut bread into hearts. Place on baking sheet at room temperature for several hours to dry out, turning once.

Preheat oven to 375F (190C). Melt butter or margarine, garlic, and curry in a microwave-safe dish in a microwave oven or in a small skillet over low heat until bubbling. Brush butter mixture on top of toasts. Bake 8 minutes. Turn and bake 2 to 5 additional minutes or until golden. Watch carefully the last few minutes.

*Makes 18 to 24 toasts, depending on size.*

**Make-Ahead Tip**   Toasts may be stored in an airtight container for several days or frozen. Defrost at room temperature. Serve warm or at room temperature.

# Salmon Wellingtons

*To make this elegant entree, cap salmon fillets with sautéed artichokes and mushrooms, and wrap them up in puff pastry. Decorate the top with pastry cutouts, your lover's initials, hearts, flowers, or whatever your romantic self desires.*

Mushroom Artichoke Filling (see below)
1 (17¼-oz.) package frozen puff pastry, defrosted until soft enough to roll, but still very cold
8 salmon fillets, ¾- to 1-inch thick, skinned (about 6 oz. each)
1 egg mixed with 1 tablespoon water for glaze
Madeira Sauce (see below)

## MUSHROOM ARTICHOKE FILLING:

1 (14⅜-oz.) can artichoke hearts, drained
8 large green onions, cut into 1-inch pieces
1 pound mushrooms, quartered
1 tablespoon olive oil
¼ cup Madeira wine
Salt and pepper

## MADEIRA SAUCE:

2 teaspoons olive oil
3 tablespoons finely chopped shallots or onion
½ cup plus 1 tablespoon Madeira wine
1½ cups clam broth
1 tablespoon cornstarch
5 teaspoons lemon juice
5 tablespoons whipping cream
Salt and pepper

**Make filling:** In a food processor with the metal blade, pulse artichoke hearts, green onions, and mushrooms until coarsely chopped. (Or chop with knife.) In a medium-size skillet, heat olive oil until hot. Add vegetables and sauté, stirring occasionally, until softened, about 5 minutes. Stir in Madeira. Cook, stirring, until liquid evaporates. Season with salt and pepper. Cool.

On a lightly floured board, roll 1 sheet of puff pastry ⅛ inch thick. Cut into quarters. Tuck thinner part of each fillet underneath to make an even thickness. Divide half the filling over the fillets and spread evenly over the top. Cover each with a rectangle of pastry. Tuck ½ inch of pastry under fillets; trim off excess dough. Place fillets at least 1 inch apart on greased rimmed baking sheet. Repeat with remaining pastry, filling, and fish. Brush top and sides of pastry with egg glaze, being careful not to let it drip onto baking sheet. Reroll scraps and cut out small decorations, if desired. Place on pastry and glaze again. Cover and refrigerate assembled Wellingtons.

**Make sauce:** In a small saucepan, heat olive oil over medium heat until hot. Add shallots or onion and sauté until they begin to soften, about 3 minutes. Add Madeira and cook until reduced by half. Mix clam juice with cornstarch to dissolve. Remove pan from heat and whisk in clam juice mixture, lemon juice, and cream. Return to heat and cook, whisking constantly, until mixture comes to a boil and thickens. Season with salt and pepper.

Preheat oven to 400F (205C). Bake chilled Wellingtons 20 to 25 minutes or until golden. If baking 2 sheets in same oven, rotate their positions after 10 minutes. Spoon a small amount of sauce onto each plate, place a Wellington on sauce, and pass remaining sauce.

*Makes 8 servings.*

**Make-Ahead Tips** The pastry-wrapped fish may be covered and refrigerated up to 8 hours before baking.

The sauce may be refrigerated overnight. Reheat before serving.

# Broccoli Bouquets

*To retain the bright green color and crisp texture of the broccoli, parboil it a day ahead and then sauté it briefly before serving. Ribbons of jarred red pepper or pimiento tie the broccoli into pretty bouquets.*

3 pounds fresh broccoli
1 tablespoon salt (optional)
1 tablespoon butter or margarine
1 tablespoon vegetable oil
3 garlic cloves, minced
2 tablespoons lemon juice
Freshly ground black pepper to taste
1 or 2 whole jarred roasted red bell peppers or pimientos, cut into strips for garnish

**C**ut tough ends off broccoli and discard. Peel stems, leaving flowerets attached. Cut the bunches into 8 to 10 serving-size portions.

Bring a large pot of water and salt, if using, to a boil. Add broccoli and boil slowly, uncovered, 10 to 12 minutes or until the thickest part of the stem can be pierced with a fork. Remove from heat and immediately plunge broccoli into a bowl of ice water to stop the cooking. When cool, remove from water and drain thoroughly on paper towels. Cover with plastic wrap until ready to use.

In a large skillet over medium heat, melt butter or margarine and oil. Add garlic, lemon juice, and broccoli. Sauté mixture, turning often with tongs, until heated through. Season to taste. Remove to serving plates and garnish each serving with a strip of bell pepper or pimiento to look like a ribbon.

*Makes 8 to 10 servings.*

**Variation** Strips of lemon peel may be substituted for roasted red bell pepper strips.

**Make-Ahead Tip** Broccoli may be refrigerated overnight after cooling. Bring to room temperature before sautéing with butter, garlic, and lemon juice.

# Poached Pears in Raspberry Sauce

*It's so easy to poach pears in a microwave oven. The trick is to microwave only four at a time. The pears look as pretty as a still life coated in a crimson raspberry sauce and garnished with a sprig of mint.*

8 ripe but firm pears, with stems
1 tablespoon sugar, divided
1 lemon
Raspberry Sauce (see below)
8 sprigs fresh mint for garnish

**RASPBERRY SAUCE:**
3 (10-oz.) packages frozen raspberries in syrup, thawed
1 tablespoon Chambord liqueur (optional)
2 tablespoons cornstarch
1 tablespoon lemon juice

**Peel** 4 of the pears, leaving stems intact. Using a melon baller and working from the base, remove the seeds, leaving the top intact. Stand the pears in a circle around the edge of a round casserole or soufflé dish. Sprinkle with ½ tablespoon sugar and juice of half a lemon. Cover with lid or sheet of waxed paper. Microwave on HIGH (100 percent) 6 to 12 minutes, rotating the dish after 5 minutes, until pears are tender when pierced with the tip of a sharp knife. Timing varies with type and ripeness of the pears. Remove to a plate. Meanwhile, peel and core remaining pears. Microwave in same manner.

**Make sauce:** Place a medium-mesh strainer over a medium-size saucepan. Add raspberries with their liquid and stir until all pulp is extracted, scraping bottom of strainer frequently. Discard seeds. Stir in liqueur, if using, cornstarch, and lemon juice. Bring to a boil over medium heat, stirring constantly, until thickened. Remove to a bowl.

Before serving, bring pears and sauce to room temperature. Dip pears in sauce to coat and place on plate. If sauce is too thick, thin with a little Chambord or water. Garnish tops with a sprig of mint. Spoon remaining sauce around the base of pears and serve immediately.

*Makes 8 servings.*

**Make-Ahead Tips** Pears may be refrigerated, covered, overnight. Sauce may be refrigerated up to 2 weeks.

# St. Patrick's Day Party

---

**M E N U**

*Artichoke Hearts with Green-Onion Marinade*
*Miniature Reubens*


*Irish Stew*
*Bread Bowls*
*Green Bean, Cabbage & Bacon Casserole*
*Boiled Irish Potatoes*
*Shamrock Beer*


*Butterscotch Baked Apples*
*Irish Coffee*

---

Whether you're Irish or not (in fact, St. Patrick himself wasn't), St. Patrick's Day is a great excuse to let your hair down and throw a lively party. This buffet-style menu features a hearty Irish stew — a great entree for a crowd. It can be refrigerated or frozen ahead, adapts to any size group, is easy to serve and eat, and is economical to prepare. In my version, the stew is served in individual scooped-out toasted bread bowls. They retain their crisp crust while sopping up every last drop of sauce.

For those who can't imagine St. Patrick's Day without corned beef and cabbage, you'll be happy to find the meat in miniature Reuben sandwich hors d'oeuvres, and the cabbage mixed with green beans in a delectable casserole. For a fiery finale, spike coffee with fragrant spices, citrus peel, and a stout splash of Irish whiskey and flambé.

Cover your table with a sheet of plastic and a field of lacy fern leaves, sod, or artificial turf. When you invite your guests, request they dress all in green.

Although this menu serves sixteen, I've prepared it for as few as eight and as many as forty-eight.

# Artichoke Hearts with Green-Onion Marinade

*These marinated artichokes bear little resemblance to the jarred store-bought variety.*
*Mixed with green olives, green onions, and chunks of cheese, this verdant medley*
*makes a light vegetarian appetizer.*

1 (9-oz.) package frozen artichoke hearts, halves
    and quarters
½ cup pitted green olives
¾ cup regular or low-fat Swiss cheese, cut into
    1-inch cubes (about 3 oz.)
½ cup green onions, sliced diagonally into 1-inch
    pieces

**GREEN-ONION MARINADE:**
1 large garlic clove, minced
⅓ cup olive oil
2 tablespoons lemon juice
1 tablespoon red wine vinegar
1 tablespoon green onion dip mix
1 tablespoon chopped fresh basil, thyme, tarragon,
    or parsley
Salt and pepper to taste

Cook artichokes as package directs. Rinse under cold water; drain. Cool and place in a medium-size bowl. Stir in olives, cheese, and green onions.

**Make marinade:** Mix garlic, oil, lemon juice, vinegar, dip mix, and herbs in a small bowl or process in a food processor with the metal blade. Pour over artichoke mixture. Season with salt and pepper. Cover and refrigerate at least 2 hours for the flavors to blend. Serve with picks.

*Makes 8 servings.*

**Make-Ahead Tip**  Artichokes may be marinated in the refrigerator overnight.

---

# Miniature Reubens

*These petite replicas of classic Reuben sandwiches are baked between two baking sheets.*
*They end up so crisp and golden, you'll think they were sautéed or grilled.*

2 (8-oz.) packages cocktail rye bread
Mustard
½ pound thinly sliced corned beef
1 (8-oz.) can sauerkraut, drained
½ pound thinly sliced Swiss cheese
Nonstick cooking spray

Preheat oven to 450F (230C). Grease a baking sheet. (Not the cushioned variety because they don't brown.) Spread half of the bread slices with mustard. Top each with a folded piece of corned beef to cover the bread completely but not extend over the edge. Spread 1 teaspoon sauerkraut over meat. Place 2 slices of Swiss cheese over sauerkraut and trim edges even with bread. Top with remaining bread.

Spray both sides of bread very generously with nonstick cooking spray. Place on greased baking sheet. Place a second baking sheet over the top to compress the sandwiches. Bake 5 to 8 minutes, turn sandwiches over, press baking sheet on top, and bake 5 to 8 more minutes or until golden. Cut into halves before serving.

*Makes 36 to 40 sandwiches.*

**Make-Ahead Tip**  If not serving immediately, place sandwiches on baking sheet and freeze. When almost frozen, cut each sandwich in half, wrap airtight, and freeze up to 2 months. Before serving, reheat, uncovered, in a preheated 400F (205C) oven 15 minutes if frozen; 8 to 10 minutes, if thawed.

# Irish Stew

*This stew is much more flavorful than other Irish stews I've sampled. The orange peel adds a delightful tang, although I can't credit the Irish for that — I borrowed the idea from the Italians. The recipe can be cut in half, but leftovers freeze well. Plan to make this at least one day in advance; the flavor improves when made ahead.*

8 pounds lean lamb leg or rump or beef round, cut into 2-inch cubes
1½ cups all-purpose flour
1 tablespoon salt
½ teaspoon pepper
¼ cup vegetable oil
4 onions, sliced
2 tablespoons sugar
6 cups dry red wine (or enough to cover two-thirds of the meat)
1 (16-oz.) can tomato puree
2 teaspoons dried leaf basil
1 teaspoon dried leaf thyme
4 teaspoons grated orange peel
4 garlic cloves, minced
2 pounds peeled and trimmed fresh or frozen baby carrots
2 pounds small fresh mushrooms

Preheat oven to 325F (165C). Dry meat thoroughly. In a plastic bag, shake flour, salt, and pepper together. Add meat in batches and shake to coat. Pat off excess. Heat oil in a wide, heavy ovenproof saucepan or Dutch oven. Sauté meat in batches over medium-high heat, one layer at a time, until browned on all sides. Remove meat as it browns.

Add onions and sugar to saucepan. Sauté, stirring constantly, until glazed and lightly browned. Add a little more oil if pan is too dry. Pour off excess fat. Add wine to pan. Cook over medium heat 2 minutes, stirring constantly and scraping up residue from bottom of pan. Stir in tomato puree, basil, thyme, orange peel, and garlic. Return meat to pan and bring to a boil.

Cover and bake 2 to 3 hours, stirring occasionally, until fork tender. If sauce boils rapidly, reduce oven to 300F (150C), so the juices do not evaporate. Remove from oven and if not serving immediately, place a clean damp dish towel directly on top of the meat to prevent it from drying out.

Cook carrots in boiling water 10 to 15 minutes or until almost tender; drain. Remove fat from top of stew. Stir in carrots and mushrooms and simmer on top of the stove or in the oven at 325F (165C), stirring occasionally, until heated through and carrots are tender, about 30 minutes. Season to taste with additional wine, salt, pepper, or orange peel.

*Makes 16 servings.*

**Make-Ahead Tip** Stew may be refrigerated before adding carrots and mushrooms up to 3 days or frozen up to 1 month.

# Bread Bowls

*Filling hollowed-out toasted rolls with stew is something like dipping bread into sauce to get up every last drop — only better.*

16 (6-inch) French or sourdough rolls
½ cup (1 stick) butter or margarine
½ cup olive oil
4 garlic cloves, crushed
¼ cup chopped parsley
Salt to taste

**Preheat** oven to 375F (190C). Cut tops off rolls. Hollow out bread, leaving a shell. Heat butter or margarine and olive oil in a small skillet until hot. Add garlic and cook over low heat 2 minutes. Stir in parsley and salt. Brush inside of rolls with butter mixture, using about 1 tablespoon per roll. Place rolls and tops separately on baking sheets. Bake 10 to 15 minutes or until lightly browned and crisp.

Place rolls and tops on a platter. Let guests help themselves to fill their bread bowls with stew.

*Makes 16 servings.*

**Make-Ahead Tip**   Rolls with tops on them may be covered with foil and refrigerated overnight or frozen. Bring to room temperature and reheat in a preheated 375F (190C) oven 5 minutes.

---

# Green Bean, Cabbage & Bacon Casserole

*One of my first cooking teachers, Jack Lirio, gave me this recipe more years ago than I care to count. It's remained one of my favorite cabbage dishes.*

3 heads cabbage (approximately 4 lbs.)
1 pound regular or turkey bacon, chopped into
   1-inch pieces
¾ cup chicken broth
3 (10-oz.) packages frozen French-style green beans
2 envelopes dry onion soup mix
1 teaspoon salt or to taste
½ teaspoon pepper or to taste

**Remove** outer leaves of cabbage, cut cabbage into quarters, and cut out core. Slice cabbage thinly; do not shred. Set aside. In a large skillet over medium heat, cook bacon until crisp. Remove to paper towels. Pour drippings into a measuring cup and reserve ⅓ cup. Pour chicken broth into skillet. Bring to a boil, add green beans, cover, and cook, stirring occasionally, until beans are thawed. Add cabbage, onion soup mix, and ⅓ cup bacon drippings. Stir well, cover, and simmer 5 to 6 minutes or until cabbage is tender but still crisp. Stir in bacon and salt and pepper. Turn into a 13″ × 9″ casserole dish.

Before serving, preheat oven to 350F (175C). Bake, covered, 25 to 30 minutes or until heated through.

*Makes 16 servings.*

**Make-Ahead Tip**   The casserole may be refrigerated overnight before baking. Bake chilled casserole at 350F (175C) 35 to 45 minutes or until heated through.

# Boiled Irish Potatoes

*A traditional side dish for Irish stew, these parsley-garnished potatoes are moist, tender, and buttery.*

6 to 8 pounds small new potatoes (about 3 per person) or large boiling potatoes
1 tablespoon salt
2 to 4 tablespoons butter or margarine to taste, at room temperature
½ cup chopped parsley
Salt and pepper to taste

Scrub potatoes. If using small potatoes, peel a small band of skin from around the center to keep them from bursting. If using large potatoes, peel, cut into serving-size pieces, and drop them into cold water until ready to use. This will prevent them from discoloring.

Put potatoes into a large saucepan. Cover with cold water and add 1 tablespoon salt. Bring to a boil over high heat, reduce heat, and boil gently 15 to 20 minutes or until tender when pierced with a fork. Drain. Return potatoes to the pan and place over medium heat about 1 minute to evaporate the remaining moisture. Add butter or margarine to taste, parsley, salt, and pepper, and toss until butter melts. Serve immediately.

*Makes 12 to 16 servings.*

---

# Shamrock Beer

Pour beer into a pitcher. Stir in a few drops of green food coloring to tint.

---

# Butterscotch Baked Apples

*These baked apples are stuffed generously with whiskey-plumped raisins and dates and then cloaked with a warm butterscotch-caramel glaze.*

½ cup raisins
½ cup chopped dates
6 tablespoons whiskey, divided
½ cup coarsely chopped walnuts or pecans (2 oz.) (optional)
16 medium-size baking apples
2 (3¾-oz.) packages instant butterscotch pudding
2 cups light corn syrup

Preheat oven to 350F (175C). In a medium-size microwave-safe bowl or 2-cup measure, stir raisins and dates with 4 tablespoons whiskey. Cover and microwave on HIGH (100 percent) 2 to 4 minutes or until mixture is hot and fruits are soft. Cool to room temperature. Stir in nuts, if using.

Peel apples. Cut out core, taking care to remove all seeds and seed pockets. Place apples in two 13″ × 9″ baking dishes. Spoon filling into the cavities. In a medium-size bowl, stir pudding with 1 cup water until pudding is dissolved. Stir in remaining 2 tablespoons whiskey, corn syrup, and 1 cup water. Pour evenly over the apples. Bake 40 to 45 minutes, basting every 10 to 15 minutes, until apples are tender when pierced with a small knife. The sauce will thicken as it cooks and frequent basting toward the end of baking time will give the apples a rich caramel coating. Serve warm or at room temperature. Spoon sauce over each apple when serving.

*Makes 16 apples.*

**Make-Ahead Tip** The baked apples may be held at room temperature 8 hours or they may be refrigerated overnight. Before serving, bring to room temperature. To serve warm, reheat in a preheated 350F (175C) oven 10 minutes.

# Irish Coffee

*What better way to end a St. Patrick's Day dinner than with Irish coffee? To make it in a chafing dish, divide the ingredients into two batches. For a less flamboyant version, make it in a large saucepan on the stove.*

Peel of 4 oranges, removed in strips with vegetable peeler
Peel of 4 lemons, removed in strips with vegetable peeler
Whole cloves
4 cinnamon sticks
6 tablespoons sugar
32 ounces (1 qt.) Irish whiskey
12 cups strong hot coffee
½ pint (1 cup) whipping cream, whipped

Cut the orange and lemon peel into 1-inch strips. Stud each strip with 2 to 3 cloves. Place peel, cinnamon sticks, and sugar in chafing dish or saucepan. Stir occasionally over medium heat until sugar melts. Pour in the whiskey, stand back, and carefully ignite. Shake the pan back and forth slowly until the flames die out. Add hot coffee all at once and simmer the mixture 3 to 4 minutes.

Ladle coffee into Irish coffee glasses or mugs. Top each with a dollop of whipped cream.

*Makes 16 servings, 8 ounces each.*

# THE JOYS OF SPRING

## Easter Feast

---

### MENU

*Molded Easter Egg Spread*
*Ham, Cheese & Green Peppercorn Pâté*

*Crown Roast of Lamb or Roast Leg of Lamb*
*Minted Lamb Gravy*
*Pear Bunnies*
*Fruited Rice Pilaf*
*Spring Peas with Lettuce*
*Ruby Glazed Carrots*
*Easter Nest Bread*

*Frozen Raspberry Meringue Torte*
*Chocolate Basket with White Chocolate Strawberries*
*Fudgy Chocolate Easter Egg*

WINE RECOMMENDATION:
*A dry and full-bodied cabernet sauvignon or a robust, dry zinfandel*

---

It was only after I moved from Los Angeles to Baltimore that I began to fully appreciate the rites of spring. With the first rays of sunshine, golden daffodils peak their heads through the earth, and melodious chirping permeates the air. At Easter time, families and dear ones gather together to celebrate rebirth, both the resurrection of Jesus Christ and the awakening of nature after its long winter sleep.

A splendid entree for this occasion is succulent spring lamb. I offer two alternatives: a regal crown roast, which the butcher makes by tying ribs into a ring; or a leg, a tasty, but less costly option. Both roasts are marinated in a zesty wine-based mixture, which is then reduced to an essence and added to the gravy. Flanking the lamb are more harbingers of spring—peas simmered with lettuce and baby carrots cloaked in a cranberry glaze.

Because eggs are the hallmark of Easter, I've incorporated them in a variety of ways. Eggs are in the hors d'oeuvre as a molded spread for crackers; depicted in the bread as a nest filled with egg-shaped rolls; and finally, in a super-fudgy dessert decorated with rosettes of whipped cream to look like a colossal Easter egg.

Set your table with pretty pastel colors and for a centerpiece, fill a shallow basket with colored eggs, daffodils, tulips, irises, and daisies. Decorate small terra-cotta pots with Easter stickers, ribbons, and lace, and fill them with flowering plants. Write a name with paints or markers on each pot to double as a place card and favor.

This Easter feast menu serves eight to twelve.

## Molded Easter Egg Spread

*Hatch an Easter hors d'oeuvre by molding chopped eggs and spiced cheese into the shape of an egg.*

8 slices regular or turkey bacon (about ½ lb.)
2 (4-oz.) packages regular or low-fat spiced cheese with garlic and herbs (such as Rondele or Boursin), at room temperature
4 whole hard-boiled eggs
4 hard-cooked egg whites
⅓ cup chopped green onion
Salt and pepper to taste
Green onion top, cut into thin strips for garnish (optional)
Parsley sprigs for garnish (optional)
Radish roses for garnish (optional)
Crackers or bread rounds for serving

**D**ice bacon and cook in microwave-safe dish in the microwave or in a large skillet over medium heat until crisp. Remove bacon and drain on paper towels. Place cheese, whole eggs, and egg whites in food processor with the metal blade. Pulse until blended, but still chunky; do not puree. Remove to a bowl and stir in bacon, green onion, salt, and pepper. Line a 3-cup mold with plastic wrap. Pack egg spread into mold. Or, mound into an egg shape with your hands. Cover with plastic wrap and refrigerate.

If molded, invert mold onto platter and remove plastic wrap. Garnish with green onion strips, small sprigs of parsley, and radishes, if desired. Serve with crackers or bread rounds.

*Makes 3 cups spread.*

**Make-Ahead Tip**   Spread may be refrigerated up to 2 days.

## Ham, Cheese & Green Peppercorn Pâté

*Green peppercorns are soft, underripe berries that are less pungent than black ones. They lend a subtle spiciness to this smoky blend of ham and cheese.*

8 ounces lean smoked ham, cut into cubes
4 ounces regular or low-fat provolone or Swiss cheese, cut into cubes or shredded (1 cup)
2 teaspoons coarsely crushed green peppercorns
¼ cup fresh basil leaves
½ cup regular or low-fat mayonnaise
¼ cup regular or low-fat sour cream
1 tablespoon Dijon mustard
1 teaspoon honey
Fresh basil leaves for garnish
Green peppercorns for garnish (soaked and drained, if dried)
Crackers or bread rounds for serving

**I**n a food processor with the metal blade, pulse ham, cheese, crushed peppercorns, and basil until coarsely chopped. Add mayonnaise, sour cream, mustard, and honey and process until well blended. Pack pâté into a crock or small bowl. Cover with plastic wrap and refrigerate at least 4 hours for the flavors to blend.

Before serving, garnish with basil leaves and green peppercorns. Serve with crackers or bread rounds.

*Makes 2½ cups.*

**Make-Ahead Tip**   Pâté may be refrigerated up to 3 days.

# Crown Roast of Lamb

*Few foods are as festive or elaborate as a crown roast. It should be presented on your loveliest platter, but that leaves the dilemma of having to carve on it. I solved the problem by having a carpenter cut and finish a piece of wood to fit my platter. I hide the rim of the board with a wreath of fresh greens.*

*The lamb is marinated before roasting for extra flavor and tenderness. The reduced marinade, accented with a hint of mint jelly and thyme, becomes an aromatic sauce.*

16- to 24-rib crown roast of lamb
Lemon Garlic Marinade (see below)
Salt and freshly ground pepper
Fruited Rice Pilaf for center of crown (page 29)
Minted Lamb Gravy (page 28)
16 to 24 glazed kumquats or paper frills for bone ends
Mint, parsley, or watercress sprigs for garnish
Pear Bunnies for garnish (page 29) (optional)

Place roast in a bowl that fits it as snugly as possible. Pour marinade over; it will cover only a small portion of the meat. Refrigerate, covered with foil, 8 to 12 hours.

About 3 hours before serving, remove lamb from marinade and bring to room temperature. Reserve marinade for gravy. Dry roast well with paper towels. Sprinkle with salt and pepper. Preheat oven to 450F (230C). Place roast on a rack in a shallow roasting pan or broiler pan. Cover the bone ends with foil to keep them from burning. Fill center with a mound of foil to help retain its shape. Put roast in oven and immediately reduce temperature to 350F (175C). Roast 45 minutes and remove foil from center. Continue roasting a total of 1 hour and 30 minutes, about 15 minutes per pound, or until a meat thermometer inserted into the meatiest part registers 140F (60C) for medium-rare or 150F (65C) for medium-well doneness.

While roast cooks, make gravy as directed. Remove roast to platter. Let rest 10 to 20 minutes. Fill center with Fruited Rice Pilaf. Remove foil from rib bones and top each with a glazed kumquat or paper frill. Garnish with greens and Pear Bunnies, if desired. Serve with gravy.

*Makes 8 to 12 servings, allowing 2 to 3 ribs per person.*

---

# Lemon Garlic Marinade

*This marinade goes especially well with lamb.*

2 cups dry white wine or imported dry vermouth
¼ cup lemon juice
2 tablespoons olive oil
3 large garlic cloves, minced
1 large onion, sliced
2 bay leaves
3 tablespoons fresh chopped mint or 1 teaspoon dried leaf mint, crumbled
1 teaspoon dried leaf thyme

Stir all ingredients together in a medium-size bowl. Use as directed in recipes.

*Makes about 3 cups or enough marinade for a 6- to 7-pound leg of lamb or a 24-rib crown roast.*

# Roast Leg of Lamb

*Marinating the meat not only adds flavor, it's a tenderizer as well. To ensure the meat is done to your liking, use a meat thermometer. If the lamb is cooked to 140F (60C), it will be juicy, pink, and very tender.*

1 (6- to 7-lb.) leg of lamb, with bone in or boned and rolled
Lemon Garlic Marinade (page 27)
3 tablespoons vegetable oil
1 teaspoon crushed dried rosemary or 2 tablespoons crushed fresh rosemary
1 teaspoon dried leaf thyme
Salt and freshly ground pepper
Minted Lamb Gravy (see below)
Mint, parsley, thyme, or rosemary sprigs for garnish
Pear Bunnies for garnish (page 29) (optional)

Place lamb in a large nonaluminum bowl or self-sealing plastic bag and add marinade. Refrigerate, covered, approximately 24 hours, turning occasionally.

Several hours before serving, remove lamb from marinade; bring to room temperature. Reserve marinade for gravy. Preheat oven to 450F (230C). Dry lamb very well with paper towels. Rub oil on all sides and sprinkle with rosemary, thyme, salt, and pepper. Place roast on a rack in a shallow roasting pan or broiler pan. Put in oven and immediately reduce heat to 350F (175C). While meat cooks, make the gravy.

Roast lamb 2 to 2½ hours (approximately 20 minutes per pound) or until a meat thermometer inserted into the meatiest part registers 140F (60C) for medium-rare or 150F (65C) for medium-well doneness. Baste lamb occasionally with pan drippings. Remove lamb to carving board and let rest 15 to 20 minutes before carving. Garnish with greens and Pear Bunnies, if desired. Serve with Minted Lamb Gravy.

*Makes 8 to 10 servings.*

---

# Minted Lamb Gravy

*Serve with either the crown roast or leg of lamb.*

Reserved marinade from lamb
1 (1-oz.) package brown gravy mix
Water or dry white wine
1 tablespoon mint jelly or to taste
¼ teaspoon dried leaf thyme
Salt and pepper

Strain marinade into a medium-size saucepan. Bring to a boil, reduce heat, and simmer until liquid is reduced by half to about 1 cup. In a separate saucepan, stir gravy mix and 1 cup cold water until blended. Add reduced marinade and bring to a boil, stirring constantly.

When lamb has finished cooking, remove excess fat from pan drippings and stir drippings into gravy. If too thick, stir in additional water or wine. Season to taste with mint jelly, thyme, salt, and pepper.

*Makes about 2½ cups.*

# Pear Bunnies

*These cute bunnies, decorated à la Peter Cottontail, will surely make you smile. It's fun garnishes like these that make holidays feel special.*

1 (1-lb. 13-oz.) can pear halves in syrup
¼ to ½ teaspoon peppermint extract
Green food coloring
Currants or snipped black raisins
Snipped golden raisins
Flaked coconut
Sliced almonds
Miniature marshmallows

**D**rain pears, reserving syrup in a medium-size bowl. Stir in peppermint extract and enough food coloring to tint a deep green. Add pear halves and marinate at room temperature 1 hour or until they become a pale shade of green. If they are not dark enough, add additional food coloring.

Remove pears from marinade and drain on paper towels. Decorate with currants for the eyes, a golden raisin for the nose, coconut for whiskers, sliced almonds for ears, and half a miniature marshmallow for the tail.

*Makes about 9 bunnies (amount varies with brand of pears).*

**Make-Ahead Tip** Bunnies may be refrigerated, covered with plastic wrap, overnight.

# Fruited Rice Pilaf

*Toss tender fluffy rice, crunchy golden almonds, and juicy chunks of apple with fragrant cinnamon and spicy cardamom and you have a sensational dish worthy of your fanciest occasion.*

½ cup chopped blanched almonds
Bouquet Garni (see below)
½ cup (1 stick) butter or margarine
1 large onion, chopped
2 cups uncooked long-grain white rice
4½ cups boiling chicken broth
1 cup golden raisins
1 large green apple, peeled, cored, and chopped into ½-inch pieces (about 1½ cups)
⅓ cup chopped green onions
Salt and pepper to taste

**BOUQUET GARNI:**
12 whole peppercorns
12 whole cloves
1 large cinnamon stick, broken into pieces
2 garlic cloves, sliced
6 whole cardamom pods, smashed lightly to expose seeds, or ¼ teaspoon ground cardamom

**T**oast almonds in a 350F (175C) oven or toaster oven 10 to 15 minutes, stirring occasionally, or until golden. Set aside.

**Make bouquet garni:** Cut a piece of cheesecloth into a 4-inch square. Place peppercorns, cloves, cinnamon stick, garlic, and cardamom in center of cloth. Bring edges together at the top to make a small pouch. Tie with string and cut off excess cheesecloth.

Melt butter or margarine in a medium-size, heavy saucepan. Sauté onion until soft. Add rice and sauté, stirring often, until lightly browned. Slowly stir in chicken broth. Add Bouquet Garni, cover, and simmer 15 to 20 minutes or until almost all liquid is absorbed. Stir in raisins and apple. Cover and simmer 5 minutes more or until all liquid is absorbed and rice is tender.

Before serving, remove Bouquet Garni. Stir almonds and green onions into rice. Season with salt and pepper.

*Makes 10 to 12 servings.*

**Make-Ahead Tip** Rice may be made ahead, cooled, covered, and refrigerated overnight. Reheat, covered, in a microwave-safe bowl in the microwave. Stir in almonds and green onions.

# Spring Peas with Lettuce

*The French method of cooking peas layered with lettuce is the best. The lettuce adds just enough moisture for the peas to steam to perfection.*

1 head iceberg lettuce (about 1½ lbs.)
1 tablespoon sugar
1 teaspoon dried chervil or fines herbs
2 chicken bouillon cubes, crumbled
½ teaspoon salt or to taste
2 tablespoons butter or margarine
4 pounds fresh peas (4 cups unshelled) or 2 (10-oz.) packages frozen petite peas
¾ cup sliced green onions

**C**ut lettuce into quarters, remove core, and slice lettuce into thin strips about 1 inch long. In a small bowl, mix sugar, chervil or herbs, chicken bouillon, and salt. Melt butter or margarine in a medium-size saucepan. Add half the lettuce. Sprinkle with half the peas. (If using frozen peas, separate them with your hands.) Sprinkle half the seasoning mixture over peas and top with half the green onions. Repeat with a second layer of lettuce, peas, seasonings, and green onions.

Cook over medium-high heat, stirring occasionally, until peas are tender, 7 to 10 minutes. Pour off excess liquid and serve immediately.

*Makes 8 servings.*

**Make-Ahead Tip**    The uncooked pea and lettuce mixture may be refrigerated up to 4 hours.

---

# Ruby Glazed Carrots

*Cranberry sauce tempered with a splash of raspberry vinegar highlights the natural sweetness of carrots.*

2 pounds carrots
1 tablespoon olive oil
1 cup Cran-Fruit or whole-berry cranberry sauce
¼ cup raspberry vinegar
½ teaspoon ground cumin
Pinch ground cinnamon
Salt to taste

**P**eel carrots and slice thinly by hand or in the food processor. Heat olive oil in a medium-size skillet over medium-high heat until hot. Add carrots and sauté 6 to 8 minutes or until softened slightly. Stir in Cran-Fruit, vinegar, cumin, cinnamon, and salt. Reduce heat to medium and cook 5 minutes more or until carrots are tender.

*Makes 8 servings.*

# Easter Nest Bread

*Part of the dough becomes a braided nest and the rest is shaped into eggs to fill it. The baked "eggs" are tinted with pastel frosting and then nestled in a bed of coconut grass. This tastes great and is decorative enough to be a centerpiece.*

## DOUGH:

1 package active dry yeast
¼ cup warm water (100–115F, 40–45C)
1 cup regular, low-fat, or nonfat milk
½ cup (1 stick) unsalted butter or margarine
5 to 5½ cups all-purpose flour
½ cup sugar
1 teaspoon salt
2 large eggs, at room temperature
¼ cup orange juice
2 tablespoons grated orange peel

## TINTED COCONUT:

Green food coloring
1 cup flaked coconut

## SUGAR GLAZE:

¾ cup powdered sugar
Red and yellow food coloring

**Make dough:** Sprinkle yeast over warm water, stirring until dissolved; let stand until foamy, 5 to 10 minutes. In a small saucepan, heat milk and butter until lukewarm. Place 2 cups flour in a large bowl. Add warm milk mixture, sugar, salt, and yeast mixture. Mix until blended. Beat in eggs, one at a time, mixing until smooth. Add orange juice and peel. Beat 2 minutes, scraping down sides of bowl occasionally. Mix in 3 cups additional flour. Dough should be fairly stiff. If it is too soft and sticky, mix in a little more flour. Knead on floured board or with dough hook, adding more flour only if dough is too sticky to work with, until it becomes smooth and elastic, 8 to 10 minutes. Shape into a ball, place in a greased bowl, and turn to grease all surfaces.

Cover with buttered plastic wrap and a damp towel and let rise in a warm place (see page 7) until double in bulk, about 2 hours. Punch dough down and let rest 10 minutes. Grease a baking sheet and a 10-inch springform pan or round cake pan.

Use one-third of the dough to make eggs. Break off small balls of dough and shape into approximately ½-inch oval egg shapes. You should have at least 20. Place on greased baking sheet.

Use remaining two-thirds dough to make nest. Divide dough in half. Spread half into bottom of greased springform pan. Roll remaining dough into a ½-inch-thick rectangle about 12 inches long. Cut into 6 (½-inch) strips. Make 2 braids, using 3 strips for each. Press one braid around side of half the pan. Place second braid around other half. Press the ends of both braids together securely. Attach braids to bottom dough by pressing them together lightly. Press braids against sides of pan and flatten bottom dough to form a nest. Cover nest and eggs with a damp towel and let rise 45 minutes to 1 hour or until nearly double.

Preheat oven to 350F (175C). Bake eggs 15 to 20 minutes and nest 30 to 40 minutes or until golden brown. Remove from oven and cool.

**Make coconut:** Mix a few drops green coloring with 1 teaspoon water. Place coconut in a small bowl, add colored water, and toss well. Repeat until desired color is obtained. Sprinkle coconut in bottom of nest for grass.

**Make glaze:** Place powdered sugar in a small bowl. Stir in 1 teaspoon hot water. Continue to add hot water a few drops at a time until mixture attains a thin spreading consistency. Divide sugar in thirds. Tint one part pink, one yellow, and leave the remainder white. Brush or spread glaze over eggs. Set aside until glaze is dry. Place as many eggs as desired into coconut in nest and serve remainder separately.

*Makes about 10 servings.*

**Make-Ahead Tip** The baked and undecorated nest and eggs may be wrapped in foil and stored at room temperature overnight or frozen up to 1 month. Decorate after thawing.

# Frozen Raspberry Meringue Torte

*Layers of crunchy meringue sandwich frozen raspberry yogurt and Chambord-flavored whipped cream. A crimson berry sauce is spooned over all. This delightful dessert reminds me of an Easter bonnet and all the goodness of spring.*

**MERINGUE LAYERS:**
4 large egg whites
Dash of salt
¼ teaspoon cream of tartar
1 cup sugar, preferably superfine
½ teaspoon vanilla extract

**FILLING:**
2 pints frozen raspberry yogurt or sherbet, softened slightly
½ pint (1 cup) whipping cream
2 tablespoons Chambord liqueur
2 tablespoons seedless raspberry preserves

**FROSTING:**
1 pint (2 cups) whipping cream
1 tablespoon Chambord liqueur

**FRESH BERRY SAUCE:**
2 cups fresh strawberries
1 (10-oz.) package frozen raspberries in syrup, thawed
3 tablespoons Chambord

**GARNISH (OPTIONAL):**
Candied violets or 12 whole strawberries
Nonpoisonous garden leaves or flowers (optional)

**Make meringue layers:** Preheat oven to 250F (120C). Line 2 baking sheets with parchment or waxed paper. Draw 3 (8-inch) circles on paper. If using waxed paper, grease and flour circles. Beat egg whites with an electric mixer on high speed until frothy. Add salt and cream of tartar and beat until soft peaks form. Add 1 tablespoon sugar. Beat 1 minute. Add another 1 tablespoon sugar and beat 1 minute more. Continue to add sugar, 1 tablespoon at a time, beating constantly, until meringue stands in firm, shiny peaks, about 10 minutes. Beat in vanilla. Divide meringue among circles and spread evenly. Bake on center rack of oven 1 hour. If baking both sheets in one oven, rotate them halfway through the baking time.

Turn oven off and cool meringues in oven 4 hours or overnight. (If meringues are thoroughly dried, they will keep well in an airtight container for at least 1 week.)

**Make filling:** Line an 8-inch round cake pan with foil or plastic wrap. Fill with yogurt and spread evenly. Freeze until firm. Whip cream until soft peaks form. Add Chambord and preserves and beat until stiff.

**Assemble torte:** Place 1 meringue on a small baking sheet. Remove yogurt from cake pan and remove paper. Place yogurt on meringue layer. Top with second meringue. Spread with Chambord cream. Top with third meringue. Wrap torte in foil and freeze until firm.

**Make frosting:** Place torte on a serving platter. Whip cream until soft peaks form. Add Chambord and beat until stiff. Spread on top and sides of torte. Pipe rosettes on top, if desired.

**Make sauce:** Hull and halve strawberries and place in a small bowl. In a small saucepan, heat raspberries to boiling. Cool slightly. Press through a strainer into strawberries, discarding the seeds. Stir in Chambord. Refrigerate for at least 1 hour.

**For garnish:** Before serving, if using, dip 12 strawberries into sauce to coat. Drain on paper towels to remove excess sauce. Place around top of torte, if desired. Garnish platter with leaves or flowers, if desired. Cut torte into wedges. Pass remaining sauce.

*Makes 12 to 14 servings.*

**Make-Ahead Tips** Unfrosted torte may be frozen up to 1 week. Wrap tightly after freezing.

Frosted torte may be frozen overnight.

Sauce may be covered and refrigerated up to 8 hours.

# Chocolate Basket

*This woven chocolate basket looks so real that one time an unassuming guest picked it up by the handle. The basket broke and the strawberries in it fell into all the other food. The guests didn't mind; they sat down and ate the basket. When you want to make a lasting impression, this chocolate showpiece will do it. The basket can be refrigerated or frozen for months, and, if someone doesn't devour it, or think it's real, it can be used over and over again. Vary the filling according to your whim.*

1 pound semisweet chocolate, chopped
White Chocolate Strawberries (page 34)

**EQUIPMENT:**
1 (2- to 4-cup) soufflé dish or 6 custard cups
Heavy-duty foil
1 small pastry bag
1 small plastic coupler to hold tips or a second small pastry bag
1 writing tip (#2 or #3)
1 small star tip (#18 or #20)

**P**lace soufflé dish or custard cups upside down on a small board or baking sheet. Press foil evenly over top and sides, letting it extend about 2 inches on bottom. Press foil tightly around bottom to make a sharp, definitive edge. Place in refrigerator or freezer.

**Make basket:** Melt chocolate in a medium-size microwave-safe bowl, uncovered, at 50 percent power until melted, stirring every minute until smooth. Let stand until thick enough to pipe. If it becomes too firm while working, remelt slightly. Fit a small pastry bag with a writing tip. Fill with some of the chocolate. Pipe a continuous drizzle of chocolate in a lacy design over bottom of dish. Overlap circles of chocolate from the sides to the bottom and continue piping up the sides of the dish. Do not be concerned if chocolate drips slightly. If it drips too much, the chocolate is too warm. Refrigerate or freeze basket 5 to 10 minutes or until chocolate is firm. Repeat with a second layer in the same manner. Refrigerate or freeze

until firm. Repeat with a third layer; refrigerate or freeze until chocolate is firm.

Remove soufflé dish or cup by carefully pulling it out from underneath the foil. Turn basket right side up and remove foil by slowly and carefully pulling small pieces of it away from sides and bottom of basket. Remove writing tip from coupler (or use another pastry bag) and replace it with a star tip. Pipe a decorative chocolate border around top edge of basket. Refrigerate while making handle.

**To make handle:** Line a baking sheet that will fit into your refrigerator or freezer with waxed or parchment paper. To make handle, measure the diameter of the basket and mark that width on the paper. Draw the curved shape of a handle. Using room-temperature chocolate (it cannot be too warm or the design won't hold) and star tip, pipe lines around the curved line, following your handle pattern. Refrigerate or freeze until firm. Turn handle over and pipe similar pattern on other side to reinforce it. Refrigerate or freeze until firm.

Attach handle to basket by using melted chocolate as glue and dabbing it on each side of the basket. Using the palm of your hand, hold handle in place until it sticks.

Before serving, fill with White Chocolate Strawberries.

*Makes 1 large basket or 6 small baskets.*

**Make-Ahead Tip** Basket may be refrigerated or frozen for several months.

# White Chocolate Strawberries

*White chocolate can be tricky to melt. I prefer to use either Tobler Narcisse, Lindt Blancor, or candy-coating chips available at cake-decorating stores and some cookware shops. When strawberries aren't available, dip fresh orange segments or dried or candied apricot or peach halves.*

16 to 20 large strawberries, with stems if available
6 ounces white chocolate, chopped

Line a small baking sheet or tray with waxed paper. Pat strawberries clean with paper towels; do not wash. Melt chocolate in top of a double boiler over hot water or in a microwave-safe bowl in the microwave at 50 percent power, stirring often.

Holding each strawberry by the leaves, dip it into the melted chocolate so that two-thirds of the berry is covered. Place on prepared baking sheet. Refrigerate until firm.

*Makes 16 to 20 strawberries.*

**Make-Ahead Tip**  Strawberries may be refrigerated, uncovered, overnight.

---

# Fudgy Chocolate Easter Egg

*Chocolate lovers, here's an extravaganza especially for you. It's so rich and fudgy it won't cut into perfect slices, so just spoon it onto the plate. It should be refrigerated for at least two days before serving, so be sure to plan accordingly.*

12 ounces semisweet chocolate
3 tablespoons instant coffee granules or powder
¾ cup water
1½ cups sugar
1½ cups (3 sticks) unsalted butter, cut into small pieces and at room temperature
6 large eggs
1 pint (2 cups) whipping cream
Candied lilacs or violets or frosting flowers for decoration (optional)

Preheat oven to 350F (175C). Line a 10-cup metal bowl with several layers of heavy-duty foil.

In a medium-size saucepan or large microwave-safe bowl, combine chocolate, coffee, and water. Cook over low heat, stirring constantly, or microwave, covered with waxed paper, on HIGH (100 percent) 3 to 5 minutes, stirring every minute, until chocolate is melted and mixture is smooth. Remove from heat and stir in sugar until dissolved. Stir in butter until melted. Whisk in eggs one at a time until mixture is smooth. Pour into prepared bowl. Bake, uncovered, 1 hour or until a thick crust has formed over the top. Remove from oven and cool. It will sink and crack. Cover with foil and refrigerate for a minimum of 2 days.

Several hours before serving, turn dessert rounded side up on a serving plate. Remove bowl and foil. Whip cream until stiff. Spread over chocolate to cover completely. Or, fit a pastry bag with a ½-inch star tip and pipe rosettes of whipped cream over chocolate to cover completely. Garnish with candied lilacs or violets, if desired.

*Makes 12 servings.*

**Make-Ahead Tip**  Undecorated dessert may be refrigerated up to 1 week or frozen up to 1 month. Defrost in refrigerator 2 days before serving.

A perfect ending to an *Easter Feast* are three wonderful desserts: Clockwise from top: Fudgy Chocolate Easter Egg (above), Frozen Raspberry Meringue Torte, (page 32), and Chocolate Basket with White Chocolate Strawberries (page 33 and above).

# Passover Seder

```
┌─────────────────────────────────────────────┐
│                    MENU                       │
│                                               │
│                   Haroset                     │
│              Gefilte Fish Loaf                │
│        Vegetable Soup with Matzo Balls        │
│   Brisket of Beef with Broccoli-Farfel Stuffing │
│      Asparagus with Lemon Matzo Crumble       │
│              Matzo Fruit Kugel                │
│                                               │
│                                               │
│            Frozen Strawberry Cloud            │
│              Chocolate Nut Torte              │
└─────────────────────────────────────────────┘
```

The beautiful ritualistic dinner known as the Seder, which commemorates the week-long celebration of the Jews' flight from bondage, is rooted in centuries of tradition and ceremony. This menu has been very popular with my cooking classes. It seems cooks across the country are looking for contemporary, easy, light dishes that maintain dietary restrictions.

A carrot-flecked ground-fish mixture baked in a loaf pan is my updated rendition of gefilte fish. Served with horseradish, it is a first cousin to classic ovals or balls. Chicken soup is the mainstay of most Jewish holiday dinners. My version incorporates a medley of fresh vegetables, and my German great-grandmother's matzo balls add the touch of tradition.

A refreshing, low-fat Frozen Strawberry Cloud is an alluring dessert for this robust meal. But for those who yearn for a richer finale, there's a fabulous Chocolate Nut Torte, too.

This Passover Seder menu serves ten to twelve.

A contemporary, yet traditional menu for the *Passover Seder*: Brisket of Beef with Broccoli-Farfel Stuffing (page 38), Vegetable Soup with Matzo Balls (page 37), and Asparagus with Lemon-Matzo Crumble (page 39).

# Haroset

*Haroset, a mixture of fruit, spices, and nuts to recall the mortar the Jews made as slaves, is a traditional offering at the Seder. It's slightly sweet and slightly tart and can be altered to your preference.*

¼ cup raisins
¼ cup chopped dates
¼ cup dry red wine
2 green apples, peeled, cored, and chopped
    (about 3 cups)
½ cup chopped walnuts (2 oz.)
1 teaspoon ground cinnamon
1 to 2 tablespoons sugar

Stir all the ingredients together in a medium-size bowl. Cover and refrigerate for at least 4 hours for the flavors to blend.

*Makes about 3 cups.*

**Make-Ahead Tip**   Haroset may be refrigerated up to 3 days.

---

# Gefilte Fish Loaf

*I've never made gefilte fish the classic way — shaped in balls and poached in stock, probably because watching my mother make it wore me out. I've taken the traditional ingredients and simplified the technique by baking them in a loaf pan. But the food processor, which replaces my mom's hand-cranked meat grinder, is the real timesaver.*

3 pounds firm, white-fleshed fish fillets such as
    whitefish, carp, pike, scrod, or halibut, skin and
    bones removed
2 medium-size onions, coarsely chopped
3 carrots, peeled and quartered
1 teaspoon salt
2 large eggs
⅓ cup ice water, divided
1 tablespoon kosher salt, divided
1 teaspoon sugar, divided
½ teaspoon white pepper, divided
2 rounded tablespoons matzo meal
2 tablespoons freshly grated horseradish or 1
    tablespoon prepared horseradish
2 to 3 tablespoons fresh chopped dill or 2 to 3
    teaspoons dried dill
Lettuce leaves for serving
Sprigs of fresh dill or parsley for garnish
Red horseradish for serving

Preheat oven to 325F (165C). Place a baking pan in center of oven and fill with about 2 inches of water. Grease a 9-inch loaf pan. Cut a piece of parchment or waxed paper to fit the bottom. Grease the paper.

Cut fish into small pieces and place in a bowl with onions. Cover and refrigerate. In a food processor with the metal blade, chop carrots into very

small dice. Place into a small saucepan, cover with water, add 1 teaspoon salt, and bring to a boil. Boil 2 minutes. Drain and run under cold water to stop the cooking. Set aside.

Divide the fish and onions in half. Place half in the food processor with the metal blade. Puree until smooth. Add 1 egg, half the ice water, ½ tablespoon kosher salt, ½ teaspoon sugar, and ¼ teaspoon white pepper. Process until pureed. Remove to a bowl. Repeat with remaining half of ingredients. Stir in matzo meal, horseradish, carrots, and dill.

Spoon mixture into prepared loaf pan, spreading top evenly. Set pan in oven in baking pan of water. Bake 50 to 60 minutes or until center feels firm to the touch. Remove from oven and cool 5 minutes. Run a sharp knife around inside edge. Invert onto a platter, or if not serving immediately, a sheet of foil. Remove the pan and the paper. Serve warm or chilled.

Slice and serve on lettuce leaves. Garnish with fresh dill or parsley and serve with horseradish.

*Makes 10 to 12 servings.*

**Make-Ahead Tip**   The fish loaf may be refrigerated up to 2 days.

# Vegetable Soup with Matzo Balls

*This savory vegetable soup is delicious made with either homemade stock or kosher canned chicken broth. It's lighter than most vegetable soups and offers a change of pace from the customary chicken soup.*

3 tablespoons vegetable oil or rendered chicken fat
2 large onions, chopped
2 carrots, peeled and chopped into ½-inch pieces
3 large leeks, white part only, cleaned and chopped
½ cup celery root, peeled and chopped into ½-inch pieces
1 small turnip, peeled and chopped into ½-inch pieces
1 small rutabaga, peeled and chopped into ½-inch pieces
1 small head green cabbage, cored and shredded
11 cups chicken broth
3 peppercorns
1 teaspoon dried leaf thyme
1 teaspoon dried leaf basil
Salt and pepper to taste
2 tomatoes, seeded and chopped
Matzo Balls (see below)

In a large soup pot over medium heat, heat oil until hot. Add onions, carrots, leeks, celery root, turnip, rutabaga, and cabbage. Sauté, stirring often, until softened, about 15 minutes.

Add chicken broth, peppercorns, thyme, and basil. Bring to a boil, reduce heat, cover, and simmer about 2 hours, stirring occasionally. Strain into a clean pot or large bowl. Stir as many vegetables as desired into broth.

Before serving, reheat and season to taste. Add chopped tomatoes and matzo balls and cook until heated through.

*Makes 8 to 10 servings.*

**Make-Ahead Tip** The soup may be refrigerated up to 2 days or frozen up to 1 month. If frozen, thaw in refrigerator overnight.

---

# Matzo Balls

*These matzo balls with their slight almond crunch are a family recipe that has been handed down through the generations.*

4 large eggs
3 tablespoons vegetable oil or rendered chicken fat
1 cup matzo meal
⅓ cup chicken broth
¼ cup finely ground almonds
1½ teaspoons salt or to taste
2 tablespoons finely chopped parsley
½ teaspoon ground ginger (optional)

In a medium-size bowl, mix eggs and oil or chicken fat until blended. Stir in matzo meal. Stir in chicken broth, almonds, salt, parsley, and ginger, if

using. Refrigerate 1 hour or more. With wet hands, form into 1½-inch balls.

Bring 4 quarts of salted water to a boil in a soup pot. Reduce to a simmer and drop in matzo balls. Cover the pot and cook at a low simmer 20 minutes. Do not lift the lid while cooking or the matzo balls will boil instead of steam and become tough. Drain. Add to soup. Heat through.

*Makes about 28 matzo balls.*

**Make-Ahead Tip** Matzo balls may be refrigerated in soup for several days or frozen up to 1 month.

# Brisket of Beef with Broccoli-Farfel Stuffing

*Brisket is a popular Seder entree because it feeds a crowd, is inexpensive, and reheats beautifully. To dress it up, cut a pocket through the center and fill it with chopped broccoli, mushrooms, and small pieces of matzo called farfel.*

## BROCCOLI-FARFEL STUFFING:
2 tablespoons vegetable oil
1 large onion, chopped
½ pound mushrooms, coarsely chopped
2 garlic cloves, minced
1 (10-oz.) package frozen chopped broccoli,
    thawed and drained
1½ cups matzo farfel
1 egg, beaten lightly
1 teaspoon dried leaf basil or 2 tablespoons
    chopped fresh basil
1 teaspoon salt or to taste
Freshly ground pepper to taste

## BRISKET:
1 (3- to 5-lb.) first-cut beef brisket
Salt and pepper
Paprika
2 onions, quartered
3 carrots, peeled and cut into 2-inch pieces
1 cup beef broth
1½ cups dry red wine
2 tablespoons Dijon mustard
1 to 2 tablespoons potato starch mixed with an
    equal amount of cold water (optional)

**Make stuffing:** In a large skillet over medium-high heat, heat oil until hot. Add onion and sauté until softened. Add mushrooms and garlic and sauté until most of the liquid has evaporated. Transfer to a medium-size bowl and cool slightly. Stir in broccoli and farfel. Stir in egg and basil. Season with salt and pepper.

**Prepare brisket:** Make a pocket in brisket by cutting horizontally through the center of the meat, leaving a ¾-inch border uncut on three sides. Loosely push stuffing into the pocket, pushing it to the back of the meat. Do not overstuff. Skewer closed with turkey lacers or sew with thread and trussing needle. Press meat with hands to distribute stuffing evenly. Sprinkle both sides of meat with salt, pepper, and paprika.

Preheat broiler. Place onions and carrots in bottom of a roaster or Dutch oven. Place brisket on vegetables. Broil until top is brown. Turn meat over and brown other side. Reduce oven temperature to 300F (150C). In a small bowl, whisk beef broth, wine, and mustard together. Pour over brisket. Cover and bake 3 to 4 hours, basting occasionally, until meat is tender when pierced with a fork. If sauce boils rapidly, reduce oven temperature to 275F (135C).

When meat is tender, remove from oven. If not serving immediately, place meat in a bowl and cover with a damp towel to prevent the top from drying out. Strain pan juices for sauce; discard vegetables.

Before serving, preheat oven to 350F (175C). Remove fat from sauce. Slice meat ¼ inch thick. Place slices overlapping on a large sheet of heavy-duty foil. Place in casserole dish or roasting pan. Pour sauce over meat. Close foil tightly and bake 45 minutes or until heated through.

Remove meat to a serving platter. Season sauce with salt, pepper, and additional wine or mustard, if desired. If a thicker sauce is desired, pour sauce into a small saucepan and stir in starch and water mixture. Cook over medium-high heat, stirring constantly, until sauce comes to a boil and thickens. Spoon a small amount of sauce over meat and pass remaining sauce.

*Makes 8 to 12 servings.*

**Make-Ahead Tip** Meat and sauce may be refrigerated separately up to 2 days or frozen up to 1 month. Wrap meat tightly in foil. Store sauce in a covered bowl.

**Variation** For a year-round version, substitute 1¾ cups herb-seasoned bread stuffing for the matzo farfel and 1 to 2 tablespoons cornstarch for the potato starch.

# Asparagus with Lemon Matzo Crumble

*Bread crumbs may be substituted for matzo meal at other times of the year, but after you taste this crumbly topping, you may not want to make any substitutions.*

4 pounds asparagus
Matzo Crumble (see below)
Salt
4 tablespoons melted pareve margarine
4 teaspoons fresh lemon juice

**MATZO CRUMBLE:**
4 tablespoons pareve margarine
3 tablespoons vegetable oil
3 garlic cloves, crushed
2 tablespoons fresh lemon juice
4 green onions, finely chopped
2 cups matzo meal
½ teaspoon salt

**Cook asparagus:** Cut off woody bottoms of asparagus, leaving spears about 6 inches long. If stalks are thick, peel with a vegetable peeler, pulling from stem end toward tip. (Thin spears do not need peeling.) Separate into bundles of about 6 to 8 spears. Tie with string. In a large skillet, bring 1 inch of salted water to a boil. Add asparagus and cook until tender, 4 to 8 minutes after water comes back to a boil. Timing depends on size and age of spears. Remove bundles, cut string, and run asparagus under cold water to stop the cooking. Blot well with paper towels.

**Make crumble:** In a large microwave-safe bowl, heat margarine and oil on HIGH (100 percent) 1 minute or until margarine is melted. Stir in garlic, lemon juice, green onions, matzo meal, and salt. Microwave, uncovered, on HIGH (100 percent) 6 to 8 minutes, stirring every 2 minutes, until dry and crisp.

**Before serving:** Arrange cooked asparagus on microwave-safe platter. Sprinkle with salt. Cover with waxed paper and microwave on HIGH (100 percent) 2 to 4 minutes or until heated through. Heat margarine and lemon juice in a small skillet on top of stove or in a microwave-safe dish in the microwave until melted. Drizzle over asparagus. Sprinkle crumble across the center.

*Makes 10 to 12 servings.*

**Make-Ahead Tips** Cooked asparagus may be refrigerated overnight, wrapped in a double thickness of paper towels. Bring to room temperature before reheating.

Crumble may be refrigerated up to 3 days or frozen up to 2 weeks. Bring to room temperature before using.

# Matzo Fruit Kugel

*This baked casserole has the consistency of a noodle pudding, but matzo replaces the noodles. It's filled with fruit and makes a delicious side dish for dinner or entree for breakfast or lunch.*

5 matzos
3 large eggs
4 egg whites
2 unpeeled red apples, shredded
1 small unpeeled pear, shredded
1 (8-oz.) can crushed pineapple, drained
¾ cup golden raisins
3 tablespoons sugar
Grated peel of 1 lemon
1 tablespoon lemon juice
1 teaspoon ground cinnamon
2 teaspoons vanilla extract
2 tablespoons pareve margarine
2 tablespoons sugar mixed with ½ teaspoon ground cinnamon
2 tablespoons red currant jelly

**Preheat** oven to 325F (165C). Break matzos into a bowl and cover with water. Soak 2 minutes and drain.

In a large bowl, mix eggs and egg whites until blended. Stir in apples, pear, pineapple, raisins, sugar, lemon peel, lemon juice, cinnamon, and vanilla. Stir in matzos.

Place margarine in a 13″ × 9″ casserole dish. Heat in oven until melted. Swirl pan to coat with margarine. Pour excess margarine into fruit mixture. Pour fruit into casserole dish, spreading evenly. Sprinkle sugar-cinnamon mixture over top. Dot with currant jelly.

Bake 45 minutes or until top is golden and kugel is solid. Cut into squares to serve.

*Makes 10 to 12 servings.*

**Make-Ahead Tip**  Unbaked kugel may be covered and refrigerated overnight. Before baking, bring to room temperature.

# Frozen Strawberry Cloud

*When you're looking for a light, fruity, impressive dessert to follow a heavy meal, this
is it. It's wonderful for entertaining because it goes directly from freezer to table.
Because the egg whites are not cooked, use fresh eggs without cracks or pasteurized
eggs, if they are available.*

**MACAROON NUT CRUST:**
5 ounces soft almond macaroons, crumbled
   (1½ cups)
2 tablespoons unsalted pareve margarine
½ cup chopped pecans or walnuts

**STRAWBERRY FILLING:**
2 large egg whites
1 cup sugar
2 cups sliced fresh strawberries
1 tablespoon lemon juice
1 teaspoon vanilla extract

**STRAWBERRY SAUCE:**
1 (10-oz.) package frozen sliced strawberries,
   defrosted slightly
3 tablespoons frozen undiluted orange juice
   concentrate or 2 tablespoons orange marmalade
1 tablespoon currant jelly
1 cup sliced fresh strawberries

**Make crust:** In a food processor with the metal
blade, process macaroons and margarine until
coarsely ground. Add nuts and process until mixture
holds together. Press into bottom of a 10-inch
springform pan.

**Make filling:** Place egg whites, sugar, strawberries,
lemon juice, and vanilla in a large bowl. With
electric mixer on low speed, mix egg-white mixture
until blended. Increase speed to high and mix until
stiff peaks form when beaters are withdrawn, 10 to
15 minutes. Pour into crust. Cover and freeze until
firm, a minimum of 6 hours.

**Make sauce:** Place slightly defrosted strawberries
and orange juice concentrate or marmalade in
food processor with metal blade. Process until pureed.
Add currant jelly and process until blended.
Remove to a bowl and stir in sliced berries. Refrigerate
until serving.

   Serve torte directly from freezer. It will not become
too frozen to cut. Cut into wedges and serve
with sauce.

*Makes 12 servings.*

**Make-Ahead Tips** The torte may be frozen up to
3 weeks, tightly covered.

   The sauce may be covered and refrigerated overnight.

# Chocolate Nut Torte

*One of the most popular desserts in my* Dessert Lover's Cookbook *is this sensational torte prepared in a flash in the food processor. It's made without flour, so it's perfect for Passover. Butter can be used for a dairy meal.*

## TORTE:
4 ounces semisweet chocolate, chopped (4 squares)
1¾ cups pecans or walnuts (about 7 oz.)
2 tablespoons plus ½ cup sugar
½ cup (1 stick) unsalted pareve margarine
3 large eggs
1 tablespoon orange juice, Grand Marnier, or rum

## CHOCOLATE GLAZE & GARNISH:
6 ounces semisweet chocolate, chopped (6 squares)
6 tablespoons unsalted pareve margarine
20 to 22 pecan halves, baked at 350F (175C) 10 to 15 minutes or until toasted

**Make torte:** Preheat oven to 375F (190C). Grease an 8-inch round layer cake pan. Cut a circle of parchment or waxed paper to fit bottom. Grease paper. Melt chocolate in microwave-safe dish in a microwave or in top of double boiler over simmering water. Cool slightly. Place nuts and 2 tablespoons sugar in food processor fitted with the metal blade. Pulse until nuts are ground. Remove to a bowl. Place margarine and remaining ½ cup sugar in food processor. Process until blended. Pour in melted chocolate and process until smooth. Add eggs and juice or liqueur. Process until combined. Scrape down sides of bowl and add nuts. Pulse 2 or 3 times to combine.

Pour into prepared pan. Bake 25 minutes. It will be soft, but will firm up as it cools. Remove to rack and cool 20 minutes. Invert onto rack. Remove paper and cool completely.

**Make glaze and garnish:** Up to 1 day or several hours before serving, line a small baking sheet with waxed paper; set aside. Place cake on a rack over another baking sheet. Melt chocolate and margarine in a microwave-safe bowl in a microwave or a small saucepan over low heat, stirring until smooth. Dip half of each pecan into chocolate and place on paper-lined pan. Refrigerate until set. If glaze is too thin to coat the cake, set it aside until it thickens slightly. Pour glaze into middle of cake, tilting the cake so the glaze runs down the sides. Use a knife dipped in hot water to smooth the sides, if necessary. Do not touch up the top or the knife marks will show. Arrange a border of chocolate-dipped pecans around the top edge of the cake.

*Makes 8 servings.*

**Make-Ahead Tips** The unglazed torte may be stored at room temperature, wrapped in foil, up to 2 days or frozen up to 1 month. Defrost wrapped cake in refrigerator.

The glazed torte may be kept at room temperature, uncovered, overnight.

Recipe reprinted from *The Dessert Lover's Cookbook*, Harper/Collins, © 1983.

# FAMILY FESTIVITIES

## Mother's Day Breakfast in Bed

---

### MENU

*Mother's Eye-Opener*
*Grapefruit Baskets with Orange-Blossom Fruit Salad*

*Maple Almond Omelet Soufflé or*
*Mexican Omelet or*
*Banana Pancakes or*
*Baked Cinnamon French Toast with Cinnamon Syrup*

*Peanut Butter & Jelly Muffins or*
*Honey-Glazed Pineapple Bran Muffins*

---

I'm sure that when Woodrow Wilson proclaimed the second Sunday in May a national holiday to commemorate mothers, he had the best intentions. He set aside one day each year to pamper those of us who work so hard to raise healthy, well-adjusted children. However, when my four children were growing up, I had serious doubts that he achieved his goal.

My kids' annual gift to me was breakfast in bed. After an hour and a half of waiting, four beaming faces would appear at my door, arms extended with food. They would peer over me while I cheerfully swallowed blackened French toast, charred muffins, and scorched omelets. Even the Cocoa Puffs were burnt, or was that merely the melted marshmallows floating on top?

Necessity being the mother of invention, I developed recipes simple enough for kids to prepare. Baked Cinnamon French Toast and Banana Pancakes are almost foolproof, and Peanut Butter & Jelly Muffins begin with buttermilk baking mix. Other recipes, such as Maple Almond Omelet Soufflé, may need Dad's assistance.

The dishes in this menu are wonderful in or out of bed, any day of the week, but especially for a relaxed Sunday brunch. The two omelets each have an original twist: one is sweetened with maple syrup and the other has the crunch of tortillas.

Each of the entrees in this menu serves two to four.

# Mother's Eye-Opener

*Turn any day into a holiday by beginning it with this frosty, thick, and fruity drink. If you're the Mom, you deserve the rum!*

1½ cups evaporated regular or skim milk
1 (6-oz.) can frozen orange or tangerine juice concentrate, defrosted slightly
1½ cups cubed fresh pineapple (about ½ pineapple)
1 ripe banana, peeled
6 to 7 ice cubes
¾ cup dark rum (optional)
Orange slices for decoration (optional)

**P**lace evaporated milk, juice concentrate, pineapple, banana, ice cubes, and rum, if using, in a blender container. Blend until thick and smooth. Pour into stemmed glasses. Decorate with an orange slice, if desired.

*Makes 4 (8-oz.) servings.*

**Variation**   To make a Champagne Eye-Opener, mix all ingredients, except rum and orange slices, in a blender. Fill glasses half full. Fill rest of glass with Champagne.

---

# Grapefruit Baskets

*Tied up with ribbons to match your theme, these fruit-filled baskets make a lovely introduction to a brunch, lunch, or shower. One grapefruit makes two baskets.*

2 medium to large grapefruit
Ribbon to tie handles
Orange-Blossom Fruit Salad (opposite)

**C**ut grapefruit in half. To make a handle, insert 2 wooden picks into the grapefruit peel about ¼ inch down from the cut edge, spacing them about ¼ inch apart. Repeat on the opposite side with two more wooden picks. Place the grapefruit on its side and cut a ¼-inch slice, stopping at the wooden picks. Repeat on opposite side. The slice should remain attached between the wooden picks. Remove picks. Using a grapefruit knife, scoop out all fruit, leaving a shell. Reserve fruit for salad.

Before serving, fill baskets with fruit salad. To make handles, pull cut strips of grapefruit up from each side and tie together at the top with ribbon.

*Makes 4 baskets.*

**Make-Ahead Tip**   Grapefruit shells may be refrigerated overnight, covered with a damp towel.

# Orange-Blossom Fruit Salad

*Most of the fruits in this salad are available year-round. Feel free to stir in seasonal fruits such as melon balls, berries, sliced peaches, or nectarines before serving.*

¾ cup seedless grapes
¾ cup 1-inch pieces fresh pineapple
½ cup orange segments, chopped into 1-inch pieces
½ cup grapefruit segments, chopped into 1-inch pieces
1 apple, peeled, cored, and chopped into 1-inch pieces
1 teaspoon grated orange peel
2 tablespoons orange juice
2 tablespoons sugar
2 tablespoons kirsch or orange-flavored liqueur (optional)
½ cup small whole or sliced strawberries

Place grapes, pineapple, oranges, grapefruit, and apples in a medium-size bowl. Mix orange peel, orange juice, sugar, and liqueur, if using, in a small bowl. Pour over fruit. Cover and refrigerate 1 hour or up to overnight.

Before serving, stir in strawberries.

*Makes 4 servings.*

# Maple Almond Omelet Soufflé

*When I was a young bride living on an army post in southern France, a very special friend and generous woman named Gisela Weidt took me under her wing. She loved to cook and became the inspiration for my career. This light-as-air combination of pancake and omelet comes from her.*

3 eggs, separated
3 tablespoons maple syrup
2 tablespoons regular, low-fat, or nonfat buttermilk or cream
½ teaspoon vanilla extract
1 tablespoon butter or margarine
¼ cup sliced almonds
Maple syrup for serving

Preheat oven to 350F (175C). In a bowl with electric mixer, beat egg yolks until thick and creamy. Mix in maple syrup, buttermilk, and vanilla. In another bowl, beat egg whites on high speed until soft peaks form. Fold whites into yolk mixture.

Melt butter or margarine in an 8- to 9-inch omelet pan with an ovenproof handle. (Or cover the handle with a double thickness of foil.) Sprinkle almonds over bottom. Spoon egg mixture over almonds. Cook over low heat until sides begin to brown and the underside is golden when lifted with a spatula, about 5 minutes. Be careful not to burn the almonds on the bottom.

Transfer pan to oven and bake 5 to 8 minutes, or until top is puffed and browned. Slide omelet onto serving plate, flipping top half over bottom to fold in half. Serve with additional syrup.

*Makes 2 servings.*

# Mexican Omelet

*This omelet has bite-size tortilla pieces in the eggs and is filled with creamy guacamole.*

**GUACAMOLE FILLING:**

½ cup chopped avocado
¼ cup regular or low-fat sour cream
1 tablespoon chopped canned green chiles
1 tablespoon chopped green onion
1 teaspoon lemon juice
Dash Tabasco sauce

**OMELET:**

3 large eggs
4 egg whites
Dash salt
4 teaspoons butter or margarine
1 corn tortilla, cut into bite-size pieces
½ cup shredded regular or low-fat Monterey Jack cheese (about 2 oz.)

**Make filling:**  In a small bowl, mix avocado, sour cream, chiles, green onion, lemon juice, and Tabasco sauce. Set aside.

**Make omelet:**  Preheat oven to 325F (165C). Mix eggs, egg whites, and salt until blended. Melt 2 teaspoons of the butter or margarine in a 7- to 8-inch omelet pan with an ovenproof handle. (Or cover handle with a double thickness of foil.) Add half the tortilla pieces and cook until soft. Pour in half the eggs and cook 2 to 3 minutes, lifting eggs to allow uncooked portion to flow underneath. Do not cook until firm; eggs should be very soft because they will continue to cook in the oven.

Sprinkle top with half the cheese. Spread half the filling over half the omelet. Place pan in oven and bake 5 to 7 minutes or until cheese is melted. Slide onto plate, folding top half over filling. Repeat for second omelet.

*Makes 2 omelets.*

# Banana Pancakes

*One morning I made these for my children, who knew I was testing them for this book. After the first bite, there was complete silence. Then my oldest, Cheryl, said, "But Mom, how will your readers know that these are not just pancakes?"*

¾ cup whole-wheat flour
¼ cup all-purpose flour
⅓ cup all-bran cereal
2 teaspoons baking powder
Dash of salt
1¼ cups regular, low-fat, or nonfat milk
2 tablespoons vegetable oil
1 medium-size banana, finely chopped (about ¾ cup)
Syrup for serving

In a medium-size bowl, stir together flours, cereal, baking powder, and salt. Stir in milk and oil. The batter will be slightly lumpy. Stir in banana. Heat a lightly greased griddle until hot. Using a scant ¼ cup per pancake, drop batter onto griddle. Cook until bubbles appear and undersides are golden. Turn and cook until bottoms are golden. Serve immediately with syrup.

*Makes 12 pancakes.*

# Baked Cinnamon French Toast

*You can soak the bread in the cinnamon-scented batter for several minutes or overnight. Either way it will bake to golden crispness on the outside with a soft and spongy interior.*

6 to 8 slices egg, French, or sourdough bread, about ¾ inch thick
2 large eggs
2 egg whites
½ cup regular, low-fat, or nonfat milk
2 tablespoons sugar
⅛ teaspoon baking powder
¼ teaspoon ground cinnamon
1 teaspoon vanilla extract
Melted butter for serving (optional)
Cinnamon Syrup for serving (see below)

**P**lace bread on a rimmed baking sheet. In a medium-size bowl, whisk together the eggs, egg whites, milk, sugar, baking powder, cinnamon, and vanilla. Slowly pour egg mixture over bread, turning to coat both sides completely. Bake immediately or cover and refrigerate overnight.

Before serving, preheat oven to 450F (230C). Generously grease a baking sheet or spray with nonstick cooking spray (not the cushioned variety because they don't brown). Place bread on baking sheet about 2 inches apart. Bake 6 to 9 minutes or until bottoms are golden. Turn and bake 6 to 9 minutes longer or until both sides are golden brown. Transfer to plates, top with butter, if desired, and drizzle with Cinnamon Syrup. Pass remaining syrup.

*Makes 6 to 8 slices.*

# Cinnamon Syrup

*You may use supermarket syrup out of habit, but once you make this version in the microwave, you may never be satisfied with the bottled variety again.*

1 cup golden-brown sugar
½ cup light corn syrup
¼ cup water
½ teaspoon ground cinnamon
½ cup regular, low-fat, or nonfat plain yogurt

**I**n a medium-size microwave-safe bowl, stir together brown sugar, syrup, water, cinnamon, and evaporated milk. Microwave, uncovered, on HIGH (100 percent) 2 to 4 minutes or until boiling.

Stir and microwave on HIGH (100 percent) 1 to 2 minutes more or until thickened slightly and bubbling gently. Whisk in yogurt. Cool at least 30 minutes. Syrup will thicken as it cools. Serve warm or at room temperature.

*Makes 1⅓ cups.*

**Make-Ahead Tip** Syrup may be poured into a jar with a lid and refrigerated up to 1 week.

# Peanut Butter & Jelly Muffins

*Peanut butter replaces butter in these soft, fluffy muffins. The jelly is spooned onto the top, but sinks to the center while they bake. My children used to make these for me every Mother's Day. I was lucky to get one, because they devoured them so fast.*

2 large eggs
1 cup water
6 tablespoons peanut butter
1 teaspoon vanilla extract
1⅓ cups buttermilk biscuit mix
⅔ cup wheat germ
½ cup sugar
6 teaspoons strawberry or raspberry jelly
Jam or jelly for serving (optional)

Preheat oven to 375F (190C). Grease or line 12 (2½-inch) muffin cups with cupcake papers. In a bowl or food processor with the metal blade, mix or pulse eggs, water, peanut butter, and vanilla until blended. Add biscuit mix, wheat germ, and sugar. Mix or process until dry ingredients are moistened. Do not overmix. Spoon batter into muffin cups, filling three-fourths full. Top each with ½ teaspoon jelly. Bake 20 to 25 minutes or until puffed and golden brown.

Serve warm or at room temperature. Top with a dollop of jam or jelly, if desired.

*Makes 12 muffins.*

**Make-Ahead Tip** Muffins may be stored, tightly covered, overnight or frozen up to 1 month.

# Honey-Glazed Pineapple Bran Muffins

*Crushed pineapple and a touch of honey make these healthful muffins very moist and a little sweet.*

1 large egg or 2 egg whites
2 tablespoons vegetable oil
2 tablespoons honey
¾ cup regular, low-fat, or nonfat buttermilk
¼ cup whole-wheat flour
⅓ cup all-purpose flour
¼ cup sugar
1½ cups all-bran cereal
¼ teaspoon salt
¼ teaspoon baking soda
Heaping ¼ teaspoon ground cinnamon
¼ cup raisins
¼ cup canned crushed pineapple, well drained
¼ cup honey for glaze
Butter for serving (optional)

Preheat oven to 400F (205C). Grease or spray 12 (2½-inch) muffin cups. In a bowl or food processor with the metal blade, mix egg, oil, honey, and buttermilk until blended. Add flours, sugar, cereal, salt, baking soda, and cinnamon. Mix or pulse until dry ingredients are moistened; do not overmix. Lightly mix or pulse in raisins and pineapple. Spoon into muffin cups, filling three-fourths full. Bake 18 to 20 minutes or until a wooden pick inserted into center comes out clean. Let cool 10 minutes and remove from pan.

Melt honey in small saucepan on top of stove or in microwave. Let stand until thickened slightly. Brush over top of warm muffins. Serve warm with butter, if desired.

*Makes 10 to 12 muffins.*

**Make-Ahead Tip** Muffins may be stored, tightly wrapped, overnight or frozen up to 1 month. Reheat before serving.

# Father's Day Seafood Supper

---

**MENU**

*Baked Blue-Cheese Spread with Chutney*

*Spinach Mushroom Salad with Amaretto Vinaigrette*

*Seafood Brochettes with Oriental Sesame Marinade or*
*Fillet of Fish in Parchment or*
*Honey-Mustard—Glazed Salmon*
*Creamy Potato Puff*
*Summer Squash with Tomatoes, Corn & Mushrooms*

*Frozen Chocolate Almond Torte*

WINE RECOMMENDATION:
*A crisp, dry sauvignon (fumé) blanc, or a spicy white wine such as a gewürztraminer*

---

For Father's Day, take the dad in your life out—outside that is—to his own backyard. Reservations are unnecessary. There are no hour-long waits. Every dish is prepared to order. You know the ingredients are fresh. Service is superb. And the price is right.

In deference to all those dads who love to fish, here are three great ways to prepare the bounty of their catch. If he fancies himself King of the Grill, then Seafood Brochettes with Oriental Sesame Marinade or Honey-Mustard—Glazed Salmon offer you an opportunity to treat him at his own game. Serve the honored guest his favorite libation, while you stoke the coals and grill the fish. For a dish that requires little cleanup, wrap fish fillets, vegetables, and a creamy tarragon sauce in parchment or foil packets. Then bake and serve right in the paper, eliminating all dirty bowls and saucepans.

If Dad is nuts over chocolate, he'll swoon over the chunky Frozen Chocolate Almond Torte. It must be prepared and frozen at least a day in advance, leaving you free to share a happy, hassle-free meal with your man of the hour.

This menu serves six to eight.

# Baked Blue-Cheese Spread with Chutney

*When you drain yogurt for three or four hours, it becomes thick like cream cheese and can be used as a low-fat or nonfat replacement for the cheese. Bake this mild, creamy blue-cheese mixture in a wide mold or dish, so you'll have room to frost it with chutney.*

1 cup plain regular, low-fat, or nonfat yogurt
8 ounces (1 cup) regular or light cream cheese
4 ounces mild blue cheese
2 large eggs
½ teaspoon Worcestershire sauce
½ teaspoon salt or to taste
Pepper to taste
½ to ¾ cup chutney such as Major Grey's Mango for serving
Crackers or bread rounds for serving

**Place** a funnel or strainer over a medium-size bowl. Line it with a double thickness of cheesecloth or a paper coffee filter. Spoon in yogurt and cover with plastic wrap. Place in refrigerator at least 4 hours or overnight. Discard liquid in bowl.

Preheat oven to 325F (165C). Grease a 2-cup shallow mold or soufflé dish. Place thickened yogurt in food processor with the metal blade. Add cream cheese, blue cheese, eggs, Worcestershire sauce, salt, and pepper. Process until smooth, scraping sides of bowl. Spoon mixture into prepared dish. Bake 35 to 40 minutes or until sides pull away slightly and top feels firm, but not solid. Cool slightly, cover, and refrigerate until chilled or up to 4 days.

Before serving, invert spread onto a platter and remove mold. Finely chop large pieces of fruit in chutney. Spread as much chutney as desired on top of cheese. Serve with bread rounds or crackers.

*Makes 2 cups spread.*

**Make-Ahead Tip**   The baked spread, in its dish and covered, can be refrigerated up to 4 days.

---

# Spinach Mushroom Salad with Amaretto Vinaigrette

*The mellow flavor of Amaretto adds a subtle sweetness to this spinach salad.*

Amaretto Vinaigrette (see below)
1 pound regular or turkey bacon, diced
10 ounces stemmed and trimmed spinach (about 8 cups packed)
½ pound mushrooms, thinly sliced
1 small red onion, thinly sliced

**AMARETTO VINAIGRETTE:**
1 seedless orange
2 medium-size garlic cloves, peeled
1 teaspoon dry mustard
¾ teaspoon Worcestershire sauce
1 tablespoon plus 1 teaspoon Amaretto liqueur
4 to 5 tablespoons fresh lemon juice
3 tablespoons vegetable oil
5 tablespoons plain regular, low-fat, or nonfat yogurt
Salt and pepper to taste

**Make vinaigrette:**   Peel orange and place segments in blender container. (There is no need to remove all the white membrane.) Add garlic and process until pureed. Add mustard, Worcestershire sauce, Amaretto, 4 tablespoons lemon juice, and oil. Mix until blended. Remove to a bowl and whisk in yogurt. Season with salt, pepper, and lemon juice to taste.

**Prepare salad:**   Cook bacon on top of stove or in microwave until crisp. Drain on paper towels. Place spinach in a large bowl. Before serving, add bacon, mushrooms, and onions. Pour over as much dressing as desired and toss well.

*Makes 8 servings.*

**Make-Ahead Tip**   Vinaigrette may be refrigerated up to 2 days. Stir well before using.

Serve a *Mother's Day Breakfast in Bed* with easy-to-prepare: Grapefruit Baskets with Orange Blossom Fruit Salad, (pages 44 and 45), Mexican Omelet (page 46), and Honey-Glazed Pineapple Bran Muffins (page 48).

# Seafood Brochettes with Oriental Sesame Marinade

*I like to keep a jar of this flavorful marinade in the refrigerator to use with any type of fish. After marinating one to three hours, the fish can be grilled or broiled for a quick dinner or important party. To make brochettes, be sure to cut the fish into pieces of the same size, so they will get done at the same time.*

## ORIENTAL SESAME MARINADE:

1-inch cube ginger root, peeled (about 1 tablespoon minced)
3 garlic cloves, peeled
¼ cup Oriental sesame oil
¼ cup vegetable oil
¼ cup soy sauce
¼ cup rice wine vinegar
2 tablespoons dry sherry
1 tablespoon honey

## SEAFOOD BROCHETTES:

12 ounces tuna, swordfish, halibut, or shark
1¼ pounds scallops (about 24 medium)
1 pound extra-large shrimp, peeled and deveined (about 24)

**Make marinade:** In a food processor with the metal blade, process ginger root and garlic until minced. Add sesame oil, vegetable oil, soy sauce, vinegar, sherry, and honey. Process until blended.

**Prepare brochettes:** Cut fish steaks into 1-inch cubes. If scallops are large, cut in half. Alternate shrimp, scallops, and fish cubes on 8 skewers, about 12 inches long. Place in a 13″ × 9″ glass baking dish. (Do not marinate in a metal pan.) Reserve ⅓ cup marinade. Pour remaining marinade over fish. Turn to coat all sides. Cover with plastic wrap and refrigerate 2 to 3 hours, turning two or three times.

Prepare coals. Place grill rack 3 to 4 inches from coals and grease rack. When coals are hot, grill brochettes 3 to 4 minutes on each side, basting with reserved marinade, until fish is almost cooked through. Don't overcook; the fish will continue to cook after it's removed from the heat. The brochettes may be broiled under a preheated broiler as close to the heat source as possible.

*Makes 8 servings.*

**Make-Ahead Tip** The marinade may be poured into a jar and refrigerated up to 1 month. Bring to room temperature before pouring over fish.

For a special father, a *Father's Day Seafood Supper:* Spinach Mushroom Salad with Amaretto Vinaigrette, (page 50), Seafood Brochettes with Oriental Sesame Marinade (above), Creamy Potato Puff, (page 53), and Summer Squash with Tomatoes, Corn & Mushrooms (page 53).

# Fillet of Fish in Parchment

*Cooking fish in a package, either wrapped in parchment or foil, produces a dramatic, moist entree. Cut an ✕ in the top and let guests open their own packet. This allows the fragrant juices to remain inside until the last possible moment.*

Tarragon Mustard Sauce (see below)
6 (4- to 6-oz.) fillets of orange roughy, sole, mahimahi, or other flaky white fish
Salt and pepper
6 ripe plum tomatoes, thinly sliced
¾ cup shredded zucchini, patted dry on paper towels
Fresh tarragon and lemon wedges for garnish (optional)

**TARRAGON MUSTARD SAUCE:**
⅓ cup plain regular, low-fat, or nonfat yogurt
¼ cup regular or low-fat mayonnaise
3 tablespoons Dijon mustard
3 garlic cloves, minced
1 tablespoon chopped fresh tarragon or ¾ teaspoon dried leaf tarragon
2 teaspoons fresh lemon juice
1½ teaspoons Pernod (optional)

**Make sauce:** In a small bowl, stir all ingredients together.

Cut 6 pieces of parchment paper or foil into about 15-inch squares. Fold each in half. Cut each into half a heart, about 15 inches high and 15 inches wide. Rinse fish and dry well. Open a heart and place a fillet on one half of the paper next to center fold. Season lightly with salt and pepper. Spread with 2 tablespoons sauce. Top with 5 to 6 tomato slices, overlapping them slightly. Sprinkle with zucchini. Season lightly with salt and pepper. Fold paper in half to cover fish. Seal by starting at round end, rolling and crimping edges tightly together, making sure the edges are tightly sealed. Repeat with remaining fish. Place packets on two large baking sheets, overlapping them slightly, if necessary.

Before serving, place one oven rack on bottom rung and the other in the lower third of oven. Preheat oven to 500F (260C). Bake packets 10 minutes, reversing positions after 5 minutes. Parchment should be puffed and browned. Cut an ✕ in the top with scissors and fold back corners of ✕. Garnish with tarragon sprigs and lemon wedges, if desired.

*Makes 6 servings.*

**Make-Ahead Tips** Sauce may be covered and refrigerated up to 2 days.

Fish packets may be refrigerated up to 4 hours before baking.

---

# Honey-Mustard–Glazed Salmon

*For fish that's caramelized and crunchy on the outside, flaky and succulent within, here is an amazingly easy means to a delectable end.*

6 (5- to 8-oz.) salmon fillets, skinned, or 1 whole salmon or piece (about 4 to 6 lbs.), skinned, butterflied, and boned
6 tablespoons butter or margarine
1 tablespoon honey
3 tablespoons coarse-grain mustard
2 tablespoons Dijon mustard

Prepare coals. Heavily grease grill rack and place 4 to 6 inches from coals. Wipe fish dry. In a small skillet or microwave-safe bowl, melt butter or margarine. Stir in honey and mustards. Brush mustard mixture on one side of fish. If using whole fish or a large piece of fish, brush mustard mixture on both sides of fish, and place fish in a hinged grill basket.

When coals are hot, grill fish mustard side down 3 to 5 minutes, basting occasionally. Turn and grill on other side 3 to 5 minutes, basting occasionally, until fish is well browned and flesh at thickest part begins to turn opaque when flaked with the tip of a sharp knife. Serve immediately.

*Makes 6 servings.*

# Creamy Potato Puff

*Whipping egg whites and cream cheese into mashed potatoes and baking them results in an exceptionally light and fluffy casserole.*

4 baking potatoes (about 10 oz. each)
1 (8-oz.) package regular or light cream cheese, cut into cubes, at room temperature
1 medium-size onion, finely chopped
3 large egg whites
3 tablespoons all-purpose flour
¼ cup regular or low-fat milk
1 teaspoon salt or to taste
¼ teaspoon pepper or to taste
1 (2.8-oz.) can French-fried onions

Grease a round 1½- to 2-quart casserole or soufflé dish. Place potatoes on a microwave-safe plate. Microwave on HIGH (100 percent) 14 to 18 minutes, rotating every 4 minutes, until tender when pierced with a knife. Or, bake in a conventional oven at 450F (230C) 50 to 60 minutes. Cool slightly and scrape potatoes into a bowl. With electric mixer, mix until mashed. Add cream cheese and beat until smooth. Add onion, egg whites, flour, milk, salt, and pepper. Mix until light and fluffy. Spoon into prepared dish. Sprinkle onion rings over the top. Cover with foil.

Before serving, preheat oven to 325F (165C). Bake casserole, covered, 20 minutes if at room temperature, 35 minutes if chilled. Remove foil and bake 20 more minutes or until potatoes are hot and top is golden and crusty.

*Makes 8 servings.*

**Make-Ahead Tip**  The unbaked casserole may be refrigerated overnight.

# Summer Squash with Tomatoes, Corn & Mushrooms

*Show off summer's bounty with this colorful vegetable medley mounded into hollowed-out zucchini or pattypan squash.*

4 medium-size zucchini (about 2 pounds) or 8 medium-size pattypan squash
1 medium-size tomato
1 tablespoon finely chopped fresh basil or 1 teaspoon dried leaf basil
1 large garlic clove, minced
¼ pound mushrooms, chopped
½ cup fresh or frozen corn kernels, thawed
2 teaspoons balsamic vinegar
Salt and pepper to taste
3 tablespoons regular or low-fat sour cream
1 cup shredded regular or low-fat Swiss cheese (4 oz.)

Place squash in a microwave-safe pie dish or large plate. Cover with vented plastic wrap and microwave on HIGH (100 percent) 4 to 8 minutes, rotating after 3 minutes, until tender, but still firm when pierced with a fork. Timing depends on microwave and size of squash. If using zucchini, cut off stem. Cut in half lengthwise. Scoop out pulp, leaving ¼-inch shells; reserve pulp. If using pattypan squash, scoop out enough pulp to make a cavity for the filling. If necessary, cut a thin slice off the bottom so they stand straight. Drain shells upside down on paper towels.

Chop squash pulp. Place in a medium-size bowl. Cut tomato in half crosswise. Squeeze out seeds and chop. Stir tomato, basil, garlic, mushrooms, corn, vinegar, salt, and pepper into chopped squash. Stir in sour cream and cheese. Spoon into shells, mounding the tops.

Before serving, preheat oven to 350F (175C). Place squash on a baking sheet and bake, uncovered, 10 to 15 minutes if at room temperature, 15 to 20 minutes if chilled.

*Makes 8 servings.*

**Make-Ahead Tip**  Stuffed squash may be refrigerated, covered, overnight.

# Frozen Chocolate Almond Torte

*When you want rave reviews, fold chunks of crisp meringue cookies and chocolate-covered almonds into partially frozen vanilla cream, spoon into a chocolate cookie crust, freeze, and serve proudly.*

**CHOCOLATE WAFER CRUST:**
16 chocolate wafer cookies, crushed
3 tablespoons melted butter or margarine

**MERINGUE COOKIES:**
4 egg whites, at room temperature
1 cup sugar, preferably superfine

**CHOCOLATE ALMOND FILLING:**
1 cup whipping cream
1 cup regular or low-fat sour cream
1 tablespoon vanilla extract
½ cup chopped almonds
8 ounces semisweet chocolate (8 squares)

**Make crust:** In a food processor with the metal blade, process cookies into crumbs (about 1 cup crumbs). Mix in butter or margarine. Press into bottom of an 8-inch springform pan.

**Make cookies:** Preheat oven to 300F (150C). Line a large baking sheet with waxed or parchment paper. In a large bowl with electric mixer on high speed, beat egg whites until soft peaks form. Gradually add sugar, 1 tablespoon at a time, beating constantly, until stiff, glossy peaks form, about 10 minutes. Drop large dollops of meringue onto paper-lined baking sheet. Spread to about 3-inch rounds, ½ inch thick. Bake 55 to 60 minutes or until firm in center. Cool and cut into ½-inch pieces.

**Make filling:** In a large bowl with electric mixer, beat whipping cream until stiff peaks form. Add sour cream and vanilla and beat on high speed until mixture is stiff. Place bowl of cream in freezer. Freeze, uncovered, until top is solid and icy, and middle is cold, but still soft, 60 to 90 minutes.

Meanwhile, toast almonds in an oven or toaster oven at 350F (175C) until golden, 10 to 15 minutes, stirring occasionally. Melt chocolate in top of double boiler over hot water or in microwave. Stir in almonds. When cream is ready, reheat chocolate until hot. Pour hot chocolate over cold cream and fold together. Small slivers of chocolate will form. Fold in meringue pieces. Pour into crust. Cover tightly with foil and freeze until firm.

Before serving, remove sides of springform pan and cut torte into wedges.

*Makes 10 to 12 servings.*

**Make-Ahead Tip** The torte may be frozen, tightly wrapped, up to 1 month.

# Saluting the Graduate

---

**M E N U**

*Golden Celebration Punch*

*Classic Pizza the Easy Way*

*Fettucine Bolognese or*
*Cheesy Spaghetti or*
*Capellini with Broccoli Sauce*

*Antipasto Salad*

*Ice Cream or Frozen Yogurt Sundae Bar*
*Assorted Ice Cream or Yogurt*
*Peanut Butter Cup Sauce*
*Blueberry Sauce*
*Fatless Fudge Sauce*

---

Graduates come in all sizes, from nursery-school toddlers to grown-up MDs, and pasta and pizza please every age. Here is a selection of entrees for you to create your own menu to fit the sophistication of the crowd. Cheesy Spaghetti is perfect for the younger set, while adult palates will appreciate the refined blend of vegetables, garlic, and prosciutto in the Bolognese sauce. For the pasta, use dried or fresh, either homemade or purchased from the refrigerator section of the supermarket or specialty store.

Pizza remains on the top of the list of Americans' favorite foods. For the easiest crust, either purchase one pre-prepared from the supermarket or make your own with hot roll mix.

If you enjoy watching adults act like kids, put out a make-your-own sundae bar. Scoop ice cream or frozen yogurt into balls, freeze them ahead, and prepare the sauces in advance. This makes such a carefree dessert, you can almost forget you're the host.

These recipes serve eight.

# Golden Celebration Punch

*Sweet, golden, and fruity, this is as popular with the younger set as it is with grown-ups.*

2 cups water
2 cups sugar
1 cup pineapple juice
2 cups apricot nectar
1 cup orange juice
½ cup lemon juice
3 pints (6 cups) ginger ale, chilled
1 pint pineapple sherbet

In a medium-size saucepan over medium heat, bring water and sugar to a boil. Simmer 5 minutes or until sugar is dissolved. Cool.

In a large bowl or pitcher, mix pineapple juice, apricot nectar, orange juice, lemon juice, and sugar syrup. Stir well and refrigerate until chilled.

Before serving, pour fruit mixture into a punch bowl. Add ginger ale and top with scoops of sherbet.

*Makes 24 (4-oz.) servings.*

**Make-Ahead Tip** Punch base may be covered and refrigerated up to 2 days. Add ginger ale and sherbet just before serving.

# Classic Pizza the Easy Way

*Top a store-bought crust with a homemade tomato sauce that's richer and zestier than anything you can buy. The sauce recipe makes enough for two large pizzas — one to eat and one to freeze. You can then enjoy delicious pizza in less time and for less money than you can have it delivered.*

**TOMATO SAUCE:**
2 tablespoons olive oil
1 onion, chopped
3 garlic cloves, crushed
1 (28-oz.) can whole tomatoes, drained and
    chopped
¼ cup tomato paste
1 teaspoon dried leaf basil
½ teaspoon dried leaf oregano
1 teaspoon salt
Freshly ground pepper to taste
Tabasco sauce to taste

1 (15-inch) unbaked pizza shell

**TOPPINGS, USE ANY OR ALL AS DESIRED:**
1 (7½-oz.) can caponata (eggplant appetizer)
½ to ¾ pound regular or low-fat mozzarella cheese,
    shredded
¼ cup thinly sliced green bell pepper
4 ounces pepperoni, thinly sliced
⅓ cup sliced ripe olives, drained
½ (2-oz.) jar roasted red peppers or pimientos,
    drained and sliced

**Make sauce:** In a medium-size saucepan over medium heat, heat olive oil until hot. Add onion and garlic, and sauté until softened. Stir in chopped tomatoes, tomato paste, basil, and oregano. Simmer over medium heat, stirring occasionally, until sauce is reduced to a thick puree, about 30 minutes. Season with salt, pepper, and Tabasco sauce. This makes enough sauce for 2 (15-inch) pizzas.

Before serving, place oven rack on bottom rung. Preheat oven to 425 (220C). Spread half the sauce over crust. (Reserve remainder for a later time.) Spoon caponata over crust and sprinkle lightly with cheese. Layer some of the green bell pepper, the pepperoni, the olives, and some of the roasted red pepper alternately with cheese, ending with some of the olives and peppers. Bake 20 to 25 minutes or until crust is golden brown and sauce is bubbling.

*Makes 8 servings.*

**Make-Ahead Tips** The sauce may be refrigerated up to 1 week or frozen up to 1 month. Divide in half before freezing. Thaw in refrigerator overnight.

Pizza may be frozen. Underbake slightly. Reheat frozen at 425F (220C) 20 to 25 minutes.

# Fettucine Bolognese

*If you keep a batch of this robust sauce in your freezer, you can defrost it in the microwave in the same time it takes to boil pasta. Add a salad, and you have a dinner fit for your most discriminating guests.*

½ pound prosciutto
2 onions, peeled and quartered
2 small carrots, peeled and quartered
4 garlic cloves, peeled
3 stalks celery, quartered
3 tablespoons olive oil
½ pound lean ground pork
½ pound lean ground veal
1⅔ cups chicken broth
1½ cups dry red wine
1 (28-oz.) can whole tomatoes, undrained and
    chopped
1 (8-oz.) can tomato paste
½ teaspoon dried leaf oregano
½ teaspoon dried leaf thyme
1 teaspoon dried leaf basil
¼ cup whipping cream, at room temperature
1½ to 2 pounds fettucine or spaghetti
Freshly grated Parmesan cheese for serving

In a food processor with the metal blade, process prosciutto, onions, carrots, garlic, and celery until finely ground. In a large saucepan over medium-high heat, heat olive oil. Add ham mixture and sauté until golden, about 10 minutes. Stir in ground pork and veal. Cook, stirring and breaking up meat, until it is browned. Pour off excess fat.

Add broth and wine, and simmer 5 minutes. Stir in tomatoes with their juice, tomato paste, and herbs. Reduce heat and simmer, uncovered, stirring occasionally, 1 hour, or until thickened slightly and reduced by about one-fourth. This makes 9 cups sauce.

Bring a large pot of salted water to a boil. Stir cream into hot sauce and simmer until heated through. Adjust seasonings. Cook pasta as package directs; drain. Ladle some of the sauce into a large bowl. Top with pasta and remaining sauce. Toss well. Serve with Parmesan cheese.

*Makes 8 main-dish servings.*

**Make-Ahead Tip** The sauce improves in flavor if covered and refrigerated overnight. It may be refrigerated up to 2 days or frozen up to 3 months. If frozen, thaw in refrigerator overnight, reheat, and add cream before serving.

# Cheesy Spaghetti

*When my children were young, they begged me to make this spaghetti for every birthday party. "You know, Mom," they would say, "the one that's not gourmet."*

3 pounds lean ground beef
2 teaspoons salt or to taste
3 garlic cloves, minced
2 teaspoons dried leaf oregano
2 teaspoons dried leaf basil
4 (10½-oz.) cans tomato soup
1 (15-oz.) can tomato sauce
2 (1-lb.) packages spaghetti
1 pound mozzarella cheese, shredded

In a large saucepan over medium heat, sauté meat, stirring and breaking it up, until it is browned. Pour off fat. Stir in salt, garlic, oregano, basil, tomato soup, and tomato sauce. Cook, stirring oc- casionally, 15 minutes or until heated through and mixed well.

Cook spaghetti in a large pot of boiling salted wa- ter according to package directions. Stir cheese into sauce and cook over low heat, stirring constantly, until melted. Drain spaghetti and toss with sauce.

*Makes 12 to 14 servings.*

**Make-Ahead Tip**   Sauce, without cheese, may be refrigerated up to 2 days or frozen up to 1 month. If frozen, thaw overnight in the refrigerator; reheat before serving and stir in cheese.

---

# Capellini with Broccoli Sauce

*This is my most frequently prepared pasta dish. It's fast, pretty, and light. To save time, purchase cut-up broccoli flowerets from the supermarket salad bar or produce section.*

2 tablespoons olive oil
4 garlic cloves, minced
1 cup plus ¼ cup chicken or vegetable broth
¼ cup chopped fresh basil or 1 teaspoon dried leaf basil
½ teaspoon dried leaf oregano
Salt and pepper to taste
1 tablespoon cornstarch
3 cups broccoli flowerets, cut into ¾-inch pieces (about 8 oz.)
12 ounces dried capellini (angel hair) pasta, broken into thirds
½ cup freshly grated Parmesan cheese, plus extra for serving (optional)

Fill a large, deep saucepan with salted water and bring to a boil. Meanwhile, heat olive oil in a medium-size saucepan. Add garlic and sauté over medium heat until softened but not brown. Stir in 1 cup broth, basil, oregano, salt, and pepper. Simmer 2 minutes and remove from heat. Stir cornstarch and remaining ¼ cup broth together until dis- solved. Stir into sauce, return to heat, and bring to a boil, stirring constantly.

When water comes to a boil, add broccoli and pasta. Cook according to package directions until pasta is tender to the bite. Drain in a colander. Transfer pasta and broccoli to a bowl, add sauce and ½ cup Parmesan cheese, and toss well. Serve with additional Parmesan cheese, if desired.

*Makes 8 side-dish servings.*

# Antipasto Salad

*An antipasto salad doesn't need a recipe. It's a great way of using up all the leftover vegetables, cheeses, and cold meats in your refrigerator. Feel free to experiment.*

**ITALIAN DRESSING:**
2 garlic cloves, peeled
6 anchovy fillets (optional), rinsed
6 tablespoons V-8 vegetable juice or tomato juice
6 tablespoons olive oil
6 tablespoons red wine vinegar
2 tablespoons lemon juice
Salt and pepper to taste

**SALAD:**
1 head iceberg lettuce (about 1½ lbs.), torn into bite-size pieces
2 bunches romaine lettuce (about 2 lbs.), torn into bite-size pieces
2 medium-size zucchini, thinly sliced
1 cup sliced celery
½ cup chopped green onions
1 (4-oz.) can sliced ripe olives, drained
1 (8¾-oz.) can garbanzo beans, drained
1 (16-oz.) can cannellini or kidney beans, drained

**Make dressing:** In a food processor with the metal blade, process garlic and anchovies, if using, until minced. Add juice, olive oil, vinegar, and lemon juice, and process until blended. Season with salt and pepper to taste. Pour into a jar.

Before serving, place lettuces, zucchini, celery, green onions, olives, and beans into a large bowl. Add as much dressing as desired to coat, and toss well.

*Makes 12 to 14 servings.*

**Make-Ahead Tip** The dressing may be refrigerated up to 1 week.

# Ice Cream or Frozen Yogurt Sundae Bar

*A sundae bar buffet is easy on the host or hostess and a treat for all ages. In addition to the sauces offered here, you might also serve Caramel Rum Sauce (with or without rum, page 6), and Fresh Berry Sauce (page 32).*

Here are some tips to set up your buffet:

- Offer two to three different types of ice cream or yogurt. Plan on 1 to 2 scoops per person.
- One quart of ice cream yields approximately 8 medium-size scoops.
- To make ice-cream balls in advance, line baking sheet with waxed paper. Scoop ice cream into balls and place on paper. Freeze until solid. Transfer to covered container, separating layers with waxed paper. Freeze up to one week.
- Serve a selection of at least three sauces.
- Plan on ¼ cup sauce per serving. If a recipe makes 2 cups sauce, it will be enough for 8 scoops of ice cream.

- Allow approximately 2 tablespoons whipped cream per serving: ½ pint whipping cream, whipped, serves 12.
- Offer a variety of condiments such as:
  Chopped walnuts or pecans
  Sliced almonds
  Coarsely crushed chocolate chip or Oreo cookies
  Toasted coconut
  M&M's candies
  Crushed English toffee

# Peanut Butter Cup Sauce

*My son Kenny is nuts about peanut butter. This outrageous sauce originated from his idea of topping an ice cream cone with a spoonful of peanut butter.*

1 pound Reese's peanut butter candies
1 cup whipping cream

**P**lace candy and cream in a medium-size microwave-safe bowl. Microwave, uncovered, on HIGH (100 percent) 2 to 4 minutes, stirring once, until melted.

*Makes 2 cups.*

**Make-Ahead Tip**    Sauce may be covered and refrigerated 1 week. Reheat in microwave until warm.

---

# Blueberry Sauce

*This is a little like eating blueberry pie à la mode, upside down.*

1 (12-oz.) package frozen blueberries or 1½ cups
    fresh blueberries
¼ cup sugar
¾ teaspoon ground cinnamon
¼ teaspoon ground nutmeg
½ teaspoon grated lemon peel

**B**ring blueberries, sugar, spices, and lemon peel to a boil in a medium-size saucepan over medium-high heat. Boil until sauce thickens slightly, stirring occasionally, about 10 minutes. Sauce will continue to thicken as it cools. Cool to room temperature.

*Makes 1½ cups.*

**Make-Ahead Tip**    Sauce may be covered and refrigerated up to 1 week. Bring to room temperature before serving.

---

# Fatless Fudge Sauce

*I developed this recipe when writing my cookbook* Entertaining on the Run. *It tastes so lush and decadent, everyone thinks it's loaded with cream and butter.*

¾ cup granulated sugar
1½ cups packed golden brown sugar
⅓ cup unsweetened cocoa powder
1¼ cups plain nonfat yogurt
Dash salt
1 tablespoon vanilla extract

**I**n a 12-cup (3-quart) microwave-safe bowl, stir granulated sugar, brown sugar, cocoa, yogurt, and salt together until thoroughly moistened. Microwave, uncovered, on HIGH (100 percent) 10 to 14 minutes without stirring, until bubbly, thickened, and syrupy. It will continue to thicken as it cools. Remove from microwave and stir in vanilla.

*Makes 2 cups.*

**Make-Ahead Tip**    Sauce may be refrigerated in a wide-mouth container up to 1 month. Reheat on top of stove or in microwave before serving.

Recipe reprinted from *Entertaining on the Run*, William Morrow and Co., © 1994.

# Sweet Sixteen Luncheon

## MENU

*Pineapple-Coconut Frappés*
*Avocado-Onion Dip*

*Mushroom-Ham Quiche Cups*
*Spinach Quiche Cups*
*Mixed-Up Salad with Salsa Dressing*

*Divine Devil's Food Cake*
*Banana Split Pie*

BEVERAGE RECOMMENDATION:
*Soft drinks and still and sparkling waters*

When I owned a cooking school/cookware shop in Los Angeles, I hosted all types of parties. The most popular were Sweet Sixteens and the most requested entree was Quiche Cups. I would demonstrate how to make and fill the crepe cups and serve them for lunch. The kids loved them and would tell me how much fun they had making them at home.

These days, many teenagers are vegetarians. The only meat in the menu is in the Mushroom-Ham Quiche Cups, and the ham can be eliminated or chicken substituted, if you like. The Mixed-Up Salad is dressed with a light but zippy dressing that has only three ingredients. The salad's name refers to more than the ingredients and the tossing!

Serve the Pineapple-Coconut Frappés and Avocado-Onion Dip as "ice-breakers" when the young guests arrive. Birthday parties call for a scrumptious birthday cake, and Divine Devil's Food Cake is designed for candles and singing. For this important occasion, gild the lily and serve the cake with a no-holds-barred Banana Split Pie.

This luncheon serves twelve.

# Pineapple-Coconut Frappés

*This frothy drink was a favorite with my teenage daughters and they served it at their own Sweet Sixteens. Make two batches.*

1½ cups pineapple juice
1 (8-oz.) can cream of coconut
1 cup fresh chopped pineapple
Ice cubes or crushed ice

Place juice, cream of coconut, and pineapple in blender container. Add enough ice to fill to 1 inch from top. Blend until smooth. Serve immediately.

*Makes 5 cups, about 8 servings.*

---

# Avocado-Onion Dip

*I thought the old standby onion soup dip had become passé until I added avocado to it and gave it a face-lift!*

3 large avocados, peeled, pitted, and chopped
½ cup regular or low-fat sour cream
2 tablespoons onion soup mix
Tabasco sauce to taste
1 medium-size tomato, chopped
Chips or raw vegetables for serving

In a medium-size bowl, mash avocados. Stir in sour cream, onion soup mix, Tabasco sauce, and tomato.

Add avocado pit in center and cover with a piece of plastic wrap directly on the surface to prevent it from turning brown. Refrigerate until chilled.

Remove avocado pit, stir well, and serve with chips or vegetables.

*Makes 2¾ cups; about 12 servings.*

---

# Mushroom-Ham Quiche Cups

*Crepes are topped with a cheesy quiche batter, pressed into muffin cups, and baked. Any type of cooked meat, seafood, or vegetables can be added to the batter. The filled cups can be frozen before they are baked, and then popped directly from the freezer into the oven.*

1 tablespoon olive oil
¼ pound mushrooms, coarsely chopped
¾ cup finely chopped green onions with tops
1 garlic clove, minced
3 egg whites
2 tablespoons all-purpose flour
½ cup regular or low-fat sour cream
½ pint (1 cup) regular or low-fat small-curd cottage cheese
¼ cup grated Parmesan cheese
½ cup shredded regular or low-fat Monterey Jack cheese (about 2 ounces)
½ cup finely chopped cooked ham
Tabasco sauce to taste
Salt and pepper to taste
12 (5-in.) Crepes for Quiche Cups (page 64)
Parmesan cheese for topping

Heat olive oil in a medium-size skillet. Add mushrooms, onions, and garlic, and sauté until soft. Set aside to cool. In a food processor with the metal blade or in a blender, mix egg whites, flour, sour cream, and cottage cheese until well blended. Remove to a bowl and stir in mushroom mixture, Parmesan cheese, Jack cheese, and ham. Season with Tabasco sauce, salt, and pepper.

Grease 12 (2½-inch) muffin cups. Lay crepes brown side up over cups. Spoon 2 heaping tablespoons cheese mixture onto center. Gently push into cups. They should be three-fourths full. Sprinkle tops with Parmesan cheese.

Preheat oven to 350F (175C). Bake cups 25 to 30 minutes or until golden brown. Do not overbake or quiche will be dry. Remove cups from muffin pans by inserting a small spatula or knife under cups and lifting them out.

*Makes 12 cups.*

**Variation**  Substitute ½ cup finely chopped smoked turkey or chicken for the ham.

**Make-Ahead Tip**  Filled crepe cups may be refrigerated, covered with foil, overnight or frozen up to 2 weeks. Do not defrost before baking. If frozen, bake 40 to 45 minutes.

## Spinach Quiche Cups

*This vegetarian quiche batter exemplifies the dynamic duo of spinach and cheese.*

3 large egg whites
2 tablespoons all-purpose flour
½ cup regular or low-fat sour cream
½ pint (1 cup) regular or low-fat small-curd cottage cheese
Dash nutmeg
¼ cup grated Parmesan cheese
½ cup shredded sharp regular or low-fat Cheddar cheese (about 2 oz.)
1 (10-oz.) package frozen chopped spinach, thawed, drained, and squeezed dry
Salt and pepper to taste
Tabasco sauce to taste
12 (5-in.) Crepes for Quiche Cups (page 64)
Additional Parmesan cheese for topping

In a food processor with the metal blade or in blender, mix egg whites, flour, sour cream, cottage cheese, and nutmeg until well blended. Remove to a bowl and stir in the ¼ cup Parmesan cheese, Cheddar cheese, and spinach. Season with salt, pepper, and Tabasco sauce.

Grease 12 (2½-inch) muffin cups. Lay crepes brown side up over cups. Spoon 2 heaping tablespoons cheese mixture onto center of each. Gently bring sides together and push into cups. They should be three-fourths full. Sprinkle tops with Parmesan cheese.

Preheat oven to 350F (175C). Bake filled cups 25 to 30 minutes or until golden brown. Do not overbake or quiche will be dry. Remove cups from muffin pans by inserting a small spatula or knife under cups and lifting them out.

*Makes 12 cups.*

**Make-Ahead Tip**  Filled crepe cups may be refrigerated, covered with foil, overnight or frozen up to 2 weeks. Do not defrost before baking. If frozen, bake 40 to 45 minutes.

# Crepes for Quiche Cups

*The addition of brandy to crepe batter is a trick I learned from a caterer many years ago. You can't taste it, but it has a magical tenderizing effect.*

1 egg
3 egg whites
1 cup regular or low-fat milk
¼ to ½ cup water
1 cup all-purpose flour
Dash salt
2 tablespoons brandy
2 tablespoons light olive oil or melted butter or
  margarine

In a blender container or food processor with the metal blade, process egg and egg whites, milk, ¼ cup water, flour, salt, brandy, and olive oil until smooth. Scrape down sides and blend again. Batter may be used immediately or covered and refrigerated overnight.

To make crepes to fit into 2½-inch muffin cups, you will need a 7-inch skillet that measures 5 inches across the bottom. If the pan is not nonstick, spray with nonstick cooking spray or brush with oil. Heat pan over medium-high heat until hot. Lift pan from heat and pour in 1 to 2 tablespoons batter, pouring out any excess. Quickly tilt pan so the batter covers the bottom in a very thin layer. If batter is too thick, thin with water. Return pan to heat and cook until underside of crepe is browned. Turn over with a spatula. Cook 1 to 2 minutes or until other side is browned slightly. Slide onto plate and continue with remaining batter.

*Makes 20 to 24 (5-inch) crepes.*

**Make-Ahead Tip** Crepes may be refrigerated 5 days or frozen. Stack with wax paper between them to keep them separate. Seal in plastic bag. Bring to room temperature before filling.

# Mixed-Up Salad with Salsa Dressing

*One day when my pantry was almost bare, my vegetarian daughter, Caryn, created this salad dressing. It only has three ingredients, but that's all it needs.*

**SALSA SALAD DRESSING:**
¾ cup mild salsa
½ cup regular, low-fat, or nonfat mayonnaise
⅓ cup V-8 vegetable juice or tomato juice

**SALAD:**
2 large heads romaine lettuce
1 head iceberg lettuce
1 large cucumber, peeled and coarsely chopped
1 pint cherry tomatoes, stemmed and halved
2 small avocados, peeled, pitted, and chopped
¾ cup sliced black olives, well drained
2 cups croutons

**Make dressing:** In a medium-size bowl, stir salsa, mayonnaise, and juice together until blended.

**Prepare salad:** Tear lettuce leaves into bite-size pieces. Wrap in paper towels, place in a plastic bag, and refrigerate until ready to use or overnight. Before serving, place lettuce in a large bowl. Add cucumber, tomatoes, avocados, olives, and croutons. Add as much dressing as desired and toss well.

*Makes 12 to 14 servings.*

**Make-Ahead Tip** Dressing may be covered and refrigerated for several days.

# Divine Devil's Food Cake

*The secret to making the richest, moistest, and greatest tasting chocolate cake is to add a can of beets (yes, beets!). This recipe first appeared in my dessert cookbook, and one reviewer described it as "the apogee of devil's food cakedom."*

## CAKE:
3 ounces unsweetened chocolate, chopped (3 squares)
1 (8¼-oz.) can sliced or chopped beets
½ cup (1 stick) unsalted butter or margarine
2½ cups packed golden brown sugar
3 large eggs
2 teaspoons vanilla extract
2 cups all-purpose flour
2 teaspoons baking soda
½ teaspoon salt
½ cup regular or low-fat buttermilk

## FROSTING:
4 ounces unsweetened chocolate, chopped (4 squares)
9 tablespoons half-and-half or whipping cream
1 tablespoon vanilla extract
3 tablespoons unsalted butter or margarine
Dash salt
3 cups sifted powdered sugar

**Make cake:** Preheat oven to 350F (175C). Grease 2 (9-inch) round layer cake pans. Dust with flour and shake out excess. Melt chocolate in double boiler or in a microwave-safe bowl in microwave. Set aside to cool slightly. Drain beet juice into small bowl. Chop beets with knife into very small pieces (do not use food processor). You should have ½ cup juice and 1 cup chopped beets. Stir beets into juice.

In a large bowl with electric mixer, cream butter, brown sugar, eggs, and vanilla on high speed until light and fluffy, about 5 minutes, scraping sides occasionally. Reduce speed to low and beat in melted chocolate.

Stir together flour, baking soda, and salt in a medium-size bowl. With mixer on low speed, alternately mix flour in fourths and buttermilk in thirds into chocolate mixture, beginning and ending with flour. Mix until incorporated, about 1 minute. Add beets and juice, and mix on medium speed until blended, about 1 minute. The batter will be thin with small pieces of beets.

Divide batter evenly between cake pans. Shake pans slightly to even out the tops. Bake in center of oven 30 to 35 minutes, or until a wooden pick inserted in center comes out clean and top springs back when lightly pressed with fingertips. To ensure even baking, it may be necessary to rotate the pans halfway through the baking time. Cool on wire racks 10 minutes. Place racks over top and invert cakes onto them. Cool completely.

**Make frosting:** In a large microwave-safe bowl, microwave chocolate, half-and-half, vanilla, butter, and salt, covered with a paper towel, on HIGH (100 percent) 2 to 4 minutes, stirring every minute until smooth. Stir in 1 cup of the powdered sugar at a time, until frosting is smooth. Use immediately; it hardens quickly. If it becomes too stiff, stir in hot water, a teaspoon at a time, until mixture is soft enough to spread.

Line a platter with 4 strips of waxed paper to catch any frosting. Place one cake layer bottom side down over waxed paper. Spread about a quarter of the frosting over cake. Top with second layer, bottom side up. Frost the sides and then the top. If you have extra frosting and wish to decorate the cake, put frosting into a small pastry bag fitted with a small star tip. Pipe a border of small rosettes around the top and bottom edge. When set, carefully remove waxed-paper strips.

*Makes 12 servings.*

**Make-Ahead Tips** Cake layers may be wrapped in foil and stored at room temperature overnight or frozen up to 1 month. Thaw, covered, at room temperature before frosting.

Frosted cake may be stored, uncovered, at room temperature overnight or refrigerated up to 2 days. Bring to room temperature before serving.

Recipe reprinted from *The Dessert Lover's Cookbook*, Harper/Collins, © 1983.

# Banana Split Pie

*This may sound like it's for kids, but I've never seen adults devour anything so fast.*
*Remember its great flavor for summer barbecues.*

1 cup vanilla wafer or shortbread cookie crumbs
2 to 3 tablespoons butter or margarine
1 pint vanilla ice cream or frozen yogurt
1 pint strawberry ice cream or frozen yogurt
1 pint chocolate ice cream or frozen yogurt
1 recipe Fatless Fudge Sauce (page 60) or 1 (10-oz.)
   jar chocolate fudge sauce
1 (10-oz.) jar strawberry ice cream topping
2 small bananas, sliced
1 cup sliced fresh strawberries
6 ounces English toffee, Heath Bars, or Skor bars

In food processor with the metal blade or in a small bowl, mix cookie crumbs and butter or margarine. Press into bottom of a 9-inch springform pan. Slightly thaw ice cream or yogurt. Alternate scoops, covering the bottom with different flavors. Drizzle heavily with fudge sauce and strawberry topping. Scatter banana and strawberry slices over and in between sauce and ice cream. Repeat with remaining ice cream, sauce, and fruit. Crush toffee coarsely with rolling pin and sprinkle over top. Cover with foil and freeze until firm.

Before serving, bring to room temperature until soft enough to cut, 30 to 40 minutes. Remove sides of springform pan and cut pie into wedges.

*Makes 14 to 16 servings.*

**Make-Ahead Tip**   Pie may be frozen up to 1 month.

1) Harvest Vegetable Patch with Ranch Dill Dip (page 110), 2) Brie en Croûte (page 68), 3) Fruited Ice Mold (page 74), 4) Vegetable Chartreuse (page 140), and 5) Easter Nest Bread ((page 31).

# SPECIAL CELEBRATIONS

## Birthday or Anniversary Buffet

---

**M E N U**

*Brie en Croûte*

*Chicken Breasts in Phyllo or*
*Veal au Vin with Fluffy Veal Meatballs*
*Marinated Garden Feast*
*White & Wild Rice Pilaf*
*Spiced Peaches with Currant Jelly*

*Chocolate Strawberry Carousel*

*Sparkling Champagne Punch with Fruited Ice Mold*

---

Life's milestones, birthdays, and anniversaries deserve special commemoration. The menu offers a choice of two elegant entrees, Chicken Breasts in Phyllo or Veal au Vin with Fluffy Veal Meatballs. Each serves sixteen, but for a larger group, serve them both. They are complementary in taste, appearance, and practicality—while the chicken bakes in the oven, the veal reheats on the stove. They are easy to multiply and divide, go from refrigerator to oven, and are effortless to dish up.

I often encounter students who are afraid to work with phyllo dough, or strudel leaves. They needn't be, because they are easy to use, unless you get a bad package. Sometimes after they're frozen, the leaves become dry and brittle and are impossible to separate. Don't even try; just run out, and buy another package. Let the package come to room temperature before opening it and don't let the sheets stand at room temperature uncovered or they will dry out and disintegrate. Work quickly and keep unused portions covered with a towel or waxed paper.

For an anniversary, love is the theme, so decorate the Brie en Croûte with pastry hearts and flowers, and arrange chocolate hearts around the top of a beautiful Chocolate Strawberry Carousel. Decorate your table with silver, gold, and chocolate kisses. Weave the ribbons around large foil-wrapped chocolate kisses. For place cards and/or favors, fill small dishes with candy kisses and tie them with a bow.

For a special *Birthday or Anniversary Buffet,* serve: Chicken Breasts in Phyllo (page 68), White & Wild Rice Pilaf (page 72), Spiced Peaches with Currant Jelly (page 72), and Marinated Garden Feast (page 71).

# Brie en Croûte

*A wheel of Brie, spread with spiced cheese and baked in pastry, makes a very impressive hors d'oeuvre for a large party. It's important to let it stand at least two hours after baking, or the cheese will be too soft to cut. It can be prepared in advance, frozen, and baked when needed.*

2 (4½-oz.) packages regular or light spiced cheese with garlic and herbs (such as Rondele or Boursin)
1 (2-lb.) Brie cheese (8 inches in diameter)
1 (17¼-oz.) package frozen puff pastry, defrosted until soft enough to roll, but still very cold
1 egg beaten with 1 tablespoon water for glaze

In a small bowl, mix spiced cheese until smooth. Spread evenly over top of Brie.

Place 1 sheet of puff pastry on a lightly floured board. Roll into a 14-inch square. Brush with egg wash. Place Brie in center. Trim pastry into a circle 2 inches larger than the cheese. Brush edges of pastry with more egg wash. Press a portion of dough against the side of the cheese. Cut along crease and place cut edge against bottom edge of cheese. Repeat with remaining pastry, covering entire sides of cheese. Roll second sheet of pastry into a 14-inch square. Brush with egg wash. Turn Brie over and place rind down in center of pastry. Trim pastry into a circle 2 inches larger than the cheese. Brush edges of pastry with egg wash. Repeat folding and cutting, covering the sides with a double thickness of pastry. Brush top and sides with egg wash. Reroll pastry scraps and cut out decorations, like hearts, flowers, and initials. Arrange on top and brush with egg glaze. Refrigerate until set.

About 2 hours before serving, preheat oven to 400F (205C). Bring Brie to room temperature. Place on an ungreased baking sheet and bake 35 to 40 minutes, or until pastry is golden. Let rest at room temperature at least 2 hours for the cheese to set. Cut into wedges to serve.

*Makes 16 to 20 servings.*

**Make-Ahead Tip** Unbaked brie may be refrigerated, covered overnight, or frozen up to 2 weeks. Bring to room temperature before baking.

---

# Chicken Breasts in Phyllo (photo on cover)

*Wrapping stuffed rolled chicken breasts in phyllo and topping them with phyllo bows makes one of the most elegant entrees I know. Coating the phyllo sheets with nonstick cooking spray instead of butter or oil reduces fat and prep time.*

Green Peppercorn & Spinach Stuffing (see below)
16 boneless skinless chicken breast halves (8 to 10 oz. each), pounded as thin as possible
Salt and pepper
2 pounds phyllo dough, at room temperature
Nonstick cooking spray
1½ cups dry bread crumbs
Watercress or parsley for garnish (optional)

**GREEN PEPPERCORN & SPINACH STUFFING:**
4 garlic cloves, minced
2 cups shredded Swiss cheese (½ pound)
1 to 2 tablespoons coarsely crushed green peppercorns or to taste
1 medium-size onion, finely chopped
4 cups chopped fresh spinach leaves, loosely packed (about 6 oz. trimmed)
1 cup whole or part-skim ricotta

4 hard-cooked eggs, coarsely chopped
1½ teaspoons salt or to taste

**PINK MADEIRA SAUCE:**
2 tablespoons cornstarch
⅓ cup Madeira
2¼ cups chicken broth
4 teaspoons tomato paste
½ cup regular or low-fat sour cream
Salt to taste
⅔ cup chopped chives or green onion tops

**Make stuffing:** In a large bowl, stir all ingredients together until thoroughly mixed. To stuff chicken, place breasts on work surface and sprinkle with salt and pepper. Spread ⅓ cup stuffing over each breast. Beginning at one long end, roll up once, fold in sides and roll as for jellyroll.

To wrap in phyllo, place 3 sheets of phyllo on work surface. Keep remainder covered so they don't dry out. Spray one sheet with nonstick cooking spray. Sprinkle with 1 tablespoon crumbs. Top with second sheet. Spray and sprinkle with 1 tablespoon crumbs. Top with third sheet, spray, and sprinkle with crumbs, leaving a 1-inch border. Cut pastry in half crosswise. Place a stuffed chicken breast in the center of each pastry half. Fold one end over, fold in sides, and roll up to enclose. Spray top and sides. If not baking immediately, place seam side down on an ungreased baking sheet and refrigerate. Repeat with remaining chicken and phyllo.

To make phyllo bows, preheat oven to 400F (205C). Spray one sheet of phyllo with nonstick cooking spray and fold lengthwise in thirds. Spray both sides. Tuck one part of each side under to make two loops. Crimp center. Cut a small strip from another phyllo sheet to wrap around center. With scissors, cut each end into a "V." Spray top of bow with nonstick cooking spray. Repeat to make one bow per breast. Place on baking sheet that has been sprayed with nonstick cooking spray and bake 4 to 8 minutes or until golden.

**Make sauce:** In a 3-quart microwave-safe bowl, stir cornstarch and Madeira until dissolved. Whisk in broth and tomato paste. Microwave on HIGH (100 percent) 1½ to 3½ minutes, whisking every minute, until sauce comes to a boil and thickens. Or cook in saucepan on stove. Whisk in sour cream, salt, and chives.

To bake chicken, preheat oven to 400F (205C). Spray 2 large baking sheets with nonstick cooking spray. Place packets on sprayed baking sheets at least 1 inch apart. (If you put them too close together, they will steam instead of brown.) Spray tops with nonstick spray. Bake 20 to 25 minutes or until golden. If baking two sheets in one oven, rotate them halfway through the baking time. Reheat bows 2 to 3 minutes. Transfer chicken to plates or platter, top each with a bow and drizzle with sauce. Garnish with greens, if desired. Pass remaining sauce.

*Makes 16 servings.*

**Make-Ahead Tips** Unbaked chicken may be refrigerated overnight or frozen up to 1 week. Defrost in the refrigerator in a single layer at least ½-inch apart. Bows may be stored at room temperature up to 3 days or frozen.

Sauce may be refrigerated, covered, up to 2 days. Before serving, reheat in microwave or on stove, stirring often, until hot. Stir in chives or green onion tops.

# Veal au Vin with Fluffy Veal Meatballs

*Some dishes fit every occasion, like this one, which is both homey and comforting, refined and elegant. Light, airy balls of pureed veal mingle with tender cubes of veal and mushrooms in a delicate white-wine sauce.*

6 pounds veal stew, cut into 1½-inch cubes
Salt and pepper
4 tablespoons olive oil
2 tablespoons tomato paste
2 tablespoons instant beef soup base (beef-flavored bouillon)
½ cup plus 1 tablespoon all-purpose flour
5 cups chicken broth
1½ cups dry white wine
1 tablespoon red currant jelly
Veal Meatballs (see below)
1 pound fresh mushrooms, thickly sliced

**VEAL MEATBALLS:**
2 garlic cloves, peeled
3 tablespoons coarsely chopped shallots or onion
3 tablespoons coarsely chopped chives or green onion tops
¼ cup chopped parsley leaves
1½ pounds lean ground veal
6 egg whites, unbeaten
1½ cups whipping cream, half-and-half, or evaporated skim milk
1½ teaspoons salt

Preheat oven to 375F (190C). Sprinkle veal cubes with salt and pepper. In a wide, heavy ovenproof saucepan or Dutch oven, heat 2 tablespoons of the oil until hot. Add veal in batches; sauté over medium-high heat until lightly browned on both sides. Transfer to a large bowl or platter. Repeat with remaining veal, adding oil as needed. If drippings begin to burn, reduce heat.

Stir tomato paste, soup base, and flour into drippings. It will be thick and grainy. Gradually stir in broth, wine, and jelly. Cook, stirring constantly, scraping up brown bits from bottom of pan, until mixture comes to a boil. Add veal. Cover and bake 1½ to 2 hours, stirring occasionally, until veal is tender when pierced with a fork. If sauce boils rapidly, reduce temperature to 350F (175C).

While veal bakes, prepare meatball mixture: In a food processor with the metal blade, process half of the garlic, shallots, chives, and parsley until minced. Add half of the veal and process until blended. Add 3 egg whites and process until incorporated. With machine running, pour ¾ cup cream through the feed tube. Mix in ¾ teaspoon salt. Remove to a bowl and repeat with remaining ingredients. Refrigerate until needed.

About 20 minutes before veal is done, dip 2 teaspoons or a meatball-size scoop into the hot gravy. Dip into meatball mixture and drop a ball onto stew. Repeat until all meatball mixture is used. Meatballs will be layered on top of each other, but will separate while cooking. Cover pan and bake 20 minutes. Stir well.

Stir in mushrooms. Bake or cook on top of stove, until heated through, about 30 minutes, stirring occasionally.

*Makes 16 servings.*

**Make-Ahead Tip** If not serving immediately, place a damp dish towel directly on top of stew, cover, and refrigerate. Veal may be refrigerated in an airtight container up to 2 days or frozen up to 2 months. Before serving, add mushrooms and heat to serving temperature.

# Marinated Garden Feast (photo on cover)

*This colorful display of vegetables is designed especially for a buffet. The fresh vegetables are blanched to retain their bright color and can stay for hours without wilting or drying out.*

2 pounds green beans
2 large heads cauliflower (about 5 lbs.)
2 large bunches broccoli (about 3 lbs.)
3 to 4 pounds peeled baby carrots
3 (8-oz.) cans artichoke hearts
2 red and/or yellow bell peppers
Lettuce leaves
3 (5½-oz.) jars baby corn
4 cans (5- to 6-oz. dry weight) pitted ripe olives, drained
1 pint cherry red and/or yellow tomatoes

### ITALIAN DRESSING:

3 (16-oz.) bottles regular or reduced-calorie Italian salad dressing
2 (0.7-oz.) packages dry Italian salad dressing mix
4 garlic cloves, minced
1 cup chopped parsley leaves

### GARNISH (OPTIONAL):

1 whole artichoke
1 or 2 ears corn on the cob, with the husk
1 small head cauliflower
1 bunch broccoli
2 tomatoes
1 bunch carrots with stems
1 red or yellow bell pepper

**Prepare vegetables:** Cut tips off green beans. Cut stems off cauliflower and broccoli and cut into serving-size flowerets.

Fill a deep skillet or wide saucepan with 2 inches of water. Bring to a boil over medium heat. Add green beans, cover, and boil gently 4 to 6 minutes or until tender, tossing with a spatula once or twice. Remove with slotted spoon or strainer to a colander. Place colander in a bowl of ice water to stop the cooking. Drain and transfer vegetables to a plastic bag. Bring water back to a boil. Repeat with carrots, cauliflower, and broccoli, cooking each until tender, about 8 to 12 minutes for carrots; 3 to 5 minutes for broccoli and cauliflower. Place each vegetable into a separate plastic bag. Cool completely.

**Make dressing:** In a large bowl or jar, mix liquid dressing, dry dressing, garlic, and parsley.

One to 2 hours before serving, pour ¾ to 1 cup dressing over cauliflower, broccoli, and carrots. Drain artichoke hearts. Pour into plastic bag and add ¾ cup marinade. Place peppers in a bag and pour ¾ cup dressing over peppers. Refrigerate bags, turning once or twice to distribute marinade.

Before serving, line one or two large platters or baskets with lettuce leaves. Remove vegetables from marinade. Arrange green beans, cauliflower, broccoli, carrots, artichoke hearts, peppers, baby corn, olives, and tomatoes on lettuce, keeping each type separate. If desired, garnish with uncooked vegetables. Spoon marinade over green beans, corn, and tomatoes.

*Makes 24 servings.*

**Make-Ahead Tip** Vegetables and marinade may be refrigerated overnight.

# White & Wild Rice Pilaf (photo on cover)

*This casserole, studded with pecans, makes a great accompaniment for poultry, meat, or fish.*

2 cups wild rice (12 ounces)
¼ cup olive oil
2 onions, chopped
1 cup chopped celery
1½ cups chopped pecans (about 6 oz.)
2 cups long-grain white rice
8 cups chicken broth
6 tablespoons soy sauce
½ teaspoon salt, or to taste

**R**inse wild rice and place in a medium-size saucepan. Cover with 2 to 3 inches of water. Bring to a boil and boil gently 20 minutes. (It will not be done.) Drain off excess water. Set rice aside.

Heat oil in a large saucepan or Dutch oven. Add onion and celery and sauté until softened. Add pecans and white rice and sauté, stirring, until lightly toasted, about 5 minutes. Stir in wild rice. Transfer to a greased 4-quart shallow casserole or baking dish, or 2 (2-quart) casserole dishes. Cover and refrigerate if making ahead.

About 1½ hours before serving, preheat oven to 350F (175C). Bring chicken broth to a boil in a large pan. Stir in soy sauce and salt. Pour over rice. Bake, covered, 60 to 75 minutes or until all liquid is absorbed. Let stand 10 minutes before serving.

*Makes 16 servings.*

**Make-Ahead Tip**   Casserole may be refrigerated overnight before adding the broth.

---

# Spiced Peaches with Currant Jelly

*Serve these broiled peach halves when you want something sweet and colorful on the plate. Because the amount of peaches varies with each can, to serve sixteen people, purchase three cans, and use the juice from only two of them.*

3 (1-lb. 13-oz.) cans peach halves
1¼ cups packed light brown sugar
1 cup white vinegar
2 cinnamon sticks
2 teaspoons whole allspice
4 teaspoons whole cloves
1 teaspoon red currant jelly per peach half

**D**rain peaches, reserving syrup from 2 of the cans in a deep saucepan. Add brown sugar, vinegar, cinnamon sticks, allspice, and cloves. Bring to a boil and simmer, uncovered, 10 minutes. Add peaches and simmer 5 minutes. Cool peaches in syrup at room temperature; cover and let stand 4 to 8 hours. With a slotted spoon, lift peaches from syrup and place in a shallow ovenproof casserole.

Before serving, bring peaches to room temperature. Fill center of each with 1 teaspoon currant jelly. Preheat broiler. Broil about 4 inches from heat source until jelly is melted and peaches are warm.

*Makes 12 to 16 peach halves (amount varies with the cans).*

**Make-Ahead Tip**   Before broiling, peaches may be refrigerated, covered, up to two days.

# Chocolate Strawberry Carousel (photo on cover)

*The crust is a big chocolate cookie. Strawberry halves encircle the sides and whole berries dot the bottom. A rich, silky, egg-free chocolate mousse covers it all.*

**CHOCOLATE ALMOND CRUST:**
⅓ cup slivered blanched almonds
½ cup sugar
2 tablespoons unsweetened cocoa
2 tablespoons all-purpose flour
2 egg whites
½ teaspoon vanilla extract

**CHOCOLATE MOUSSE:**
1 pound semisweet chocolate, chopped
¼ cup Amaretto liqueur or coffee-flavored liqueur such as Kahlua
⅔ cup evaporated whole or skimmed milk
1 (8-oz.) package regular or light cream cheese
1 cup (½ pint) whipping cream
1 cup regular or low-fat sour cream
2 pints fresh strawberries

**DECORATION (OPTIONAL):**
1 cup whipping cream, whipped
Chocolate hearts (see below)
10 to 12 strawberries

**Make crust:** Preheat oven to 425F (220C). Place rack in center of oven. Generously grease or spray the bottom of a 9-inch springform pan with non-stick cooking spray. In a food processor with the metal blade, process almonds and sugar until finely ground. Add cocoa, flour, egg whites, and vanilla and pulse 3 or 4 times to mix; the batter will be very runny. Spoon into springform pan. Using the back of a spoon or spatula, spread the batter to cover the bottom of the pan. Place pan on a baking sheet and bake 12 to 13 minutes or until the edges look crisp and pull away from rim of pan. Remove from oven. Cool completely.

**Make mousse:** In a small saucepan over low heat, stir chocolate, liqueur, milk, and cream cheese until smooth and melted. Cool to room temperature. In a large bowl with electric mixer, beat whipping cream until stiff peaks form. Add sour cream and continue beating to soft peaks. On low speed, mix cooled chocolate into cream until incorporated.

To assemble, cut a small slice off stem end of each berry. Slice 10 to 12 berries in half through the stem end. Place around edge of crust, pointed side up, cut sides against sides of pan. Arrange remaining whole berries about ½ inch apart over crust. Pour chocolate mixture over berries. Smooth top. Refrigerate several hours.

Several hours before serving, remove sides of springform pan. Smooth sides of mousse and place on a serving platter. If desired, fill a pastry bag fitted with a large rosette tip with whipped cream and pipe rosettes around the top. Garnish with chocolate hearts and strawberries.

*Makes 12 servings.*

**Make-Ahead Tip** Baked crust may be held at room temperature overnight or frozen. Mousse may be refrigerated overnight.

---

# Chocolate Hearts

*Make these hearts for decorating desserts.*

12 ounces semisweet chocolate chips or chocolate candy coating chips from cake-decorating shop or cookware shop

**Heat** chocolate in a microwave-safe bowl or on top of stove in double boiler until melted and smooth. Line the back of a baking sheet with waxed paper. Spread the chocolate into a ¼-inch-thick rectangle. Freeze 2 to 5 minutes or refrigerate until it begins to set but is still soft enough to cut. Using a heart-shaped cookie cutter, cut out hearts. Or, purchase chocolate heart molds from cake decorating shop, fill with melted chocolate, freeze firm, then pop out. Store in cool place. Avoid handling hearts with your fingers; they will melt the chocolate and leave prints. Handle hearts with a spatula or hold by the edges.

*Makes about 20 hearts, depending on size of cutter.*

**Make-Ahead Tip** Hearts may be refrigerated or frozen up to 1 month.

# Sparkling Champagne Punch with Fruited Ice Mold

*Not too sweet nor too dry, this punch is a great champagne stretcher.*

## ICE MOLD:

1 bunch green grapes, preferably seedless, cut into small sprigs
1 bunch red grapes, preferably seedless, cut into small sprigs
1 box strawberries
Nonpoisonous garden leaves, such as lemon, rose, or grape

## CHAMPAGNE PUNCH:

1 (750-ml.) bottle sauterne
1 cup brandy
¼ cup sugar
1 (1-liter) bottle club soda, chilled
2 (750-ml.) bottles dry Champagne, chilled

**Make ice mold:**   Fill a ring mold, heart-shaped mold, or cake pan two-thirds full of water. Freeze solid. When frozen, place small clusters of grapes over the top. Add strawberries and leaves to cover the top almost completely. Carefully pour in enough water to half cover fruit. Return to freezer. When frozen, add more water, if needed. Freeze solid. To unmold, dip mold briefly in warm water and unmold onto freezer foil. Wrap in foil and freeze until ready to use.

**Make punch:**   In a large bowl, combine sauterne, brandy, and sugar, stirring until sugar dissolves. Refrigerate until chilled or overnight.

Before serving, pour sauterne into a large punch bowl. Add ice mold. Pour in club soda and champagne.

*Makes 24 (4-oz.) servings.*

**Make-Ahead Tip**   Ice mold may be frozen up to 1 month.

# Chicken Salad with Oranges and Sweet & Spicy Pecans

*This salad offers two serving options: The chicken, vegetables, and sliced oranges can be tossed in the creamy orange-yogurt dressing, or the ingredients can be artfully arranged on a platter or individual plates and the dressing passed separately. Candy-coated peppery pecans are sprinkled over all.*

**FRESH ORANGE VINAIGRETTE:**

2 medium-size seedless oranges, peeled and quartered
4 small green onions (white part only)
¼ cup vegetable oil
¼ cup raspberry vinegar
6 tablespoons orange juice
1 tablespoon honey
½ cup plain regular, low-fat, or nonfat yogurt
Salt and pepper to taste

**SALAD:**

1 recipe Sweet & Spicy Pecans (see below)
3 medium-size heads romaine lettuce
3 pounds boneless, skinless chicken breast halves
Nonstick cooking spray
2 cups chopped cucumber, preferably European type
½ cup chopped green onions with tops
4 seedless oranges, peeled, sliced, and cut into ¾-inch pieces
3 avocados, peeled, pitted, and sliced or chopped

**Make vinaigrette:**  In a blender container, puree oranges. Add green onions, oil, vinegar, orange juice, and honey. Mix until blended. Remove to a bowl and whisk in yogurt. Season with salt and pepper.

**Prepare salad:**  Make pecans as directed. Wash and dry lettuce and tear into bite-size pieces. Wrap in paper towels, place in a plastic bag, and refrigerate until serving. Preheat grill or broiler. Spray tops of chicken breasts with nonstick spray. Place in a baking pan. Season with salt and pepper. Grill or broil as close to the heat source as possible, 3 to 4 minutes per side. Cool and refrigerate.

Before serving, slice chicken. Place lettuce, cucumbers, and onions in a large bowl. Add oranges, avocado, and chicken. Toss with vinaigrette. Sprinkle with nuts. Or, assemble ingredients on lettuce leaves and pass dressing.

*Makes 12 to 14 servings.*

**Make-Ahead Tips**  Vinaigrette may be refrigerated up to 2 days.

Lettuce, cucumber, onions, and chicken may be covered and refrigerated separately overnight.

# Sweet & Spicy Pecans

*Toss these in salads or stir-frys, serve them for hors d'oeuvre, or wrap them up for gifts.*

¼ cup sugar
¼ cup plain regular, low-fat, or nonfat yogurt
¾ teaspoon salt
¾ teaspoon red (cayenne) pepper
1½ cups pecan halves or pieces

Preheat oven to 300F (150C). Line a baking sheet with heavy-duty foil. Grease or spray the foil with nonstick cooking spray. In a 2-quart (8-cup) microwave-safe bowl, stir together sugar, yogurt, salt, and cayenne. Microwave on HIGH (100 percent), uncovered, 2 to 3 minutes or until sugar melts. Stir in nuts. Transfer to baking sheet, spreading out into single layer. Bake 30 minutes or until crisp and dry. Stir to separate.

*Makes 1½ cups.*

**Make-Ahead Tip**  Nuts may be stored airtight 1 week.

# Oriental Tuna Salad

*When you want to dress up canned tuna, combine it with water chestnuts, snow peas,
and fresh pineapple chunks, and toss it with a gingery sesame-oil vinaigrette.
Attractively presented in a pineapple shell, it makes a glorious main-dish salad.*

1 large, whole pineapple with leafy top

**ORIENTAL DRESSING:**
2 garlic cloves, peeled
1 piece peeled gingerroot, about the size of a quarter
2 tablespoons Oriental sesame oil
½ cup reserved chopped pineapple
2 tablespoons lemon juice
1 cup plain regular, low-fat, or nonfat yogurt
2 tablespoons plus 2 teaspoons soy sauce
1 tablespoon plus 1 teaspoon honey

**SALAD:**
1 (3-oz.) package Ramen noodles (reserve
    seasoning packet for another use) or 1 (5-oz.) can
    chow mein noodles
2 (12½-oz.) cans oil- or water-packed tuna, drained
2 (10½-oz.) packages frozen snow peas or sugar
    snap peas, thawed and drained on paper towels
1 cup green onions, sliced diagonally into ½-inch
    pieces
2 cups chopped celery
2 (8-oz.) cans sliced water chestnuts, drained
1 cup reserved chopped pineapple

Cut pineapple in half through top, leaving top attached. Using a grapefruit knife, cut out the fruit. Cover the shells with plastic wrap and refrigerate. Cut fruit into chunks; measure 1 cup for dressing and ½ cup for salad. Reserve remaining pineapple for another use.

**Make dressing:**  In a food processor with the metal blade, process garlic and gingerroot until minced. Add sesame oil, pineapple, lemon juice, yogurt, soy sauce, and honey. Process until blended.

**Make salad:**  If using Ramen noodles, crumble them with your hands. Place noodles on a small baking sheet. Preheat toaster oven or regular oven to 350F (175C). Bake noodles until golden, 10 to 15 minutes, stirring once. (The noodles may be stored in an airtight container at room temperature up to 2 days.)

Before serving, in a large bowl, flake tuna with a fork. Add peas, green onions, celery, water chestnuts, pineapple, and noodles. Add dressing and toss well. Spoon into pineapple shells. Serve immediately.

*Makes 14 servings.*

**Make-Ahead Tips**  Pineapple shells for salad can be prepared the day before, covered, and refrigerated.

Dressing may be refrigerated overnight. Bring to room temperature and shake well before using.

# Lemon Pecan Popovers with Lemon-Honey Butter

*When cooking teacher Richard Nelson taught cooking classes in Seaside, Oregon, he introduced me to these popovers. For years I served them for showers in my cooking school — all puffed and warm and slathered with lemon-honey butter.*

**POPOVERS:**
2 cups all-purpose flour
¼ cup very finely chopped pecans
2 cups regular or low-fat (2%) milk
4 large eggs
¼ teaspoon salt
2 teaspoons finely grated lemon peel

**LEMON-HONEY BUTTER:**
½ cup (1 stick) unsalted butter, at room temperature
2 tablespoons honey
2 teaspoons lemon juice
2 tablespoons finely grated lemon peel

**Make popovers:**  In a bowl with electric mixer, mix flour, pecans, milk, eggs, salt, and lemon peel until well blended. Batter will be slightly lumpy.

**Make honey butter:**  Beat butter until smooth. Add honey, lemon juice, and lemon peel and mix until blended.

Preheat oven to 425F (230C). Heavily butter 12 (6-oz.) custard cups, popover pans, or 2½-inch muffin cups. Fill two-thirds full of batter. Bake 30 to 35 minutes or until puffed and browned. Serve immediately with honey butter.

*Makes 12 popovers.*

**Make-Ahead Tip**  Batter may be covered and refrigerated overnight. Bake as above.

Butter may be covered and refrigerated up to 4 days or frozen up to 1 month. Serve at room temperature.

---

# Sweet & Sour Cucumber Chips

*These crunchy marinated cucumber slices have all the flavor of pickles, but are lighter and crispier. They can be served as a condiment or a side-dish salad.*

2 large cucumbers (about 1¾ lbs.)
¾ teaspoon salt
½ cup ¼-inch-diced green bell pepper
½ cup thinly sliced onion
½ cup white vinegar
½ cup plus 2 tablespoons sugar
1½ teaspoons celery seeds

**Peel** cucumbers and cut crosswise into ¼-inch-thick slices. Place in a colander in the sink and sprinkle with the salt. Let stand 2 hours. Drain well. Place in a medium-size bowl with bell pepper and onion. In a small bowl, stir together vinegar, sugar, and celery seeds until sugar is dissolved. Pour over vegetables. Cover and refrigerate at least 24 hours.

To serve, remove vegetables with a slotted spoon.

*Makes about 3½ cups or 8 servings.*

**Make-Ahead Tip**  Cucumber chips may be refrigerated up to 1 month.

# Buckets of Frozen Fruit

*This fluffy frozen cherry mousse could be molded in a loaf pan, but that wouldn't be as much fun. Shape it into one large sand bucket or several smaller ones, serve it with a shovel, and relive a little of your childhood.*

**FROZEN FRUIT MOLD:**

1 (4-oz.) package whipped cream cheese, at room temperature

1 (4½-oz.) carton frozen whipped topping, thawed

1 (21-oz.) can cherry pie filling

2 (11-oz.) cans mandarin orange segments or mandarin orange segments with pineapple tidbits, drained

**DECORATIONS:**

1 large or several small sand buckets with detachable handles

Wooden picks

Gumdrops

In a large bowl, stir together cream cheese and dessert topping. Stir in pie filling and mandarin orange segments until blended. Pour mixture into a 5-cup bucket or mold or divide among smaller ones. Cover and freeze until firm.

Go around inside edge of mold(s) with tip of a sharp knife. Dip briefly in warm water and unmold onto platter. Turn right side up. Return to freezer until ready to serve.

To decorate, insert a wooden pick at an upward angle into each side where the handle will be attached. Place plastic handle(s) from bucket(s) over wooden picks and secure in place with a gumdrop.

Leave at room temperature until just soft enough to cut. A large bucket will take about an hour, smaller ones, about 30 minutes. Slice large bucket in half crosswise and then into wedges to serve.

*Makes 12 servings.*

**Make-Ahead Tip**   Mold(s) may be frozen up to 1 month.

# Raspberry & Chocolate-Almond Ice Cream Bombe

*Joann Roth, owner of the successful catering company, Someone's in the Kitchen, in
Los Angeles, gave me the recipe for this molded ice-cream dessert called a bombe.
Grand Marnier, chocolate-coated almonds, and vanilla ice cream packed inside a
raspberry sherbet shell make the best bombe I've ever tasted.*

1 quart raspr    herbet
3 ounces sem.       chocolate, chopped or chips
½ cup slivered a.       toasted at 350F (175C) 10 to
   15 minutes, stirring       nally
1½ pints good-quality v.      cream
½ pint (1 cup) whipping c.
3 tablespoons Grand Marnie.
Strawberries for decoration (op..
Mint or lemon leaves for decoratio.       1)

Lightly oil or spray a 2-quart (8-cup) sta.      el
bowl or ring mold with nonstick cooking
Reserve 2 cups sherbet and return to freezer. L
the back of a spoon, spread remaining sherb
around the sides of the mold, coating it evenly.
Freeze until firm.

Melt chocolate in a double boiler over simmering water or in a microwave-safe bowl in microwave until smooth. Stir in almonds. Place ice
cream in a bowl with electric mixer and mix on low
speed until softened, but not melted. In another
bowl, beat cream and Grand Marnier until soft
peaks form. Fold chocolate mixture into ice cream.
Fold in the whipped cream.

Spoon into sherbet-lined mold. Freeze until
firm. Spread reserved sherbet over the top. Cover
with foil and freeze overnight.

To unmold, go around edge of mold with the tip
of a knife. Dip mold briefly in warm water several
·mes and invert onto serving plate. Return to
      ·er. Before serving, if desired, decorate with
          ·rries and mint or lemon leaves.

*Ma.       ·4 servings.*

**Make-..**              Bombe may be frozen up to 2
weeks.

# Baby Carriage Apricot Cake

*This is a simple sheet cake shaped into a baby carriage, decorated and trimmed with candies. It's very whimsical and adds a touch of fun to a happy occasion.*

**CAKE:**
1 (18½-oz.) package yellow cake mix
1 (3¾-oz.) package vanilla instant pudding
4 large eggs
1 cup regular or low-fat sour cream
¾ cup Amaretto liqueur or water
7 canned apricot halves, drained and chopped

**FROSTING & DECORATIONS:**
2 to 3 cups whipping cream
Red or blue food coloring
Red licorice whips
M&M's candies or other candies

Preheat oven to 350F (175C). Grease and flour a 13" × 9" baking pan. Make cake: In a bowl with electric mixer on low speed, beat cake mix, pudding, eggs, sour cream, and Amaretto or water until blended. Increase speed to high and beat 2 minutes. Add chopped apricots and mix until incorporated. Pour batter into prepared pan and bake 40 to 45 minutes or until a wooden pick inserted in center comes out clean. Cool in pan 10 to 20 minutes. Turn out onto rack to cool.

To decorate, draw a paper diagram of a baby carriage about 12 inches long and 9 inches wide. Use a 2½- to 3-inch round cookie cutter to outline arc for wheels in diagram. Place diagram on cake and cut cake around it. Cut out 2 wheels with cookie cutter.

Place cake and wheels on platter. Whip cream until soft peaks form. Tint pink or blue and beat until stiff. Frost cake and wheels. Outline carriage and wheels with candy. Place licorice whips radiating out from center of wheels as spokes. Place a candy in the center of the spokes. Decorate with additional candies as desired.

*Makes 18 to 20 servings.*

**Variation**   Cake may be baked in a greased and floured 10-inch fluted tube pan or Bundt pan in preheated 350F (175C) oven 45 to 55 minutes. While still warm, brush top and sides with ¾ cup hot apricot preserves, which have been heated and strained.

**Make-Ahead Tips**   Undecorated cake may be stored at room temperature overnight or frozen.

Decorated cake may be refrigerated several hours before serving.

# Gala Wedding Reception

---

**MENU**

*Golden Sausage Rings*
*Feta Shrimp Triangles*
*Warm Salsa Dip in a Baked Tortilla Bowl*

*Butter Lettuce & Walnut Salad*
*Filets of Beef Chasseur*
*Champagne Rice Pilaf with Vermicelli*
*Cauliflower with Puree of Peas & Watercress*

*Chocolate-Filled Cream Puff Heart*
*Grand Marnier Apricot Trifle*

*Sparkling Champagne Punch with Fruited Ice Mold (page 74)*
*Pink Pastel Punch*

---

We are inclined to spend more time and money on a wedding than on any other single event in our lives. We want it to be perfect. Preparing the food for your own or a friend's reception is a labor of love. To ensure success, you need elegant dishes that can be prepared ahead, reheated without a hassle, and served with ease.

This menu serves twenty-four, but the recipes are extremely flexible and adapt well to being multiplied or divided. For a large celebration, you'll want a selection of hot hors d'oeuvre to pass, such as Golden Sausage Rings and Feta Shrimp Triangles. You'll also want to set some dips and spreads on a central table or in different spots throughout the room. You might wish to add Smoked Oyster Roll (page 124), Southwestern Guacamole Wreath (page 122), and a selection of cheeses and crackers.

Once you've made Beef Chasseur for a party, it will become one of your favorite entrees. Often students tell me they are hesitant to try it, thinking that steaks that cook in a sauce will come out brown and steamed. But they don't. They are beautifully pink and juicy — and go from refrigerator to oven to table, just like your favorite casserole. The Cauliflower with Puree of Peas & Watercress is a colorful and tasty side dish.

The menu also includes two glorious desserts. They may be served with pride along with a wedding cake, or even in place of one.

Champagne adds a sparkle to weddings, so pour it from the bottle, or mix it into an effervescent Champagne punch. Nonalcoholic Pink Pastel Punch is the right choice for a group that includes children.

# Golden Sausage Rings

*Bulk sausage is shaped into a log and wrapped inside mustard-coated puff pastry. You can control the spiciness by using mild or hot sausage, or combining some of each.*

1 (17¼-oz.) package frozen puff pastry, defrosted until pliable, but still cold
2 pounds bulk pork or turkey sausage, mild or hot
4 tablespoons Dijon or grainy mustard
1 egg mixed with 1 tablespoon water

**Preheat** oven to 375F (175C). Grease 2 rimmed baking sheets. On a lightly floured board, roll 1 sheet of pastry into a 12-inch square. Cut in half. Divide sausage into 4 portions. On a lightly floured board, shape one sausage portion into a 12″ × 1″ log. Spread 1 tablespoon mustard in a 1-inch band along center of pastry. Place sausage on mustard. Brush one long edge of pastry with egg. Roll around sausage to enclose it. Brush top and sides with egg. Repeat with remaining puff pastry and sausage to make 4 logs. Slice into 12 (1-inch) pieces.

Place slices seam side down on greased rimmed baking sheets. Bake 20 minutes or until golden.

*Makes 48 rings.*

**Make-Ahead Tip** Rings may be refrigerated overnight or frozen in an airtight container. Underbake slightly. Remove to paper towels and blot off excess fat. Bring to room temperature and reheat at 375F (190C) for 10 minutes or until heated through.

# Feta Shrimp Triangles

*Crisp pita bread triangles are the base for a cheesy Middle Eastern shrimp spread accented with cumin, mint, and a sprinkling of sesame seeds.*

4 (5- to 6-inch) pita breads
8 ounces feta cheese
8 ounces peeled baby shrimp or medium-size shrimp, chopped
2 large garlic cloves, minced
½ cup regular, low-fat, or nonfat mayonnaise
½ teaspoon chili powder
½ teaspoon ground cumin
2 tablespoons chopped fresh mint or 1 to 2 teaspoons dried mint, crumbled
Sesame seeds
Paprika

**Preheat** oven to 300F (150C). Slip knife into edge of pita breads and divide them in half horizontally. Cut each half into 5 or 6 triangles. (If bread is large, cut it into 8 to 10 triangles.) Place triangles on baking sheet and bake 15 to 20 minutes or until lightly browned.

Preheat broiler. Crumble feta cheese into a medium-size bowl. Stir in shrimp, garlic, mayonnaise, chili powder, cumin, and mint with a fork until blended. Spread generously on toasted triangles. Sprinkle tops with sesame seeds and dust with paprika. Place on broiler pan and broil until tops are brown and bubbly.

*Makes about 40 triangles.*

**Make-Ahead Tip** Triangles may be frozen. Reheat on baking sheet in a preheated 450F (230C) oven 5 to 10 minutes or until heated through.

# Warm Salsa Dip

*No one will guess that the secret ingredient of this creamy, warm dip is pureed lima grands, also called butter beans.*

2 garlic cloves, peeled
4 ounces Monterey Jack cheese, cut into cubes
  (1 cup)
1 (8-oz.) package regular or light cream cheese
1 (16-oz.) can lima beans, rinsed and drained
1 cup mild or medium-hot salsa
1 Baked Tortilla Bowl (see below, optional)
½ cup salsa for topping
Tortilla chips or raw vegetables for dipping

**In** a food processor with the metal blade, process garlic until minced. Add Jack cheese and pulse until finely chopped. Add cream cheese, lima grands, and salsa and process, scraping sides, until blended and smooth. Remove to a microwave-safe bowl.

Microwave, covered, on HIGH (100 percent) 2 to 4 minutes, stirring every 60 seconds, until hot. If desired, spoon into Baked Tortilla Bowl. Top with additional salsa. Serve with tortilla chips or vegetables.

*Makes 3 cups.*

**Make-Ahead Tip** Dip may be covered and refrigerated up to 2 days.

# Baked Tortilla Bowl

*To eat or not to eat, that is the question. Fill this fluted bowl with any thick, creamy dip, and if guests want to, they can break off pieces to use as dippers.*

3 (10-inch) burrito-style flour tortillas
1 egg white mixed with 1 tablespoon water

**Preheat** oven to 225F (105C). Place 1 tortilla over one-third of a 9½-inch, deep-dish pie plate. Press tortilla into the bottom and up the side, extending about 2½ inches over the rim. Brush with egg white, being careful not to let it drip onto the plate. Place second tortilla overlapping the first to cover a third of the plate and come up the sides. Brush with egg white. Place last tortilla overlapping to cover bottom of pie plate. Brush with egg white. The tortillas should cover the bottom of the dish and extend in a fluted pattern up the sides to form a bowl.

Bake 1 hour or until tortillas are very dry and crisp and sides are lightly browned. Remove from oven and gently remove tortilla bowl from pie plate. The bottom will be slightly soft, but will crisp up as it cools.

*Makes 1 tortilla bowl.*

**Make-Ahead Tip** Bowl may be kept at room temperature, uncovered, up to 2 days.

# Butter Lettuce & Walnut Salad

*When the occasion calls for a sophisticated salad, choose this simple blending of soft butter lettuce (also called Boston lettuce) leaves dressed with rich, smooth walnut oil and a sprinkling of toasted nuts. Store walnut oil in the refrigerator after opening.*

**WALNUT VINAIGRETTE:**
¾ cup walnut oil
6 tablespoons olive oil
¾ cup raspberry wine vinegar
2 tablespoons Dijon mustard
3 tablespoons orange juice
3 tablespoons plain regular, low-fat, or nonfat yogurt

**SALAD:**
1 cup chopped walnuts (about 4 oz.)
4 heads butter or Boston lettuce (about 1½ lbs. total)
2 (14-oz.) cans hearts of palm, drained and sliced
¾ cup sliced green onions (1 bunch)

**Make vinaigrette:**   In a small bowl, whisk together walnut and olive oils, vinegar, mustard, orange juice, and yogurt until smooth. Cover and refrigerate.

**Make salad:**   Preheat a regular or toaster oven to 350F (175C). Place walnuts in a shallow baking pan. Bake for about 8 minutes or until golden. Cool and store in an airtight container. Wash and dry lettuce. Tear into bite-size pieces. Wrap in paper towels and refrigerate until ready to use.

**Before serving:**   Place lettuce, hearts of palm, green onions, and walnuts in a large salad bowl. Add as much dressing as needed and toss well.

*Makes 14 to 16 servings.*

**Make-Ahead Tips**   Vinaigrette may be refrigerated up to 2 days. Whisk well before using.

The washed and dried lettuce may be refrigerated overnight.

---

# Filets of Beef Chasseur

*This dish is easy, can be prepared ahead, is foolproof, and delicious. The steaks are quickly sautéed first and the drippings that stick to the bottom of the pan become the essence of a delicious sauce. That's why it's important that you don't use a nonstick pan. Don't crowd the meat while sautéing or baking, or it will steam instead of brown.*

24 (6- to 8-oz.) filet mignon steaks, cut 1 inch thick
3 large garlic cloves, minced
1½ tablespoons seasoned salt or to taste
¾ teaspoon seasoned pepper or to taste
3 to 4 tablespoons olive oil

**SAUCE CHASSEUR:**
½ cup brandy
½ cup plus 2 tablespoons olive oil
½ cup plus 1 tablespoon all-purpose flour
2 tablespoons tomato paste
3 garlic cloves, minced
2¼ cups dry red wine
3 cups chicken broth
2¼ cups beef broth
1½ cups water
1 teaspoon Worcestershire sauce
6 tablespoons red currant jelly
1½ pounds mushrooms, sliced

**Prepare filets:**   Place steaks on a work surface. In a small bowl, make a paste of the garlic, seasoned salt, and seasoned pepper. With hands, rub seasoning on both sides of meat. Heat 1 tablespoon of the oil in a large, heavy skillet (not nonstick) over high heat until very hot. Add 5 or 6 steaks at a time; sauté until brown on each side, but still raw in the center. Do not crowd. If oil begins to burn, decrease heat slightly. Repeat with remaining steaks, adding oil as needed. Divide steaks between 2 or 3 casserole dishes, leaving at least 1 inch space between them.

**Make sauce:**   Add brandy to skillet. Cook over medium heat, stirring constantly, scraping up all brown bits that stick to the bottom of the pan. Stir in oil and flour. Reduce heat to low and cook, stirring constantly, until mixture is golden. Stir in tomato paste and garlic; it will be thick and grainy. Remove pan from heat and whisk in wine, chicken broth, beef broth, water, Worcestershire sauce, and jelly. Return to medium heat and bring to a boil, stirring constantly. Reduce heat and simmer, stirring occasionally, 10 minutes or until reduced by about one-third and thick enough to coat a spoon. Stir in mushrooms. Adjust seasonings. Cool completely. Pour sauce over steaks in casserole dishes. The sauce should not come more than half-way up the meat.

**To serve:** Preheat oven to 400F (205C). Bake, uncovered, 15 to 20 minutes for medium-rare done-ness, 20 to 25 minutes for medium to medium-well doneness. If baking two casseroles in the same oven, rotate them halfway through the baking time. Spoon some of the sauce over each filet when serving.

*Makes 24 servings.*

**Make-Ahead Tip** Filets may be refrigerated, covered with foil, overnight. Bring to room temperature 1 hour before baking.

**Variation**

### FILETS OF BEEF CHASSEUR FOR 8:
1 large clove garlic, minced
1½ teaspoons seasoned salt
¼ teaspoon seasoned pepper
2 tablespoons olive oil

### SAUCE CHASSEUR:
2 tablespoons brandy
2 tablespoons olive oil
3 tablespoons flour
2 teaspoons tomato paste
1 garlic clove, minced
¾ cup dry red wine
1 cup chicken broth
¾ cup beef broth
½ cup water
¼ teaspoon Worcestershire sauce
2 tablespoons red currant jelly
½ pound mushrooms, sliced

## Champagne Rice Pilaf with Vermicelli

*Rice with Champagne? Not the usual marriage, but it turns out extraordinary. An electric fry pan is a good choice for cooking rice. The temperature remains constant, and your oven and stove top will be free for other dishes. It's easiest to cook this amount of rice in 2 pans.*

1 cup (2 sticks) butter or margarine
6 cups uncooked long-grain white rice
4 cups fine noodles, such as vermicelli, broken into small pieces
9 cups chicken broth
4 cups Champagne
1 tablespoon salt or to taste

**D**ivide butter between 2 large wide saucepans, Dutch ovens, or electric fry pans. Melt over medium-high heat. Add rice and noodles. Sauté, stirring constantly, until rice is golden brown, 7 to 10 minutes.

Pour chicken broth and champagne over rice. Add salt. Bring to a boil. Reduce heat to low, cover, and simmer slowly 20 to 25 minutes or until all liquid is absorbed.

*Makes 24 to 30 servings.*

**Variation** Sauté rice as directed. Transfer to ovenproof casserole(s), and bake at 350F (175C) until liquid is absorbed, 45 to 60 minutes.

**Make-Ahead Tip** Cooked rice may be refrigerated overnight. Reheat in microwave, covered, on HIGH (100 percent) until hot.

# Cauliflower with Puree of Peas & Watercress

*Whole cooked cauliflower blanketed with a vivid emerald sauce of pureed peas and watercress makes a pretty vegetable dish.*

4 medium-size heads cauliflower (about 8 lbs. total)
Salt and white pepper
3 pounds frozen petite peas
3 cups loosely packed watercress leaves
2 cups chicken broth
Watercress sprigs for garnish

**Trim** outer leaves from cauliflower and cut out core. Rinse under running water.

To steam, place heads in a steamer or on a rack that can be placed over water. A large roasting pan with a rack works well for cooking several at once. Cover and bring to a boil. Reduce heat to a simmer and steam 10 to 20 minutes or until just tender when pierced with a fork.

To microwave, cook one head at a time. Place in a pie plate with ¼ cup water. Microwave, covered, on HIGH (100 percent) 8 to 10 minutes, rotating plate halfway through the cooking time.

Do not overcook or heads will fall apart. Drain. If not serving immediately, place in a sink or large bowl of cold water to stop the cooking. When cool, remove from water and dry on paper towels.

**Make puree:** In a 3-quart microwave-safe bowl, microwave peas, watercress, and chicken broth, covered, on HIGH (100 percent) until peas are tender, 8 to 12 minutes, stirring after 6 minutes. Cool slightly. Puree in batches in food processor with metal blade. Remove to a bowl and season to taste.

Before serving, spread a layer of puree on a very large platter. Arrange cauliflower on puree and, with a fork, break flowerets open. Spoon puree over the top, filling in the openings, leaving some cauliflower exposed. Garnish with watercress sprigs.

*Makes 16 servings.*

**Make-Ahead Tip** Cooked cauliflower may be refrigerated overnight, wrapped in plastic wrap. Reheat in steamer over boiling water or in microwave.

Pureed pea mixture may be covered and refrigerated up to 2 days. Reheat in microwave until hot.

---

# Chocolate-Filled Cream Puff Heart

*This beautiful heart-shaped cream puff is made up of sixteen smaller puffs filled with a chocolate cream filling and drizzled with a dark, satiny chocolate glaze. You can make this as one large heart, or divide the dough in half and make two smaller hearts.*

**CREAM PUFF PASTRY:**
1½ cups water
¾ cup (1½ sticks) unsalted butter, cut into small pieces
¾ teaspoon salt
1½ cups all-purpose flour
1½ teaspoons sugar
6 large eggs

**CHOCOLATE CREAM FILLING:**
3 cups whipping cream
¾ cup plus 2 tablespoons powdered sugar
½ cup unsweetened cocoa
2 teaspoons vanilla extract or 4 tablespoons Kahlua or crème de cacao

**CHOCOLATE GLAZE:**
4 ounces unsweetened chocolate, chopped
3 tablespoons butter or margarine
1⅓ cups sifted powdered sugar
4 tablespoons water

**Preheat** oven to 400F (205C). Lightly grease and flour a baking sheet or line it with parchment. Draw a heart approximately 10 inches high and 10 inches wide on the parchment or trace it with the tip of a knife onto the flour-lined pan.

**Make pastry:** In a heavy saucepan over medium heat, bring water, butter, and salt to a boil. When mixture boils and butter melts, remove from heat. Immediately stir in flour and sugar. Using a wooden spoon, stir vigorously until mixture leaves sides of saucepan. Return to heat and continue stirring 1 to 2 minutes to dry out the dough. Remove from heat and transfer to a large bowl. Add 1 egg and mix well. Continue adding remaining eggs, 1 at a time, beating after each addition, until well incorporated. The dough should be smooth and shiny.

Drop dough by spoonfuls into 3-inch-wide mounds, touching each other and following the lines of the heart. Bake 25 to 35 minutes or until pastry is puffed and golden. Remove from oven, but leave temperature at 400F (205C). Cut heart in half horizontally. (Some of the puffs will break apart. Don't be concerned; the filling and frosting will cover all cracks.) Bake both halves, cut side up, for an additional 10 to 15 minutes, or until dry. Remove from oven and cool.

**Make chocolate cream filling:** Beat cream until soft peaks form. Add sugar, cocoa, and vanilla or liqueur, and beat until stiff. Place bottom half of heart cut side up on a platter. Spoon or pipe filling through a large star tip onto heart. Place top over cream, letting filling show in the middle.

**Make glaze:** Melt chocolate and butter or margarine in a small saucepan on top of the stove or in a microwave-safe bowl in the microwave, covered, on HIGH (100 percent) 1 to 3 minutes or until melted. Stir in sugar and water. Cool slightly. If glaze becomes stiff, thin with additional water. Spoon over top of heart. Refrigerate for several hours.

*Makes 14 to 16 servings.*

**Make-Ahead Tips** Unfilled pastry heart may be frozen up to 2 weeks. Defrost at room temperature.

Filled and frosted heart may be refrigerated overnight.

# Grand Marnier Apricot Trifle

*Another great choice for a buffet. If you have a pretty crystal bowl, show it off with this creamy layering of cake, apricots, and lemony custard. Plan to make this at least one day before serving. The recipe can be doubled or tripled.*

Apricot Custard (see below)
1 (16-oz.) pound cake
5 tablespoons Grand Marnier mixed with 3
    tablespoons apricot syrup
1 (16-oz.) can apricot halves in syrup, drained,
    reserving syrup
Dried apricots for garnish (optional)
Mint leaves for garnish (optional)

### APRICOT CUSTARD:
½ cup fresh lemon juice
½ cup reserved apricot syrup
2 large eggs
1 cup sugar
4 teaspoons cornstarch
½ cup dried apricots, chopped into ¼-inch dice
⅓ cup whipping cream
⅓ cup regular or low-fat sour cream

**Make custard:** In a medium-size heavy saucepan, stir together lemon juice, apricot syrup, eggs, sugar, and cornstarch. Cook over medium heat, whisking constantly, until mixture comes to a full

boil and thickens. Remove from heat and stir in dried apricots. Place plastic wrap directly on the top and cool completely in refrigerator. (Or, to hasten cooling, place pan in a large bowl of ice water and stir occasionally until chilled.) Whip cream until stiff peaks form. Add sour cream and continue beating until stiff. Fold in custard.

**To assemble:** Slice cake into ½-inch-thick slices. Place on work surface and drizzle with Grand Marnier/apricot syrup. Cut cake slices into quarters. Arrange one-third of cake slices over bottom of an attractive 1½- to 2-quart (6- to 8-cup) glass bowl. Coarsely chop canned apricots and sprinkle one-third over cake. Spread with one-third of custard. Repeat layers twice, ending with custard. Cover with plastic wrap and refrigerate 24 to 36 hours.

**Before serving:** If desired, cut dried apricots into petal shapes. Arrange in daisy pattern on custard. Garnish with mint leaves.

*Makes 10 servings.*

# Pink Pastel Punch

*Here's a pretty nonalcoholic punch that freezes well before the ginger ale is added. You might make an extra batch, freeze it in a decorative mold, and unmold it to float in the punch bowl. That way the punch won't get diluted with melting ice.*

2 pints raspberry sherbet
1 (12-oz.) can pink lemonade concentrate, thawed
2 (10-oz.) packages frozen raspberries in syrup, thawed
4 cups water
1 (33.8-fl. oz.) bottle of ginger ale or 7-Up, chilled

**So**ften 1 pint raspberry sherbet. In punch bowl, combine softened sherbet and lemonade concen- trate. Stir in raspberries and water. Refrigerate until chilled. The mixture may be refrigerated overnight or frozen.

Before serving, stir in ginger ale or 7-Up. Scoop remaining sherbet into balls and float on top of punch.

*Makes 24 (4-oz.) servings.*

# PATRIOTIC PARTIES

## Fourth of July Barbecue

---

**M E N U**

*Smoked-Salmon Spread*
*Blue-Cheese Garden Dip*
*Gin-Fizz Cooler*

*Grilled Chicken with Panhandle or Firecracker Barbecue Sauce*
*Grilled Chuck Roast with Soy-Ginger Marinade*
*Old-Fashioned Potato Salad*
*Santa Fe Slaw*
*Sweet Bourbon Baked Beans*
*New-Fangled Garlic Bread*

*Blueberries 'n' Cream Torte*
*Stars & Stripes Cake*

---

Mix some warm summer sun with a soft breeze, add family and friends, combine with great food, and you have the recipe for a high-flying, flag-raising Fourth. All the tried-and-true traditional favorites are here, with a few savory twists—chicken with a choice of barbecue sauces, marinated sliced beef, coleslaw with a New Mexican twist, and garlic bread with a light, but lush, buttery cream-cheese topping.

The Stars & Stripes Cake is a fitting tribute to Old Glory and is large enough to feed a crowd. As an alternative, I also offer a Blueberries 'n' Cream Torte. Garnish the sour cream topping on the torte with rings of strawberries, raspberries, and fresh blueberries for a pretty, patriotic finish.

Most of the recipes in this menu serve eight, but if you serve the chicken and beef, you will have enough meat for twelve. Don't forget, when you serve a large assortment of dishes, you won't need as much of any one kind.

# Smoked-Salmon Spread

*The many toppings usually heaped on bagels are packed into this pinkish-orange spread for mini-bagels or toasted bagel slices. For a patriotic theme, mold the spread into a star-shaped mold, and garnish it with smoked-salmon stars and green-onion stripes.*

1 small garlic clove, crushed
1 medium-size green onion, finely chopped
4 ounces smoked salmon (coarsely chopped)
1 (8-oz.) package regular or low-fat cream cheese, at room temperature
2 tablespoons regular or low-fat sour cream
2 teaspoons lemon juice
1 tablespoon fresh dill or 1 teaspoon dried dill
⅛ teaspoon pepper
2 smoked salmon slices and 1 green onion for garnish (optional)
Mini-bagels, crackers, bread rounds, and/or cucumber slices for serving

Line a 2-cup mold or bowl with plastic wrap. In food processor with metal blade, process garlic until minced. Add green onions and pulse until chopped. Add salmon, cream cheese, sour cream, lemon juice, dill, and pepper, and pulse until blended. Spoon salmon into the mold, cover, and refrigerate until firm, at least 4 hours.

Before serving, invert salmon mold on a serving platter, and pull off plastic. If you like, cut salmon slices into stars, using small aspic cutter, and cut top of green onion into thin strips. Arrange on top of spread. Serve with mini-bagels, crackers, bread, and/or cucumber.

*Makes 1⅔ cups, serves 8 to 10.*

**Make-Ahead Tip**   Spread may be refrigerated in the mold for 2 days.

---

# Blue-Cheese Garden Dip

*A crunchy confetti of radish, celery, onion, and pepper add texture and color to this creamy blue-cheese dip. Serve with raw vegetables.*

1 garlic clove, peeled
¼ cup coarsely chopped radishes
¼ cup coarsely chopped celery
¼ cup coarsely chopped green onion
¼ cup coarsely chopped green bell pepper
1 (3-oz.) package regular or low-fat cream cheese at room temperature
½ cup regular or low-fat small-curd cottage cheese
2 tablespoons regular or low-fat sour cream
Tabasco sauce to taste
½ teaspoon dried dill
1 (½-oz.) package blue-cheese dip mix
Assorted raw vegetables for dipping

In a food processor with the metal blade, process garlic until minced. Add radishes, celery, green onion, and bell pepper; pulse until finely chopped. Add cream cheese, cottage cheese, and sour cream; process until well blended. Add Tabasco sauce, dill, and dip mix. Pulse to mix. Refrigerate at least 4 hours for flavors to blend before serving.

Serve with vegetables for dipping.

*Makes 1½ cups, serves 8.*

**Make-Ahead Tip**   Dip may be refrigerated up to 3 days. If too thick, thin with additional sour cream.

# Gin-Fizz Cooler

*Here's a great way to keep cool in the heat of summer. Make the beverage mixture ahead and freeze it. Before serving, defrost it slightly, and blend until thick and frothy.*

1 (6-oz.) can frozen lemonade concentrate, defrosted slightly
1 (6-oz.) can frozen pineapple concentrate, defrosted slightly
2 cups club soda, chilled
1½ cups gin
4 cups ice cubes

**Place** half the ingredients at a time in blender; blend until smooth. Repeat with remaining ingredients.

*Makes 12 (4-oz.) servings.*

**Make-Ahead Tip**  Mixture may be frozen up to 1 month. Remove from freezer about 1 hour before serving and blend until smooth.

# Grilled Chicken

*Barbecuing chicken is no mean feat. It's a real challenge to get the inside cooked through without burning the outside. If you partially prebake the chicken and then grill it, the results will be chicken that is moist and juicy on the inside and beautifully browned on the outside.*

2 (3½- to 4-lb.) broiler-fryer chickens, cut into serving pieces
1 recipe Panhandle Barbecue Sauce (page 94) or Firecracker Barbecue Sauce (page 94)

**Place** chicken in a self-sealing plastic bag or a bowl. Pour half the cooled barbecue sauce over chicken. Refrigerate 8 to 12 hours, turning once or twice.

About 1 hour before serving, preheat oven to 375F (175C). Place chicken in a shallow roasting pan. Bake chicken 20 minutes. (If making mainly thighs and legs, bake 5 minutes longer.)

Meanwhile prepare coals. Place grill rack about 4 inches from coals and grease rack. Remove chicken from oven and brush with barbecue sauce. Grill 20 to 25 minutes, turning and basting frequently. Bring remaining sauce to a boil and serve with reserved sauce.

*Makes 8 servings.*

# Panhandle Barbecue Sauce

*Here's an all-purpose barbecue sauce with so much pizzazz that it even gives oven-baked meats a rich flavor.*

¼ cup vegetable oil
1 small onion, finely chopped
2 garlic cloves, minced
1 (10-oz.) can tomato soup
1 (8-oz.) can tomato sauce
½ cup dark molasses
½ cup cider or white vinegar
½ cup packed golden brown sugar
1 tablespoon dry mustard
1 tablespoon Worcestershire sauce
2 teaspoons paprika
1 tablespoon seasoned salt
½ teaspoon pepper
1 teaspoon grated orange peel (optional)

In a medium-size saucepan over medium-high heat, heat oil until hot. Add onion and garlic and sauté until softened, stirring occasionally. Add tomato soup, tomato sauce, molasses, vinegar, brown sugar, dry mustard, Worcestershire sauce, paprika, seasoned salt, pepper, and orange peel, if using. Bring to a boil, reduce heat, and simmer, uncovered, stirring occasionally, 20 minutes or until thick enough to coat a spoon. Pour into a bowl, cover, and refrigerate until used or several weeks.

*Makes 1½ cups, enough for 2 to 3 chickens.*

# Firecracker Barbecue Sauce

*Spicy and robust, a little of this sauce goes a long way.*

1 tablespoon ketchup
2 tablespoons Worcestershire sauce
2 tablespoons soy sauce
4 tablespoons plum jam
1½ teaspoons salt or to taste
4 teaspoons sugar
2 teaspoons ground pepper
2 teaspoons dry mustard
2 teaspoons ground ginger
1 teaspoon curry powder
4 tablespoons fruit chutney
Tabasco to taste

Process all ingredients together in food processor with metal blade or in blender. Remove to a medium-size saucepan and bring to a boil. Reduce heat and simmer, uncovered, 5 minutes. Pour into a bowl, cover, and refrigerate until used or several weeks.

*Makes 1¼ cups or enough for 3 to 4 chickens.*

# New-Fangled Garlic Bread

*For a creamier, thicker topping for time-honored garlic bread, substitute light cream cheese for part of the butter.*

1 (8-oz.) oval loaf French or sourdough bread, unsliced
2 tablespoons low-fat cream cheese
¼ cup (½ stick) butter or margarine
1 garlic clove, minced
1 teaspoon finely chopped green onion tops
½ teaspoon dried leaf basil
1 tablespoon grated Parmesan cheese

Cut bread in half horizontally. Place cream cheese, butter, garlic, green onion, basil, and Parmesan cheese in a medium-size microwave-safe bowl. Microwave, covered with waxed paper, on HIGH (100%) 1 to 2 minutes, stirring after each minute until melted. Divide in half and spread over cut side of bread.

Before serving, preheat oven to 400F (205C). Place bread cut side up on baking sheet. Bake 12 to 15 minutes or until browned and crisp.

*Makes 8 servings.*

**Make-Ahead Tip** After spreading with garlic topping, the unbaked bread may be wrapped in foil and refrigerated overnight or frozen.

# Blueberries 'n' Cream Torte

*The layers of textures make this so special—plump juicy blueberries on a crunchy cookie crust under a silken blanket of sour cream custard.*

**PASTRY:**
1¾ cups all-purpose flour
⅓ cup sugar
Dash of salt
¾ cup (1½ sticks) cold unsalted butter, cut into pieces
1 egg

**FILLING:**
4 cups blueberries
½ cup sugar
¼ cup quick-cooking tapioca
½ teaspoon grated lemon peel
¾ teaspoon ground cinnamon
⅛ teaspoon ground nutmeg

**SOUR CREAM TOPPING:**
1 large egg
2 cups regular or low-fat sour cream
½ cup sugar
1½ teaspoons vanilla extract

**Make pastry:** Preheat oven to 400F (205C). In a food processor with the metal blade or in a bowl with electric mixer, pulse or mix flour, sugar, and salt to combine. Add butter and pulse or mix until crumbly. Add egg and pulse or mix until dough holds together and begins to form a ball. Press two-thirds of the pastry into the bottom of a 9-inch springform pan. Bake 12 to 15 minutes or until lightly browned. Remove from oven and cool. Press remaining dough 1½ inches up the sides of the pan. (You might not use all of the dough.) Reduce oven temperature to 350F (175C).

**Make filling:** In a medium-size saucepan, combine blueberries, sugar, tapioca, lemon peel, cinnamon, and nutmeg. Let stand 15 minutes. Place saucepan over medium heat and cook, stirring, until mixture reaches a full rolling boil. Remove from heat and cool slightly. Pour into pastry.

**Make topping:** In a small bowl, mix egg slightly. Stir in sour cream, sugar, and vanilla. Spoon over blueberries.

Bake torte 45 minutes. Cool completely on a rack. Cover with foil and refrigerate, if desired. Before serving, place springform pan on a bowl that is smaller than the circumference of the springform. Open side of pan and let rim slip down. Place torte on a serving platter.

*Makes 8 to 10 servings.*

**Make-Ahead Tip** Torte may be refrigerated up to 2 days. Serve chilled or at room temperature.

# Stars & Stripes Cake

*Earn a reputation as a baking Betsy Ross by making this grand old flag cake. If you're not inclined to bake a cake from scratch, use 1½ packages (18.5 oz. each) cake mix, following package directions and baking them in two jellyroll pans until a wooden pick inserted in the center comes out clean.*

## SPONGE CAKE:

12 large eggs, separated
¾ cup plus 1½ cups sugar
2 teaspoons vanilla extract
2¼ cups all-purpose flour
3 teaspoons baking powder
1 teaspoon salt
¼ cup Grand Marnier or orange juice

## STRAWBERRY FILLING:

1 cup (½ pt.) whipping cream
¼ cup powdered sugar
1 pint (1 lb.) strawberries, hulled and chopped

## FROSTING & DECORATION:

2 cups (1 pt.) whipping cream
¼ cup powdered sugar
2 pints (2 lbs.) strawberries, the smallest berries available, or raspberries
1 (1-lb. 5-oz.) can blueberry pie filling, drained, or 1 cup fresh blueberries

**Make cake:** Preheat oven to 375F (175C). Grease 2 (15" × 10") jellyroll pans. Line the pans with parchment or waxed paper. Grease the paper. If using waxed paper, dust with flour and shake out the excess.

In a small bowl with electric mixer, beat egg yolks until thick and light. Gradually beat in ¾ cup sugar and vanilla, beating 2 to 3 minutes. In a large bowl, beat egg whites until soft peaks form. Gradually add remaining 1½ cups sugar, 1 tablespoon at a time, beating until stiff peaks form. In a small bowl, stir together flour, baking powder, and salt. Fold flour and yolks into whites. Divide batter between pans, smoothing tops. Bake 13 to 18 minutes or until tops are lightly golden and spring back when pressed with finger tips. If baking both pans in one oven, rotate them after 6 minutes. Remove from oven and immediately invert onto racks or foil. Lift off pans and peel off paper. Cool completely.

Place cake layers on work surface. Sprinkle tops with Grand Marnier or orange juice. Place one layer on a large platter or a piece of heavy cardboard cut 1 inch larger than the cake and covered with plastic-coated doilies.

**Make filling:** Beat 1 cup cream until soft peaks form. Add powdered sugar and strawberries and beat until mixture turns pink. Spread over cake layer. Top with second layer. Cut cake as pictured (between pages 146 and 147) to resemble a flag "waving."

**Make frosting:** Up to 4 hours before serving, whip 2 cups cream until soft peaks form. Add powdered sugar and beat until stiff. Frost top and sides of cake.

**To decorate:** Place remaining frosting in a pastry bag fitted with a ¼-inch star or ribbon tip. If using strawberries, hull and slice through the stem end. Using wooden picks, mark a 5½-inch square on the upper left corner of the cake. Alternate rows of sliced strawberries or raspberries and piped whipped cream on rest of cake, to make 13 stripes. Fill the left-hand square with as much blueberry pie filling as needed, or cover it with fresh blueberries. Pipe desired number of whipped-cream stars on the patch of blueberries.

Refrigerate cake up to 4 hours.

*Makes 18 to 20 servings.*

**Make-Ahead Tips** Cakes may be wrapped in foil and stored at room temperature overnight or frozen up to 1 month.

Filled cake may be refrigerated overnight.

Celebrate with a *Fourth of July Barbecue:* Grilled Chicken with Panhandle Barbecue Sauce (pages 93 and 94), Old-Fashioned Potato Salad (page 95), and Santa Fe Slaw (page 96).

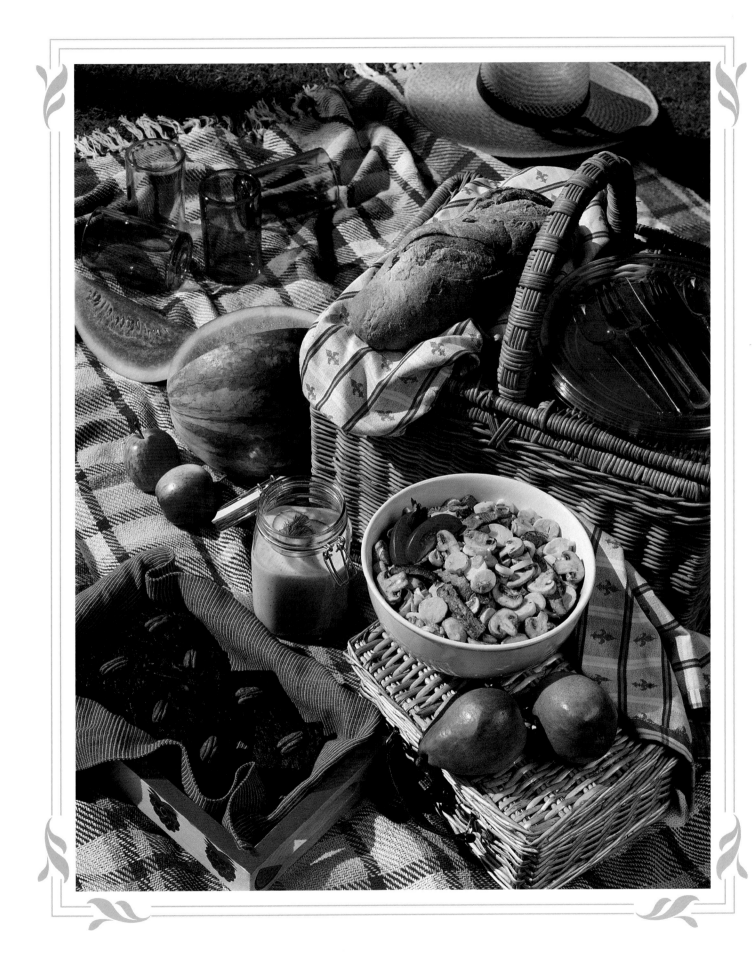

# Labor Day Picnic

---

**M E N U**

*Chilled Cucumber & Avocado Soup*

*Steak & Mushroom Salad with Mustard Vinaigrette*
*Rice Salad with Curried Artichoke Vinaigrette*

*Fresh Fruit with Fluffy Pineapple Dip and/or*
*Strawberry-Ginger Dip*
*Fudgy Caramel Brownies*

---

Labor Day signifies the passing of summer and all its glory before the crisp days of autumn. Take advantage of the last warm days of the season with these carefree picnic dishes.

Tote the creamy green velvet cucumber-avocado soup in a Thermos and pack paper or plastic bowls or cups for serving.

For beef lovers, there's a hearty steak salad and for vegetarians a curry-flavored rice salad.

For an easy, attractive, and refreshing dessert, offer an assortment of fresh fruits with either one or two rich, creamy dips. And for the dessert lover who believes that fruit doesn't count as dessert, I offer decadent Fudgy Caramel Brownies.

End the summer season with a *Labor Day Picnic:* Chilled Cucumber & Avocado Soup (page 100), Steak & Mushroom Salad with Mustard Vinaigrette (page 100), and Fudgy Caramel Brownies (page 102).

# Chilled Cucumber & Avocado Soup

*This soup is as welcome served from a Thermos on a picnic blanket as it is in balloon wine glasses at a sophisticated summer dinner. For a touch of elegance, top each serving with a slice of cucumber and a dollop of sour cream and caviar.*

1 large ripe avocado, peeled, pitted, and coarsely chopped
6 to 8 ounces European cucumber, halved and seeded
1 large green onion, coarsely chopped
1½ cups chicken broth
3 tablespoons fresh lemon juice
1 tablespoon fresh chopped dill or 1 teaspoon dried dill
Dash of sugar
½ cup regular or low-fat sour cream
Salt and white pepper to taste
Sour cream for garnish (optional)

Place avocado in a food processor with the metal blade or in a blender; process until pureed. Cut cucumber into chunks. With the motor running, drop 1 piece of cucumber at a time through the feed tube. Add green onion and process until smooth. Add chicken broth, lemon juice, dill, sugar, and sour cream. Blend well. Season with salt and pepper. Pour into a bowl, cover, and refrigerate until serving. Garnish with sour cream, if desired.

*Makes 6 servings.*

**Make-Ahead Tip**   Soup can be refrigerated up to 6 hours.

---

# Steak & Mushroom Salad with Mustard Vinaigrette

*When I found out with very little notice that James Beard would be visiting my cooking school in Los Angeles, I made him this salad for lunch. It's a great way to use up leftover roast beef, but well worth the time it takes to cook a steak.*

**MUSTARD VINAIGRETTE:**
1 tablespoon plus 1 teaspoon balsamic vinegar
4 teaspoons Dijon mustard
1 teaspoon Worcestershire sauce
Dash of Tabasco sauce
¼ cup regular or low-fat sour cream
⅓ cup olive oil
Salt and pepper to taste

**SALAD:**
1 (2-lb.) boneless beef sirloin steak, cut 2 inches thick
Salt and pepper
½ pound mushrooms, sliced
½ cup sliced green onions
1 (14-oz.) can hearts of palm, drained and sliced
2 tablespoons chopped chives
2 tablespoons chopped parsley
2 tablespoons chopped fresh dill or 2 teaspoons dried dill
2 medium-size tomatoes, sliced, for garnish (optional)

**Make vinaigrette:**   In a small bowl, whisk together vinegar, mustard, Worcestershire sauce, Tabasco sauce, sour cream, and oil. Season with salt and pepper.

**Make salad:**   Preheat broiler or grill. Season steak with salt and pepper. Broil or grill until medium rare, 8 to 10 minutes per side. An instant-read thermometer should register about 130F (55C). Cool steak slightly. To slice in food processor, cut steak into pieces as wide and high as the feed tube. Place on foil and freeze until slightly firm, but soft enough to pierce with the tip of a knife. (Or freeze solid, and defrost to the right consistency.) Slice with slicing disk of food processor to about 1⅛-inch thickness. If slicing by hand, freeze steak slightly for ease in cutting. Place slices in large bowl.

Add mushrooms, green onions, hearts of palm, chives, parsley, and dill. Pour dressing over salad and toss well. Garnish with tomato slices, if desired.

*Makes 8 servings.*

**Make-Ahead Tips**   Vinaigrette may be refrigerated for several days.

Salad may be refrigerated 6 to 8 hours. Bring to room temperature before serving.

# FALL FARE

## Treats for Halloween

---

**M E N U**

*Caramel Nut Corn*
*Spice Cookie Goblins*
*Chocolate-Almond Toffee*
*Ginger Spice Cake with Lemon Glaze*


*Hot Mulled Wine*
*Witches' Brew*

---

Trick-or-treating is not what it used to be when I first developed Halloween recipes. Then, we would hand out home-baked cookies and hand-dipped candies to the pint-sized witches and goblins who rang our doorbells. Now all treats have to be factory wrapped and hermetically sealed for safety.

We may have lost some of the innocence of the old days, but there is an upside to this New Age version of Halloween. The holiday that was once strictly for kids has become a real family affair. Adults are out strolling the streets with their offspring, meeting each other with conviviality and sharing the evening with a festive common purpose.

What a hauntingly perfect occasion to throw open your doors to friends and neighbors for a good old-fashioned family block party. Since you may not even know some of the neighbors' names to call or mail out invitations, try writing the party particulars on a scroll of orange paper tied with black ribbon. Insert it into a store-bought plastic pumpkin and hang it on each family's doorknob. Or buy a slew of miniature 3-inch pumpkins at the market and write the party plans on them with an indelible black marker. Leave them like calling cards on each neighbor's front steps.

Fill punch bowls with Hot Mulled Wine for the adults and Witches' Brew for the kids. Put out the cookies, candies, and cake in this menu and supplement them with a cauldron of steaming soup, like Puree of Pumpkin Soup (page 111), Country Minestrone (page 8) or Mushroom Barley Soup (page 8). Different-size hollowed out pumpkins make super holders for Halloween-inspired foods like sliced black bread, orange crackers, and black olives.

Just add some bewitching costumes, spooky lighting, and a background of eerie sound effects from the local party shop and you've got yourself an event the neighbors will be cackling about for a long time to come.

# Caramel Nut Corn

*This is the real thing — popcorn and nuts baked in a syrupy brown-sugar glaze until crunchy and golden.*

12 cups popped popcorn (½ cup unpopped corn)
1 cup (2 sticks) unsalted butter
2 cups golden brown sugar, packed
1 teaspoon salt
½ cup light corn syrup
½ teaspoon baking soda
1 teaspoon vanilla extract
6 ounces whole unblanched almonds (1½ cups)
6 ounces pecan halves (1½ cups)

**P**lace popcorn in a large shallow roasting pan or 2 (13″ × 9″) baking pans. Set aside. Preheat oven to 250F (120C).

In a large heavy saucepan (about 4 qt.), melt butter over low heat. Stir in brown sugar, salt, and corn syrup. Bring to a boil, stirring constantly.

Insert candy thermometer and boil without stirring until thermometer reaches 285F (140C), or syrup reaches the soft-crack stage. Immediately remove from heat; stir in soda and vanilla. The baking soda will cause the mixture to foam up and become frothy.

Pour syrup over popped corn; using 2 wooden spoons, mix well. Bake 15 minutes; stir well. Bake 15 minutes more. Stir in nuts. Bake 30 minutes more, stirring well every 10 minutes. Turn out onto waxed paper. Cool completely. Break apart. Store in airtight containers.

*Makes 12 cups.*

**Make-Ahead Tip** Nut Corn may be stored in airtight containers up to 3 months.

# Spice Cookie Goblins

*One batch of this fragrantly spiced dough makes lots of cookies. Divide the dough in thirds and roll between sheets of waxed paper and freeze. The dough is ready to cut into shapes, and it's much easier to cut out cookies from frozen cookie dough. Pint-sized volunteers love to help bake and eat these cookies.*

## SPICE COOKIE DOUGH:

1 cup (2 sticks) butter or margarine, at room temperature
½ cup sugar
½ cup dark corn syrup
3 cups all-purpose flour
1½ teaspoons ground ginger
1½ teaspoons ground cinnamon
½ teaspoon ground cloves

## DECORATIONS (OPTIONAL):

Nuts such as pecan halves and sliced almonds
Mini chocolate chips
Silver ball decorations
1 egg white, lightly beaten

**Make cookie dough:** In a large bowl with electric mixer, cream butter or margarine and sugar until light and fluffy. Mix in corn syrup. On low speed, slowly beat in the flour and spices. Remove to work surface and knead into a ball. Divide into three parts and shape each into a flat disk. Wrap in plastic wrap and refrigerate until firm.

Remove a third of the dough from refrigerator about 5 minutes before rolling. Place a sheet of waxed paper on work surface. Lightly flour the paper. Place dough in center of paper. Lightly flour another sheet of waxed paper and place on top of dough. Roll dough between sheets of waxed paper until it is approximately ⅛ inch thick. Place dough in waxed paper on baking sheets and place in freezer. Repeat with remaining 2 balls of dough.

When dough is firm, preheat oven to 350F (175C). Line baking sheets with parchment paper or spray with nonstick cooking spray. Remove 1 piece of dough to work surface. Pull off top sheet of waxed paper. Turn over and pull off remaining waxed paper. Cut dough into desired shapes, using 2-inch to 4-inch cookie cutters. Decorate as desired, dabbing egg white on the back of decorations to hold them in place. Place cookies on prepared baking sheets. Repeat with remaining dough.

Bake cookies 8 to 10 minutes or until lightly browned. If baking 2 sheets at a time, reverse positions halfway through baking time. Cool slightly before removing from pans.

*Makes about 72 (2-inch) cookies.*

**Make-Ahead Tips** Dough may be refrigerated up to 2 days or frozen, tightly wrapped, up to 1 month.

Cookies may be stored in airtight containers for 2 weeks or frozen up to 1 month.

# Chocolate-Almond Toffee

*Every so often I hear a lamentable story about a favored toffee recipe that all of a sudden won't set up. Is there a jinx? Just in case, try this one. I've been told it always works because it's made with both butter and margarine. Be sure to harden the toffee in a metal baking pan, so that you can bang it against the counter to remove the toffee.*

1 cup (2 sticks) unsalted butter
1 cup (2 sticks) unsalted margarine
2 cups sugar
6 tablespoons water
2 tablespoons light corn syrup
1 pound milk or semisweet chocolate, coarsely chopped
2 cups chopped almonds (8 oz.), toasted at 350F (175C) 10 to 15 minutes, stirring occasionally

**Grease** a 13″ × 9″ metal baking pan with butter or shortening. In a large heavy saucepan (about 4 qt.), combine butter, margarine, sugar, water, and corn syrup. Bring to a boil over medium heat, stirring occasionally. Insert a candy thermometer and boil over medium-high heat without stirring until the thermometer reaches 250F (120C). Continue to boil, stirring to prevent scorching, until the temperature reaches 300F (150C) or syrup reaches the hard-crack stage. If the candy begins to turn dark around the sides of the pan, reduce the heat.

Immediately pour the toffee into the prepared pan. Refrigerate until firm.

Remove toffee from pan by turning the pan upside down and rapping it once or twice on a countertop. Melt the chocolate in a double boiler over hot water or in a microwave oven. Spread half of it on one side of toffee. Sprinkle with half the almonds, pressing them in with the palm of your hand. Refrigerate until chocolate hardens. Turn uncoated side up, spread with remaining chocolate, and press in remaining almonds. Refrigerate until chocolate hardens. Break into pieces by inserting the tip of a knife at the points where you want the candy to break. Store in airtight containers.

*Makes 1½ pounds toffee.*

**Make-Ahead Tip** Toffee may be stored at room temperature up to 1 month or refrigerated up to 3 months or frozen.

# Ginger Spice Cake with Lemon Glaze

*Although the texture and color of this dessert are reminiscent of a spice cake, the mouthwatering, sweet and spicy flavors of gingerbread predominate.*

**GINGER SPICE CAKE:**
½ cup (1 stick) unsalted butter or margarine
1 cup packed golden brown sugar
¾ cup dark molasses
¾ cup light corn syrup
½ cup regular, low-fat, or nonfat milk
1 teaspoon baking soda
2 tablespoons hot water
2½ cups all-purpose flour
1 teaspoon ground ginger
1 teaspoon ground cloves
1 teaspoon ground cinnamon
1 large egg
2 egg whites

**LEMON GLAZE:**
1½ cups powdered sugar, sifted
2 to 4 tablespoons lemon juice
Dash of yellow food coloring (optional)

**Make cake:** Preheat oven to 325F (165C). Grease a 13″ × 9″ baking pan. Line bottom with waxed paper and grease the paper.

In a medium saucepan, heat butter, brown sugar, molasses, corn syrup, and milk until butter melts. In a small bowl, dissolve baking soda in hot water.

Stir into butter mixture in saucepan. Place flour, ginger, cloves, cinnamon, egg, and egg whites in food processor with the metal blade or in a bowl. With motor running, slowly pour in warm butter mixture through feed tube. Process, scraping down sides, until well blended. Or add warm butter mixture to flour mixture in bowl; beat until combined. Pour batter into prepared pan. Bake 40 to 45 minutes or until skewer or wooden pick inserted in center comes out clean. Cool 10 minutes. Invert cake onto a wire rack, remove from pan, and cool thoroughly.

**Make glaze:** Place powdered sugar in bowl. Stir in 2 tablespoons lemon juice. If too thick to spread, add additional lemon juice a teaspoon at a time, until mixture is the correct consistency. Tint with food coloring if desired. Spread or drizzle glaze over smoothest side of cake. Cut into squares to serve.

*Makes 16 servings.*

**Make-Ahead Tip** Cake may be stored, covered, at room temperature up to 1 week or frozen up to 3 months.

# Hot Mulled Wine

*This is a popular recipe from my "Gifts from the Kitchen" classes. It makes a welcome gift when given with a bottle of wine and a card inscribed with directions for using. It's easy and a warming treat to have on hand for a cold day.*

**MULLED WINE MIX:**
1½ cups sugar
1½ teaspoons ground cinnamon
½ teaspoon ground cloves
½ teaspoon ground allspice

**FOR 1 SERVING:**
1½ teaspoons Mulled Wine Mix
⅓ cup water
⅔ cup dry red wine
Cinnamon stick

**FOR 9 SERVINGS:**
¾ cup Mulled Wine Mix
3 cups water
1 (1½-liter) bottle dry red wine
Cinnamon stick

**To make mix:** Stir all ingredients together. Store in airtight container.

**For 1 Serving:** In a small saucepan, bring mix and water to a boil. Add wine and heat until hot; do not boil. Serve in mug with cinnamon stick stirrer.

*Makes 1 cup.*

**For 9 Servings:** In a large saucepan, bring mix and water to a boil. Add wine and heat until hot; do not boil. Serve in punch cups or mugs with cinnamon stick stirrers.

*Makes 9 (1-cup) servings.*

**Make-Ahead Tip** Wine mix may be stored at room temperature for several months.

---

# Witches' Brew

*Steaming mugs of spiced cider warm body and soul after a cold night of trick-or-treating.*

2 quarts (8 cups) apple cider
½ cup packed golden brown sugar
1 teaspoon whole allspice
1 teaspoon whole cloves
¼ teaspoon salt
1 lemon, sliced
1 orange, sliced
1 cinnamon stick
1 small orange, cut into 8 wedges, studded with cloves

In a large saucepan, combine cider, brown sugar, allspice, cloves, salt, lemon and orange slices, and cinnamon stick. Slowly bring to a boil over medium heat. Cover and simmer 20 minutes. Strain; add orange and lemon slices back, if desired.

Pour warm cider into punch bowl or mugs. Garnish with clove-studded orange wedges.

*Makes 8 (1-cup) servings.*

**Make-Ahead Tip** Brew may be refrigerated overnight and reheated.

# A Bountiful Thanksgiving

## MENU

*Harvest Vegetable Patch with Ranch Dill Dip*

*Puree of Pumpkin Soup*

*Marinated Roast Turkey*
*Traditional Giblet Gravy*
*Sausage-Apple Stuffing or*
*Chestnut-Oyster Stuffing*
*Green Beans with Cashews*
*Orange Praline Yams or*
*Apricot-Glazed Sweet Potatoes*
*Cranberry-Raspberry Relish or*
*Fresh Cranberry Sorbet*

*Sugar-&-Spice Yam Muffins*

*Pumpkin Cream-Cheese Roll*
*Cranberry-Pear Tart*

### BEVERAGE RECOMMENDATION:
*A dry and spicy wine with a hint of sweetness, such as a gewürztraminer*
*Sparkling apple cider*

Thanksgiving is truly a time of gratitude in my home. It is the only holiday for which all my children and grandchildren come from every part of the country to celebrate together. The mere mention of the holiday evokes memories of sweet and spicy aromas wafting from the kitchen and the family reminiscing joyfully around a bountiful table. Of course, there's too much food, too much fat, and too many carbohydrates. But that's all part of the holiday's glorious theme of abundance. Everyone should leave the table feeling as stuffed as a turkey.

Even though this menu is meant for overindulgence, it doesn't mean you need to set aside a big block of time to make it. With a little organization and advance planning, you can get it done without exhausting yourself. Begin by going through each of the recipes and listing the ones that can be prepared ahead and frozen. Then list those that can be refrigerated one or two days in advance. The more you get done ahead, the more relaxed your Thanksgiving will be.

I like to keep the table decorations free-form by arranging fall leaves, gourds, pumpkins, nuts, and votive candles down the center of the table. Miniature pumpkins make terrific holders for candles and/or place cards.

Each recipe states the number of people it serves. However, if you prepare every dish in the menu, the recipes will go a lot further.

# Harvest Vegetable Patch

*Raw vegetables and dip become a conversation piece when guarded by a smiling corn scarecrow.*

**VEGETABLES FOR DIPPING:**
Carrots, peeled
Celery
Radishes
Cauliflower
Broccoli flowerets
Turnip or jcama, peeled
Green onions
Snow peas

**SCARECROW & PATCH:**
2 ears untrimmed corn on the cob
Whole cloves
Twine or string
Wooden bamboo skewers
1 potato
Wooden picks
Seed packets (available from nurseries)
Ranch Dill Dip (see below)
Fresh parsley

**C**ut vegetables into dipping-size pieces. Place in a bowl of ice water for at least 4 hours to crisp.

**Make scarecrow:** Remove husk and silk from one ear of corn; set aside. Make a face in the corn, using 2 cloves for eyes and 4 or 5 for mouth. For each arm, overlap 2 or 3 pieces of reserved husk on work surface. Place some silk in the center, allowing a portion to hang over 1 end. Place a bamboo skewer on the silk. Wrap the husk around tightly and secure with string. Attach arms to each side of corn with bamboo skewers. Slice a piece off each side of the potato so it lies flat. Using wooden picks, attach scarecrow to potato to stand it up. Place on a large platter. Surround with assorted vegetables and dip. Cover potato with parsley.

**Variation** Substitute some trimmed mushrooms, zucchini in slices or wedges, drained baby corn, and olives for some of the above vegetables. These require no soaking.

# Ranch Dill Dip

*A simple blend of ingredients makes a super dip.*

1 cup regular or low-fat mayonnaise
1 cup regular or low-fat sour cream
1 tablespoon ranch salad dressing mix
2 tablespoons chopped fresh dill or 2 teaspoons dried dill
2 teaspoons lemon juice
2 tablespoons Dijon mustard
1 small pumpkin or acorn squash for serving (optional)
Assorted vegetables and/or chips for dipping

**In** a medium-size bowl, stir together mayonnaise, sour cream, dressing mix, dill, lemon juice, and mustard until blended. Refrigerate, covered, at least 4 hours.

If desired, scoop out pumpkin or squash, leaving a shell. Fill with dip. Serve with vegetables and/or chips.

*Makes 2¼ cups.*

**Make-Ahead Tip** Dip may be refrigerated up to 2 days.

# Puree of Pumpkin Soup

*I have a friend and colleague who is a purist. He loves this soup, but insists it would be better made with fresh pumpkin instead of canned. One day I took two batches to Elmer Dills, a popular Los Angeles restaurant critic, who has a Sunday radio show. I asked him, on the air, which soup he liked better. He pointed to the canned one. For those skeptics who remain purists, a three-pound pumpkin, cut into cubes, cooked in water, and drained yields one pound of pumpkin puree.*

1 tablespoon olive oil
1 large onion, chopped
1 medium-size leek, white part only, chopped
1 pound canned or pureed cooked fresh pumpkin
4 cups chicken broth
½ teaspoon salt or to taste
¾ teaspoon curry powder
¼ teaspoon ground nutmeg
½ teaspoon ground white pepper
½ teaspoon ground ginger
1 bay leaf
¾ to 1 cup half-and-half to taste
Pumpkin seeds (also called pepitas) or sunflower seeds, toasted at 350F (175C) until lightly browned, about 10 minutes, for garnishing

Heat olive oil in a medium-size soup pot over medium heat. Add onion and leek and sauté 1 minute. Cover with waxed paper and a lid and cook 15 minutes or until softened but not brown, stirring occasionally. Stir in pumpkin, chicken broth, salt, curry powder, nutmeg, pepper, ginger, and bay leaf. Bring to a boil. Reduce heat and simmer, uncovered, 15 minutes, stirring occasionally. Remove bay leaf. Puree the mixture in batches in a blender or in a food processor with the metal blade for a smoother texture.

Return soup to pot. Add half-and-half and cook over medium heat, stirring occasionally, until heated through. Adjust seasonings. Garnish each serving with a sprinkling of pumpkin or sunflower seeds.

*Makes 6 to 8 servings.*

**Make-Ahead Tip**  Soup may be refrigerated, covered, up to 2 days or frozen up to 1 month. Thaw frozen soup in refrigerator overnight. Add half-and-half and heat until hot.

# Marinated Roast Turkey

*Before I knew much about cooking, I would crawl out of bed at 6:00 A.M. Thanksgiving morning so I could stuff my 24-pound turkey and get it into a slow oven in time for dinner. I have since learned that you can cook a turkey at any temperature, as long as you don't overcook it. I am including a timetable, but a meat thermometer is a more accurate measurement. An unstuffed turkey should be cooked to 165 degrees and a stuffed one to 175. According to the USDA Meat and Poultry Hotline, that is a safe temperature to kill bacteria and produce moist and juicy meat.*

*If you roast the turkey breast side down for the first half of the baking time, the juices will accumulate in the breast and it will be juicier. To do this, you need a rack that's shaped like a V. One year I tried turning a 24-pound bird and it landed on the floor. Since the juices are better off in the turkey than on the cook, if the turkey is too heavy to handle, roast it breast side up the entire time.*

1 (12- to 20-lb.) turkey (allow about 1 pound per serving)
1 cup vegetable oil
1 teaspoon poultry seasoning
2 garlic cloves, minced
2 teaspoons seasoned salt
½ teaspoon pepper
Sausage Apple Stuffing (page 114) or
Chestnut Oyster Stuffing (page 114)
Traditional Giblet Gravy (page 113)
Greens such as parsley, watercress, or fresh herbs for garnish

Remove giblets and fat from inside both turkey cavities. Dry inside and out with paper towels. In a small bowl, mix together oil, poultry seasoning, garlic, seasoned salt, and pepper. Rub over outside of turkey. Place in a baking pan and refrigerate, covered with foil, for several hours or overnight.

Preheat oven to 325F (165C). Remove turkey from refrigerator at least 1 hour before cooking. Lightly spoon desired stuffing into cavity; do not pack. Skewer opening closed with turkey lacers or trussing needle. Tie legs together. Place turkey breast side down on a V-shaped rack in a roasting pan that is no more than 2 inches deep. Bake 20 to 25 minutes per pound for a bird up to 16 pounds; 15 to 20 minutes per pound for 16 pounds and over. Baste every 30 minutes. If roasting breast side down, turn breast up halfway through the roasting time. If skin gets too brown, cover loosely with a tent of foil, pressing it lightly into the drumstick and breast ends, making sure it does not touch the top and sides. Two-thirds through the roasting time, untie drumsticks so heat can reach the stuffed cavity.

When turkey is almost done, insert an instant-read thermometer into the thickest part of the thigh, but not touching the bone. Turkey is done when the temperature reaches 175F (80C) and drumstick moves freely in its socket. There should be at least 1 cup of cooking juices in pan. Remove turkey to carving board. Let rest 20 minutes before carving.

While turkey rests, make gravy as directed. Remove skewers and string from turkey. Carve and place on serving platter. Serve with gravy.

---

**Turkey Roasting Timetable in a 325F (175C) Oven**

| Weight | Stuffed | Unstuffed |
| --- | --- | --- |
| 9 to 12 pounds | 3½ to 4 hours | 3 to 3½ hours |
| 12 to 16 pounds | 4 to 4½ hours | 3½ to 4 hours |
| 16 to 20 pounds | 4½ to 5 hours | 4 to 4½ hours |
| 20 to 24 pounds | 5 to 6 hours | 4½ to 5 hours |

# Traditional Giblet Gravy

*Gravy making can send inexperienced or nervous cooks into a panic when their guests are waiting and the turkey's growing cold. To make gravy ahead, substitute butter or oil for the fat skimmed from the turkey drippings. Stir in enough giblet broth to make a thick gravy, and when the turkey is done, thin it down with some of the turkey juices.*

*Thick gravies are out, along with thick waistlines. The proportions in my recipe give you a "coat-the-spoon" sauce. If you prefer it thicker, use 2 tablespoons fat and flour to each cup of liquid.*

**GIBLET STOCK:**
Turkey giblets and neck
1 large onion, sliced (about 1 cup)
¼ cup celery leaves
½ cup sliced carrots
½ cup dry white wine
2 cups chicken broth

**GRAVY:**
Turkey drippings
All-purpose or instant-blending flour
Salt and pepper

**Make stock:** Cut turkey neck and heart in half. If using liver, refrigerate until ready to use. Place giblets in a medium-size saucepan. Add onion, celery leaves, carrots, wine, and chicken broth. Bring to a boil, reduce heat, and simmer, covered, 2 to 2½ hours. If using liver, add it the last half hour. Remove giblets. Strain the stock into a bowl, pressing on vegetables to extract juices. Chop giblets and meat from neck.

When turkey is done, pour drippings from roasting pan into gravy separator or pitcher. Place in freezer 10 to 15 minutes for fat to rise to top; skim off fat. For each cup of gravy, measure 1 tablespoon fat back into roasting pan. Stir in 1 tablespoon flour for each tablespoon fat. Cook, stirring constantly over low heat, scraping up brown bits from bottom of pan, until mixture is golden. Slowly whisk in pan juices and enough giblet broth to make 1 cup. Increase heat to medium and bring to a boil, stirring and scraping up all brown bits from bottom of the pan. Stir in chopped giblets. Season to taste with salt and pepper.

*Makes about 1 cup gravy.*

**Make-Ahead Tip** Stock and giblets may be refrigerated separately overnight.

# Sausage-Apple Stuffing

*Apples add sugar; sausage adds spice; sour cream, Madeira, and nuts add everything
nice to this super-special stuffing.*

1 (24-oz.) loaf egg bread
3 tablespoons olive oil, divided
½ pound chicken livers (optional), cleaned and cut
    in half
1 pound bulk pork sausage
2 medium-size onions, chopped
½ cup finely chopped celery
2 medium-size apples, peeled, cored, and
    chopped (about 1½ cups)
3 garlic cloves, minced
½ cup chopped fresh parsley
1 teaspoon dried leaf thyme
2 eggs or ½ cup frozen egg substitute, thawed
    (½ cup)
1 cup regular or low-fat sour cream
¼ cup Madeira wine
½ cup chicken broth
Salt and pepper to taste

**P**reheat oven to 250F (120C). Cut crusts off bread
and cut bread into ½-inch cubes. You should have
8 cups. Place cubes on baking sheets and toast until
dry, stirring occasionally, about 25 minutes. Remove to a large bowl.

If using chicken livers, heat 1 tablespoon olive oil
in a large skillet until hot. Add livers and sauté until
brown on the outside, but pink within, 3 to 5 minutes. Do not overcook. Remove with a slotted

spoon, place on a chopping board, cool slightly,
and chop into small pieces. Add to bowl with bread
cubes.

Add sausage to same skillet and cook, stirring,
until all pink is gone. Transfer to bowl with bread
cubes. Add remaining 2 tablespoons olive oil to
skillet. Add onions, celery, apples, and garlic, and
sauté, stirring often, until soft, about 8 minutes.
Remove to bowl with bread cubes. Stir in parsley
and thyme.

In a small bowl, combine eggs, sour cream, wine,
and broth. Pour over stuffing and toss lightly, but
thoroughly. Season to taste.

Either use to stuff turkey (page 112), or bake in a
large shallow casserole at 350F (175C), covered, 30
to 45 minutes. Uncover and bake 30 minutes
longer or until top is crisp, basting with turkey
drippings, if desired.

*Makes enough stuffing for a 14-pound turkey, serves 10
to 12.*

**Make-Ahead Tip** Before the addition of eggs,
sour cream, wine, and broth stuffing mixture may
be refrigerated, covered, overnight, or frozen up to
2 weeks. Thaw thoroughly overnight in refrigerator; stir in remaining ingredients before cooking.

Serve these special *Treats for Halloween:* Spice Cookie Goblins (page 105), Ginger Spice Cake with Lemon Glaze (page 107),
Hot Mulled Wine (page 108), and Witches' Brew (page 108).

# Chestnut-Oyster Stuffing

*Peeling chestnuts is not my idea of fun. No matter how I attempt it, my fingers get blistered and my temper gets fried. Now I keep both my sanity and fingers intact by using canned chestnuts. I may lose a little of the texture, but not a drop of the flavor.*

¼ cup olive oil
2 medium-size onions, chopped
2 large garlic cloves, minced
1½ cups chopped celery
1 cup chopped pecans (about 4 oz.)
1 (12-oz.) box melba toasted cornbread stuffing mix
1 (8-oz.) can oysters, chopped, with the liquid
1 (20-oz.) can chestnuts in water, drained and crumbled
1 teaspoon salt
1 teaspoon dried sage
1 teaspoon poultry seasoning
¾ cup chicken broth
2 large eggs or ½ cup frozen egg substitute, thawed
¼ cup dry sherry

In a large skillet, preferably nonstick, heat olive oil over medium-high heat. Add onion, garlic, and celery, and sauté 1 minute. Cover with a sheet of waxed paper and a lid and cook 8 to 10 minutes, stirring occasionally, until softened. Stir in pecans and sauté until toasted. Remove to large bowl. Add stuffing mix, oysters with liquid, chestnuts, salt, sage, and poultry seasoning. In a small bowl, mix together chicken broth, eggs, and sherry. Pour over stuffing and toss well to coat.

Use to stuff turkey (see page 112) or bake in a large shallow casserole at 350F (175C), covered, for 30 to 45 minutes. Uncover and bake 30 minutes longer or until top is crisp, basting with turkey drippings, if desired.

*Makes enough stuffing for a 20-pound turkey, serves 14 to 16.*

**Make-Ahead Tip** Stuffing mixture before adding broth, eggs, and sherry may be refrigerated, covered, overnight. Stir in remaining ingredients before cooking.

# Green Beans with Cashews

*Green beans retain their vivid color and crisp texture when steamed in a skillet with a little bit of water. They are then tossed with olive oil, butter, and salty cashews.*

3 pounds fresh green beans, ends trimmed
2 tablespoons olive oil
2 tablespoons butter or margarine
2 teaspoons lemon juice
1 cup coarsely chopped salted cashews
Salt and pepper to taste

To cook beans, fill a wide shallow pan with ¾ inch of water. Bring to a boil over high heat. Add beans, cover, and cook until tender but still crunchy, 7 to 10 minutes, tossing after 4 minutes. Drain off any remaining water, but leave beans in pan.

Add oil, butter, and lemon juice. Cook over medium heat, tossing beans to combine, until well coated.

Before serving, stir in cashews and salt and pepper.

*Makes 10 servings.*

**Make-Ahead Tip** Cooked beans may be refrigerated, covered, overnight. To serve, reheat in skillet with oil or butter. Add cashews, salt, and pepper.

Give thanks for family and friends with *A Bountiful Thanksgiving:* Marinated Roast Turkey (page 112), Traditional Giblet Gravy (page 113), Sausage Apple Stuffing (page 114), Green Beans with Cashews (page 115), and Cranberry-Raspberry Relish (page 117).

# Orange Praline Yams

*The most sensational yams I have ever eaten were served to me one Thanksgiving at Alan and Barbara Shefter's home in Washington, D.C. Thanks to the Shefters, my family, friends, and classes have been enjoying the recipe ever since. If you want to double the recipe, bake it in two separate casseroles, so the proportion of filling to topping remains the same.*

**YAMS:**
2 (2-lb. 8-oz.) cans yams, drained, or 4 pounds cooked, peeled, and sliced fresh yams or sweet potatoes
⅔ cup orange juice
1 tablespoon grated orange peel
5 tablespoons brandy
⅓ cup golden brown sugar, packed
1 large egg
2 egg whites
1 teaspoon ground ginger
2 teaspoons salt or to taste
Freshly ground pepper to taste

**PRALINE TOPPING:**
⅔ cup packed golden brown sugar
1 cup chopped pecans (about 4 oz.)
1 teaspoon ground cinnamon
4 tablespoons (½ stick) butter or margarine, melted

**Prepare yams:** Grease a 12-inch porcelain quiche dish or 11" × 7" (2-qt.) casserole dish or spray with nonstick cooking spray. In a bowl with electric mixer or food processor with the metal blade, mix or pulse yams or sweet potatoes until smooth. Mix or pulse in orange juice, peel, brandy, brown sugar, egg, egg whites, ginger, salt, and pepper. Pour in yam mixture, smoothing top evenly.

**Make topping:** In a small bowl, stir together brown sugar, pecans, and cinnamon until blended. Slowly stir in butter until mixed. Sprinkle evenly over the yams.

Preheat oven to 350F (175C). Bake 40 to 50 minutes or until yams are heated through and topping is bubbly. Remove from oven and let stand 15 minutes before serving.

*Makes 10 to 12 servings.*

**Make-Ahead Tip** Unbaked casserole may be refrigerated, covered, overnight.

# Apricot-Glazed Sweet Potatoes

*Sliced sweet potatoes are layered with a tangy puree of dried apricots for a not-too-sweet potato casserole. The top is richly glazed with apricot nectar and brown sugar and studded with pecan halves.*

1 pound dried apricots
1 (12-oz.) can apricot nectar
1 cup water
4 pounds sweet potatoes or yams
½ cup packed golden brown sugar
3 tablespoons butter or margarine, melted
2 tablespoons orange juice
1 tablespoon grated orange peel
½ cup pecan halves

**P**lace apricots in a medium-size saucepan. Add apricot nectar and water to cover. Let stand 1 hour for fruit to soften. Place over medium heat and simmer, uncovered, until apricots are very tender, about 40 minutes. Cool and drain well, reserving the liquid.

Preheat oven to 400F (205C). Scrub sweet potatoes or yams. Place on baking sheet and bake 30 to 40 minutes or until tender when pierced with a fork. Cool; peel and cut lengthwise into slices about ¼ inch thick. Lightly grease an 11" × 7" (2-qt.) baking dish. Arrange a layer of sweet potatoes over bottom of dish. Spread a layer of apricot puree to cover sweet potatoes. Repeat, alternating layers of potatoes and apricots. Sprinkle top with brown sugar.

In a small bowl, mix ½ cup reserved apricot

liquid with melted butter, orange juice, and orange peel. Pour over the layers.

Preheat oven to 375F (175C). Bake, uncovered, 40 minutes, basting occasionally with liquid in bottom of dish. Remove from oven and place pecan halves on top. Return to oven and bake until sides are bubbling and top is well glazed, 5 to 10 minutes. Let stand 10 minutes before cutting into squares.

*Makes 12 to 14 servings.*

**Make-Ahead Tip**  Unbaked casserole may be refrigerated, covered, up to 2 days. Bring to room temperature before baking.

## Cranberry-Raspberry Relish

*This uncooked relish is made very special with the addition of frozen raspberries. It goes together quickly if you chop the apples and the cranberries in a food processor.*

1 pound fresh cranberries, finely chopped
2 tart green apples, peeled, cored, and finely diced
1 cup sugar
½ cup orange marmalade
1 (10-oz.) package frozen raspberries, thawed and drained
1 teaspoon lemon juice or to taste

In a medium-size bowl, mix all ingredients. Refrigerate until serving. Spoon relish into serving bowl.

*Makes 6 cups, or 12 servings.*

**Make-Ahead Tip**  Relish may be refrigerated up to 1 week.

## Fresh Cranberry Sorbet

*Sweetly tart and icy, this makes a refreshing counterpoint to a heavy Thanksgiving dinner. Serve it in place of cranberry sauce, as an intermezzo, or for dessert.*

1 pound fresh cranberries (about 4 cups)
4 cups water
1¾ cups sugar
1 teaspoon lemon juice
Fresh cranberries for decoration
Sugar for decoration
Mint sprigs for decoration

Wash the 1 pound of cranberries in a colander under cold running water. Place them in a medium-size saucepan with the 4 cups water. Bring to a boil over high heat. Reduce heat to low, cover tightly, and simmer 10 to 12 minutes or until the berries can be easily mashed against the side of the pan with a spoon. Stir in sugar and lemon juice.

Puree cranberries and cooking liquid in batches in a food processor with the metal blade. Strain into a bowl; discard the skins. Pour the mixture into 2 or 3 ice cube trays. Freeze until solid.

Place a few cubes of cranberry ice into food processor with the metal blade. Process until broken up. With motor running, drop cubes one at a time through feed tube. You will need to do this in batches. As each batch becomes finely pureed and snowy, remove to a bowl and place in freezer. When the sorbet is firm enough to scoop, but not frozen solid, scoop into 8 small ramekins, custard cups, or soufflé dishes. Or place scoops on foil-lined baking sheets. Cover loosely with foil and return to freezer.

Several hours before serving, place whole cranberries on a wire rack placed over a baking sheet. Brush berries lightly with water and sprinkle with sugar. Set aside until sugar dries. Before serving, arrange sugar-coated berries on sorbet and decorate with mint.

*Makes about 1 quart, 8 servings.*

**Make-Ahead Tips**  Cranberry puree may be frozen up to 1 week.

Sorbet may be frozen overnight.

# Sugar-&-Spice Yam Muffins

*In my house Thanksgiving wouldn't be complete without these moist, fragrant muffins.*

¼ cup (½ stick) butter, margarine, or vegetable oil
1 cup sugar
1 (1-lb.) can yams, drained, or 1¼ cups cooked, mashed fresh yams or sweet potatoes
3 egg whites
1¼ cups regular, low-fat, or nonfat milk
2½ cups all-purpose flour
1½ tablespoons baking powder
¾ teaspoon ground nutmeg
½ teaspoon salt
1 heaping teaspoon ground cinnamon
½ cup chopped walnuts or pecans
¼ cup sugar mixed with 1 tablespoon ground cinnamon for topping
Butter for serving (optional)

Preheat oven to 400F (205C). Grease 24 (2½-inch) muffin cups. In a bowl with electric mixer or food processor with metal blade, cream butter or oil and sugar until light and fluffy. Beat in yams or sweet potatoes. Add egg whites, one at a time, beating well after each addition. Mix in milk. Add flour, baking powder, nutmeg, salt, and cinnamon. Mix until incorporated; do not overmix. Mix in nuts.

Spoon batter into muffin cups, filling three-fourths full. Sprinkle sugar-cinnamon mixture over the tops. Bake 20 to 25 minutes or until lightly browned and a skewer or wooden pick inserted in center comes out clean. Turn out onto a rack and cool.

Serve warm with butter.

*Makes 24 muffins.*

**Make-Ahead Tip** Muffins may be stored airtight for several days or frozen up to 1 month. Reheat before serving.

# Pumpkin Cream-Cheese Roll

*No matter how hard I try, I can't come up with a Thanksgiving dessert that surpasses this spicy pumpkin cake rolled around a fluffy cream-cheese filling.*

## PUMPKIN CAKE ROLL:

3 large eggs
1 cup sugar
⅔ cup canned or mashed, cooked fresh pumpkin
1 teaspoon lemon juice
¾ cup all-purpose flour
1 teaspoon baking powder
2 teaspoons ground cinnamon
1 teaspoon ground ginger
½ teaspoon ground nutmeg
½ teaspoon salt
1 cup finely chopped walnuts
Powdered sugar

## CREAM-CHEESE FILLING:

2 (3-oz.) packages regular or light cream cheese, at room temperature
¼ cup (½ stick) unsalted butter or margarine, at room temperature
1 cup powdered sugar, sifted
½ teaspoon vanilla extract

**Make pumpkin roll:** Preheat oven to 375F (190C). Grease a 15″ × 10″ jellyroll pan. Line with parchment or waxed paper, letting it extend 2 inches over narrow ends. Grease the paper, dust with flour, and shake out excess.

In a bowl with electric mixer, beat eggs and sugar until thick, light, and creamy, 3 to 4 minutes. Mix in pumpkin and lemon juice. In a separate bowl, stir together flour, baking powder, cinna-mon, ginger, nutmeg, and salt. Fold into pumpkin mixture. Pour into prepared pan; smooth top evenly. Sprinkle nuts over top. Bake 12 to 15 minutes or until top springs back when lightly pressed with fingertips and cake begins to pull away from sides of the pan.

While cake is baking, place a clean dish towel on countertop. Sprinkle powdered sugar through a strainer or sifter over towel. Remove cake from oven and immediately turn it upside down onto sugared towel. Remove cake pan and paper. Beginning with a narrow end of cake, roll towel and cake up together. Set aside seam side down until cooled to room temperature.

**Make filling:** In a bowl with electric mixer, blend cream cheese and butter until light and fluffy. Slowly beat in powdered sugar until smooth. Mix in vanilla.

When cake is cool, unroll and remove towel. Spread cheese filling over top and roll up. The nuts will be on the outside. Refrigerate for several hours.

*Makes 8 to 10 servings.*

**Make-Ahead Tip** Cake may be refrigerated, covered, overnight or frozen, wrapped in foil, up to 1 month. Defrost in refrigerator overnight.

# Cranberry-Pear Tart

*A crunchy cookie crust, mounded with smooth almond cream and crowned with juicy glistening fruit, is the apogee of fruit tartdom. It's too good to be relegated to once a year, so vary the fruit with the season and glaze it with strained apricot preserves.*

### SWEET TART PASTRY:
¾ cup (1½ sticks) unsalted butter or margarine, at room temperature
1¼ cups all-purpose flour
½ cup powdered sugar

### ALMOND FILLING:
4 ounces almond paste
1 (8-oz.) package regular or light cream cheese, at room temperature
¼ cup sugar
1 large egg
½ teaspoon vanilla extract
¼ teaspoon almond extract

### CRANBERRY PEAR TOPPING:
1 (1-lb. 13-oz.) can pear halves
¾ cup sugar
1 tablespoon cornstarch
½ cup plus 1½ cups fresh cranberries

**Make pastry:** In a food processor with the metal blade or in a bowl with electric mixer, mix or process butter, flour, and powdered sugar until blended. Press dough into the bottom and up the side of an 11- or 12-inch tart pan with a removable bottom, an 11- or 12-inch quiche dish, or an 11- or 12-inch pizza pan. Prick bottom with fork. Refrigerate 30 minutes or longer to minimize shrinkage. Preheat oven to 350F (175C). Bake 20 minutes or until pale golden. The sides will shrink slightly. Remove and cool completely before filling. (Pastry may be held at room temperature overnight or frozen.) Increase oven temperature to 375F (190C).

**Make filling:** In a food processor with the metal blade or in a bowl with electric mixer, mix or process almond paste until it is broken up. Add cream cheese, sugar, egg, vanilla, and almond extract; mix or process until smooth. Pour into pastry, spreading evenly. Bake 10 minutes. Cool.

**Make topping:** Several hours before serving, drain pears, reserving ½ cup syrup. Cut pears into thin slices; set aside. In a small saucepan, mix sugar and cornstarch. Slowly stir in reserved pear syrup until cornstarch is dissolved. Bring to a boil over medium-high heat, stirring constantly. Add ½ cup cranberries. Cook until cranberries pop and glaze turns pink. Stir in remaining 1½ cups cranberries and cook just until they become soft, about 2 minutes. Remove from heat and cool.

Leaving a 1½-inch border around outer edge of tart, arrange pear slices in an overlapping circle around top. Fill outside border with cranberries. Spoon remaining cranberries in center of pears. Gently brush pears with the juices remaining in the bottom of the pan. Refrigerate until firm.

*Makes 10 to 12 servings.*

**Make-Ahead Tips** Tart without fruit topping may be refrigerated, covered, overnight or frozen up to 1 month. Thaw frozen tart in refrigerator overnight.

Finished tart may be refrigerated, uncovered, for several hours.

# SEASON'S GREETINGS

## Holiday Open House

---

**MENU**

*Baby Potatoes with Creamy Artichoke Salsa*
*Southwestern Guacamole Wreath*
*Salmon Soufflé Torte*
*Smoked Oyster Roll*
*Sweet & Sour Chicken Wing Drumsticks*
*Greek Meatballs with Cucumber Yogurt Sauce*
*Fiesta Nacho Chips*

*Orange-Honey–Glazed Ham with Cornbread-Pecan Stuffing*
*Waldorf Cinnamon Mold*
*Winter Gazpacho Salad*

*Chocolate Mocha Cheesecake*
*Luscious Lemon Tarts*

*Cranberry Christmas Punch with Cranberry Ice Wreath*
*Tropical Rum Punch Bowl*

---

In our hectic, fast-paced lives, the traditional cocktail party is quickly becoming passé. And that's fine, as long as we replace it with a contemporary way of entertaining that fits our casual and fast-paced life-style. An open-house buffet can be a pleasure to host when you throw out old rules of etiquette, and choose recipes that can be made ahead, require a minimum of last-minute fuss, and can sit out with little attention. Leave your starched table cloth, china, and crystal in the cupboard, and purchase pretty paper or plastic ones instead. Serve buffet style and forget about the hot hors d'oeuvre that need heating and passing.

All of the dishes in this menu can be prepared ahead and served chilled or at room temperature. I offer a ham, stuffed with pecans and cornbread and served warm or at room temperature. Many of the hors d'oeuvre, like the Salmon Soufflé Torte, Southwestern Guacamole Wreath, Fiesta Nacho Chips, and Smoked Oyster Roll, can be beautifully garnished in the red and green of the holiday.

And should you wish to serve dessert, this menu includes a selection of very special ones: a delicious mocha cheesecake made with yogurt and individual bite-size lemon tarts.

# Baby Potatoes with Creamy Artichoke Salsa

*Scooped out potato shells mounded with a cheesy tomato and marinated artichoke filling look terrific and taste spectacular. No matter how many you make, it won't be enough.*

15 baby red-skinned potatoes (2 inches in diameter), scrubbed
Nonstick cooking spray
Salt
½ cup regular or low-fat mayonnaise
½ cup thick and chunky tomato salsa, preferably medium heat, drained
½ cup marinated artichoke hearts, drained and diced
½ cup shredded regular or part-skim mozzarella cheese
About ¼ cup grated Parmesan cheese, for topping

**Bake potatoes:** Place rack in center of oven and preheat to 500F (260C). Cut potatoes in half crosswise. Cut a small slice off each end so they sit flat. Place on baking sheet, flat side up, and spray with nonstick spray. Sprinkle with salt. Turn flat-side down, spray, and sprinkle with salt. Bake 15 to 20 minutes or until soft when tested with a sharp knife.

Cool slightly. Using a melon baller or teaspoon, scoop out insides, leaving a ¼-inch shell. Place potato centers in a medium-size bowl. Stir in mayonnaise, salsa, artichokes, and mozzarella cheese. Spoon into shells, mounding the tops. You might not use all of filling.

Preheat oven to 450F (230C). Sprinkle tops with Parmesan cheese. Bake 5 to 10 minutes or until heated through.

*Makes 30 potatoes.*

**Make-Ahead Tip** Filled potatoes may be refrigerated, covered, overnight. Bake just before serving.

---

# Southwestern Guacamole Wreath

*This wreath with bows of roasted red peppers is a festive change of pace from traditional guacamole.*

2 medium-size avocados, peeled and pitted
2 (8-oz.) packages regular or light cream cheese, at room temperature
2 tablespoons lemon juice
½ cup chopped onion
½ cup chopped jarred roasted red bell peppers, drained
1 cup tomato salsa, mild or medium heat
1 cup frozen whole-kernel corn, thawed
1 teaspoon salt or to taste
Green food coloring (optional)
Chopped parsley or cilantro for garnish (optional)
1 whole roasted red bell pepper or pimiento, drained, for garnish
Tortilla chips, crackers, or bread rounds, for serving

In a food processor with the metal blade, process avocados, cream cheese, lemon juice, and onion until blended. Remove to a bowl and stir in chopped peppers, salsa, corn, salt, and food coloring, if using.

Spoon guacamole onto platter in a wide circle to resemble a wreath. Sprinkle with chopped parsley or cilantro, if using. Cut roasted pepper into strips and small circles; arrange strips in bows on top of wreath. Dot with roasted pepper circles to resemble holly berries. Serve with tortilla chips, crackers, or bread rounds.

*Makes about 3 cups, serves 10 to 12.*

**Variation** Guacamole may be divided and shaped into 1½-inch-diameter logs. Sprinkle with finely chopped parsley, cilantro, or paprika.

**Make-Ahead Tip** Guacamole may be refrigerated overnight, covered with plastic wrap directly on the surface to prevent it from turning dark. Stir well before serving.

# Salmon Soufflé Torte

*Soufflé batter is baked in a jellyroll pan, cut into strips, and layered with a chunky vegetable and smoked-salmon cream cheese. The torte looks beautiful garnished with smoked salmon and olive flowers with green onion stems and leaves. Slice and serve on lettuce leaves as a first course, or cut into squares for an impressive hors d'oeuvre.*

## SOUFFLÉ LAYERS:

4 tablespoons (½ stick) butter or margarine
½ cup all-purpose flour
2 cups regular, low-fat, or nonfat milk
4 egg yolks
1 teaspoon sugar
Dash salt
4 egg whites

## SMOKED SALMON FILLING:

1 (8-oz.) package regular or light cream cheese
⅔ cup regular or low-fat sour cream
2 tablespoons lemon juice
¼ pound smoked salmon, coarsely chopped
½ cup peeled, chopped, and seeded cucumber, drained and patted dry
3 tablespoons chopped green onion
1 tablespoon fresh chopped dill or ½ teaspoon dried dill
Dash of Tabasco sauce

## GARNISH (OPTIONAL):

1 slice smoked salmon (reserved from filling, if desired)
Pitted sliced ripe olives
Green onion tops, cut into thin strips
Sprigs of fresh parsley or dill

**Make soufflé layers:** Preheat oven to 325F (165C). Grease the bottom of a 15″ × 10″ jellyroll pan. Line with waxed or parchment paper, letting 1 inch extend over short sides for handles. Grease or spray paper with nonstick cooking spray.

Melt butter or margarine in a small saucepan. Stir in flour and cook over low heat until blended, about 2 minutes; do not brown. Whisk in milk and continue cooking over medium-high heat, stirring, until sauce comes to a boil and thickens. In a small bowl, lightly whisk egg yolks, sugar, and salt. Stir a small amount of hot mixture into yolks. Return to saucepan. Cook 1 minute, stirring constantly. Remove from heat. Meanwhile beat egg whites until stiff, but not dry. Fold sauce into whites. Pour into prepared pan. Bake 15 to 18 minutes or until the top is pale golden and springs back when lightly pressed with fingertips. Cool in pan. Go around sides with a sharp knife and, using the paper as handles, lift out to flat surface.

**Make filling:** In a food processor with the metal blade, process cream cheese until smooth. Add sour cream and lemon juice and process to combine. Add smoked salmon and pulse into small pieces. Add cucumber, green onions, dill, and Tabasco sauce and pulse until incorporated but still chunky.

**To assemble:** Cut soufflé crosswise into 4 slices, each about 3½ inches wide. Place one slice on platter. Spread with a thin layer of filling. Alternate remaining soufflé with thin layers of filling. Spread a thick layer of filling over the top.

Before serving, cut flowers from smoked salmon and olives. Make stems and leaves from green onions. Arrange across top of torte. Garnish with sprigs of parsley or dill. To serve, cut into thin slices.

*Makes about 24 appetizer servings.*

**Make-Ahead Tip** Torte may be refrigerated, covered with plastic wrap, overnight. Garnish before serving.

# Smoked Oyster Roll

*When I first taught this spread to my classes, the students were skeptical. But one taste and they were converted. Pureed smoked oysters are spread over garlic-flavored cream cheese, rolled up, and sliced into brown and white spirals.*

1 medium-size garlic clove, minced
1 medium-size shallot, chopped, or 1 tablespoon finely chopped onion
2 (8-oz.) packages regular or light cream cheese, at room temperature
2 tablespoons regular or low-fat mayonnaise
2 teaspoons Worcestershire sauce
Salt and pepper to taste
Dash of Tabasco sauce
2 (3¾-oz.) cans smoked oysters, drained
½ cup finely chopped pistachio nuts, pecans, or walnuts
Crackers or bread rounds for serving

In a food processor with the metal blade or in bowl with electric mixer, process or mix garlic, shallot or onion, cream cheese, mayonnaise, Worcestershire sauce, salt, pepper, and Tabasco sauce until blended. Spoon mixture onto a sheet of foil and spread into a 10" × 8" rectangle. In same bowl, puree or mash oysters. Spread over cream cheese. Cover loosely with plastic wrap and refrigerate for several hours or overnight until firm.

Using a long, narrow spatula to help release cream cheese from foil, roll up like a jellyroll. Don't be concerned if it breaks and cracks. Shape into a long log. Roll in nuts, covering log completely.

Serve with crackers or bread rounds.

*Makes 8 to 10 servings.*

**Make-Ahead Tip** Log may be refrigerated, wrapped in plastic wrap, up to 3 days.

# Sweet & Sour Chicken Wing Drumsticks

*If you take the thickest, meatiest bone of the wing and push the meat to the top, you have what is called a chicken wing drumstick or drumette. Many markets sell them, but you can make them yourself or substitute regular wings. These bake until they are deeply glazed, crisp, and sticky, so be sure to supply plenty of napkins.*

60 chicken wing drumsticks
1 (12-oz.) bottle chili sauce
1 (10-oz.) jar grape jelly
2 tablespoons lemon juice
3 garlic cloves, minced
1 (16-oz.) can sweet and sour sauce
1 (7½-oz.) jar junior baby-food peaches
½ teaspoon ground ginger

Preheat oven to 350F (175C). Line a large shallow roasting pan with heavy foil. Place wing drumsticks in pan. In a medium-size microwave-safe bowl or saucepan, combine chili sauce, jelly, lemon juice, garlic, sweet and sour sauce, peaches, and ginger. Microwave, uncovered, on HIGH (100 percent) or cook over medium heat, stirring occasionally, until mixture comes to a boil and jelly melts. Pour three-fourths of the sauce over the drumsticks. Bake 1½ to 2 hours or until brown and crispy, basting and turning often.

*Makes 60 drumsticks.*

**Variation** Substitute Panhandle Barbecue Sauce (page 94) or Firecracker Barbecue Sauce (page 94) for sweet and sour sauce.

**Make-Ahead Tip** Drumsticks may be refrigerated, covered, up to 2 days or frozen up to 1 month. Refrigerate or freeze extra sauce separately. Thaw frozen sauce and drumsticks in refrigerator overnight. Brush drumsticks with reserved sauce. Bake in a preheated 350F (175C) oven 20 to 30 minutes or until heated through.

# Greek Meatballs with Cucumber Yogurt Sauce

*These delicious garlic- and mint-scented meatballs are adapted from my friend Jim Nassikas' mother's recipe. She makes the authentic Greek version and fries them, but because I don't like to fry, I bake them instead. The Cucumber Yogurt Sauce can be used for dipping or spooning over the meatballs in petite pita pockets.*

**MEATBALLS:**
1 large onion, finely chopped
½ cup chopped fresh mint leaves, packed
3 slices white bread with crusts, toasted and crumbled
3 large garlic cloves, minced
2 large eggs or 3 egg whites
2 heaping tablespoons tomato paste
½ pound lean ground lamb
½ pound lean ground beef
1 teaspoon salt
¼ teaspoon ground pepper
Toaster-size pita bread, cut in half, for serving, if desired

**CUCUMBER YOGURT SAUCE:**
1 cucumber
½ teaspoon salt
1 cup plain regular, low-fat, or nonfat yogurt
1 small onion, chopped
1 tablespoon chopped fresh mint leaves
Salt and pepper to taste

**Make meatballs:** Preheat oven to 400F (205C). Spray a shallow rimmed baking sheet with non-stick cooking spray or line with heavy foil. In a food processor with the metal blade or in a large bowl with electric mixer, process or mix onion, mint, toasted bread, garlic, eggs, and tomato paste until well blended. Remove to a large bowl and mix in meat. Season with salt and pepper. Shape into 2-inch balls. Place on prepared pan and bake 12 to 15 minutes or until golden brown.

**Make sauce:** Peel, seed, and grate cucumber. Place in a colander in sink, sprinkle with salt, and drain 1 hour. Squeeze in dish towel to remove excess juices. In a medium-size bowl, stir together ¾ cup of the yogurt, onion, and mint. Season with salt and pepper. Stir in cucumber and refrigerate for at least 1 hour.

Before serving, drain off excess liquid. Stir in remaining ¼ cup yogurt. Makes about 2 cups.

Serve meatballs with picks and Cucumber Yogurt Sauce for dipping. Or, place a meatball in each pita half and top with dip.

*Makes about 20 meatballs.*

**Make-Ahead Tip** Meatballs may be refrigerated overnight or frozen up to 1 month. Thaw meatballs in refrigerator overnight. Reheat in a preheated 400F (205C) oven until heated through.

Sauce may be refrigerated overnight.

# Fiesta Nacho Chips

*Crunchy chips and spicy cheese, glistening with dollops of red and green jalapeño jelly, are a tasty way to say Merry Christmas.*

1 (8-oz.) package tostitos or tortilla chips
2 cups (8 oz.) shredded hot pepper Monterey Jack cheese
½ cup (2 oz.) shredded Cheddar cheese
½ (8- to 10-oz.) jar red jalapeño jelly
½ (8- to 10-oz.) jar green jalapeño jelly

**Place** chips on a baking sheet or flameproof serving platter. In a small bowl, mix Jack and Cheddar cheeses together. Sprinkle a small amount in the center of each chip. Spoon a scant teaspoon of red and green jelly over cheese on each chip.

Before serving, broil until cheese is melted and bubbling.

*Makes about 48 chips.*

**Make-Ahead Tip** Chips may be refrigerated, covered, overnight.

# Orange-Honey–Glazed Ham with Cornbread-Pecan Stuffing

*A tunnel of stuffing through the center of the ham bakes until soft and moist. The remaining stuffing is spread over the top and basted with honey and orange juice to make a crisp, crunchy, and golden crust.*

1 (6- to 8-lb.) boneless fully cooked ham

### CORNBREAD-PECAN STUFFING
6 tablespoons butter or margarine
2½ cups chopped onions
1½ cups packaged cornbread stuffing mix
¾ cup chopped fresh parsley
2½ cups coarsely chopped pecans
3 teaspoons prepared mustard
3 eggs, lightly beaten

### ORANGE-HONEY GLAZE
¾ cup honey
3 tablespoons frozen orange juice concentrate, thawed

Cut all skin and fat from ham. Make a cavity through the entire ham by cutting a 2-inch cylindrical tunnel through the center. Remove ham center and reserve for another use.

**Make stuffing:** In a large skillet, melt butter or margarine. Add onion and sauté until softened.

Remove to bowl and add stuffing mix, parsley, pecans, mustard, and eggs; toss lightly.

Preheat oven to 325F (175C). Fill cavity of ham with two-thirds of the stuffing, packing it in lightly. Refrigerate remaining stuffing. Score top of ham in diamond pattern, making cuts about ¼ inch deep. Place on rack in roasting pan. Bake 1½ hours.

**Make glaze:** In a small bowl, mix honey and juice concentrate together. Pour glaze over ham. Bake 20 minutes. Remove ham from oven and spread remaining stuffing evenly over the top. Baste with pan juices. Return to oven and bake 20 to 30 more minutes or until brown and crusty. Slice and serve.

*Makes 18 to 24 servings.*

**Make-Ahead Tip** Stuffing may be refrigerated overnight, but add eggs just before using to stuff ham.

---

# Waldorf Cinnamon Mold

*This red-hot cinnamon mold, highlighted with fresh apples and oranges, is a beautiful and refreshing complement to ham.*

½ cup red-hot cinnamon candies
¼ cup sugar
1½ cups water
1 (6-oz.) package cherry gelatin
2 cups diced peeled apple
1 cup diced peeled orange
½ cup chopped walnuts or pecans

In a medium-size saucepan, bring candies, sugar, and water to a boil, stirring occasionally, until melted. Place gelatin in a large bowl. Pour boiling mixture over gelatin and stir until dissolved. Stir in 2 cups cold water. Refrigerate until thickened and partially set, but not firm. Stir in apple, orange, and nuts. Pour into a 6-cup mold. Refrigerate until firm.

Before serving, go around edge of mold with tip of a sharp knife. Dip mold in warm water several times and invert onto a serving plate.

*Makes 12 to 14 servings.*

**Make-Ahead Tip** Mold may be refrigerated, covered with plastic wrap, up to 2 days.

# Winter Gazpacho Salad

*Using the ingredients for summer gazpacho, here's a layered salad resplendent with tomatoes, cucumbers, mushrooms, and red onions. It's a sensible choice for a buffet; it can sit out without wilting.*

## BASIL VINAIGRETTE:

⅓ cup olive oil
2 tablespoons white wine vinegar
¼ cup chopped fresh basil or 2 tablespoons dried basil
1 garlic clove, minced
1 tablespoon fresh lemon juice
Tabasco sauce to taste
3 tablespoons orange juice
Salt and pepper to taste

## SALAD:

1 large European cucumber, thinly sliced
1 teaspoon salt
½ pound mushrooms, thinly sliced
1 green bell pepper, seeded and sliced into thin strips
1 medium-size red onion, thinly sliced
3 medium-size tomatoes, thinly sliced
Tomato wedges for garnish (optional)
Green pepper for garnish (optional)
Ripe olives, pitted and halved, for garnish (optional)

**Make vinaigrette:**  In a food processor with the metal blade, process all the ingredients until blended.

**Make salad:**  Place cucumber slices in a colander in the sink. Sprinkle with salt, toss lightly, and let drain 1 hour. Dry cucumbers with paper towels. In a large bowl, preferably glass, layer cucumbers, mushrooms, bell peppers, and onions. Sprinkle with half the vinaigrette. Arrange tomato slices over the top and pour on remaining dressing. Cover with plastic wrap and refrigerate for several hours.

Before serving, if desired, place tomato wedges in a circle around top. Cut bell pepper into triangles to resemble leaves and place them next to tomatoes. Insert a strip of green pepper into the center of each olive and arrange around tomatoes.

*Makes 8 servings.*

**Make-Ahead Tips**  Vinaigrette may be refrigerated up to 4 days.

Salad may be refrigerated, covered, overnight.

# Chocolate Mocha Cheesecake

*One taste of this incredibly rich cake defies the fact that it's substantially lower in calories and fat than your average cheesecake. The idea for using drained yogurt and pureed low-fat cottage cheese for a cheesecake comes from Nancy Baggett's book.*

**CRUST:**
1 cup chocolate wafer cookie crumbs
3 tablespoons butter or margarine, melted

**CHOCOLATE MOCHA FILLING:**
1 (12-oz.) package chocolate chips
2 cups low-fat cottage cheese
1½ cups plain nonfat yogurt, strained in a strainer
   lined with cheesecloth or a paper coffee filter 1 to
   2 hours in refrigerator
1 (8-oz.) package light cream cheese, cut into
   chunks and at room temperature
1¼ cups sugar
2 large eggs
4 large egg whites
2 teaspoons vanilla extract
¼ cup Kahlua or strong coffee

**Make crust:** Place crumbs in a food processor with the metal blade. Add butter or margarine and process until blended. Press into bottom of 9-inch springform pan. Refrigerate while preparing filling.

**Make filling:** Preheat oven to 350F (175C). Reserve ½ cup chocolate chips and set aside. Place remaining chips in a 2-quart microwave-safe bowl.

Microwave, uncovered, on HIGH (100 percent) 1 to 2 minutes or until melted; set aside.

In a food processor with the metal blade, process cottage cheese until pureed. Measure strained yogurt and add ¾ cup to processor. Add cream cheese and process until blended. Add sugar, eggs, egg whites, vanilla, Kahlua or coffee and process until mixed. Add to melted chocolate, stirring until mixture is smooth. Pour into crust. Sprinkle reserved ½ cup chocolate chips over top. Place on a baking sheet and bake 1 hour. Turn off oven and leave in oven to cool at least 2 hours. The cake will sink and crack as it cools. Cover and refrigerate several hours before serving.

Before serving, go around edge of cheesecake with a sharp knife and remove side of springform pan.

*Makes 12 servings.*

**Make-Ahead Tip** Cheesecake may be refrigerated up to 1 week or frozen up to 1 month. Thaw in refrigerator overnight.

# Luscious Lemon Tarts

*A simple-to-prepare cream-cheese pastry is pressed into small muffin cups, baked, and filled with a tangy lemon curd. The curd can also be made with lime juice, and if you tint it pale green, it's pretty to alternate lemon and lime tarts on a platter.*

## FLAKY PASTRY:

½ cup (1 stick) unsalted butter, cold and cut into pieces for food processor; at room temperature for mixer

1 (3-oz.) package regular or light cream cheese, cold and cut into pieces for food processor; at room temperature for mixer

1 cup all-purpose flour

Dash salt

## LEMON CURD:

1 cup sugar

4 teaspoons cornstarch

1 large egg

1 egg white

2 teaspoons grated lemon peel

½ cup fresh lemon juice

2 tablespoons butter, at room temperature

## GARNISH (OPTIONAL):

½ cup whipping cream

**Make pastry:** In a food processor with the metal blade or in a bowl with electric mixer, pulse or mix butter and cream cheese until smooth. Add flour and salt and pulse or mix until incorporated. Divide into small balls. Press balls into 1½-inch miniature muffin cups or tartlet pans, making thin shells. Prick the bottoms with the tines of a fork. Refrigerate 30 minutes to minimize shrinkage. Preheat oven to 350F (175C). Bake 22 to 30 minutes or until golden. Remove to racks and cool completely. Remove each shell by inserting the tip of a small knife into an edge and lifting out shells.

**Make curd:** In a medium-size, heavy saucepan, whisk sugar, cornstarch, egg, egg white, lemon peel, and lemon juice until blended. Cook over medium heat, whisking constantly and making sure to get into the edges of the pan, until mixture comes to a boil and thickens, about 3 minutes. Immediately remove from heat, stir in butter, and pour into a bowl. Refrigerate until cool, stirring occasionally. Spoon into baked shells, mounding the tops. Refrigerate for several hours before serving.

Before serving, if desired, whip cream until stiff peaks form. Spoon cream into a pastry bag fitted with a ½-inch rosette tip. Pipe rosettes of cream on each tart.

*Makes 24 tarts.*

**Variation** Lime Tarts: Substitute lime juice and peel for the lemon. Stir in a few drops of green food coloring, if desired.

**Make-Ahead Tips** Pastry shells may be refrigerated overnight or frozen up to 1 month.

Curd may be refrigerated, covered, up to 1 week.

Tarts may be refrigerated overnight or frozen up to 1 month. Defrost in a single layer in refrigerator.

# Cranberry Christmas Punch with Cranberry Ice Wreath

*This sweet nonalcoholic punch is a sparkling holly-berry red color. Cranberry juice is frozen in a ring mold and garnished with whole berries and leaves to float in the punch.*

**CRANBERRY ICE WREATH:**
3 cups cranberry juice
2 cups water
10 to 12 fresh nonpoisonous garden leaves, such as lemon or camellia (optional)
½ cup fresh cranberries

**CRANBERRY CHRISTMAS PUNCH:**
1 (3-oz.) package cherry-flavored gelatin
1 cup boiling water
1 (6-oz.) can frozen lemonade concentrate
3 cups cold water
1 (1-qt.) bottle cranberry juice cocktail, chilled
Cranberry Ice Wreath
1 (1-liter) bottle ginger ale, chilled

**Make wreath:** Mix cranberry juice with water. Pour half into a 6-cup ring mold. Freeze solid. Place leaves, shiny side up, on frozen ring. Carefully pour enough cranberry water over leaves to hold them in place. Freeze until solid. Add fresh cranberries and enough cranberry juice mixture to fill to top. Freeze until solid. To unmold, dip bottom of mold in cold water and turn out on heavy foil. Turn leaf side up, wrap in foil, and freeze.

**To make punch:** Dissolve cherry gelatin in boiling water. Stir in lemonade concentrate. Stir in the cold water and the cranberry juice cocktail.

Place ice wreath leaf side up in a large punch bowl. Pour in punch. Slowly pour in chilled ginger ale.

*Makes about 25 (4-oz.) servings.*

**Make-Ahead Tips** Ice wreath may be frozen up to 2 weeks.

Punch may be refrigerated overnight before adding ginger ale.

# Tropical Rum Punch Bowl

*Here's a terrific punch for a bunch. You can freeze the fruit-juice base in one-quart milk cartons and defrost them right in your punch bowl.*

1½ cups water
1 cup sugar
1 (24-oz.) can pineapple juice
¼ cup lemon juice
1½ cups orange juice
2 ripe bananas, mashed
1 (1-liter) bottle 7-Up, chilled
1 cup vodka
1 cup dark rum
Ice cubes or Ice Mold (Sparkling Champagne Punch, page 74)

**Place** water and sugar in a small saucepan. Bring to a boil and simmer, stirring occasionally, 3 minutes or until sugar is dissolved. Cool. If not using immediately, refrigerate almost indefinitely.

In a large pitcher or bowl, stir together sugar syrup, pineapple juice, lemon juice, orange juice, and bananas.

Before serving, pour fruit mixture into punch bowl. Stir in 7-Up, vodka, and rum. Add ice or ice mold.

*Makes 32 (4-oz.) servings.*

Invite friends to a *Holiday Open House:* (clockwise from left) Southwestern Guacamole Wreath (page 122), Sweet & Sour Chicken Wing Drumsticks (page 124), Baby Potatoes with Creamy Artichoke Salsa (page 122), Salmon Soufflé Torte (page 123), and Smoked Oyster Roll (page 124).

# Hanukkah Candle-Lighting Party

---

**M E N U**

*Herring Salad Spread with Apples*

*Potato Pancakes (Latkes)*
*Ratatouille Cheese Casserole*
*Blueberry Star Mold*

*Cookie Menorah*
*Hanukkah Star Cookies*
*Hanukkah Cutout Cookies*

W I N E   R E C O M M E N D A T I O N :
*A light, medium-dry white wine such as a chenin blanc or reisling*

---

Hanukkah is one of the prettiest and most festive of the Jewish celebrations, and I hope that my dinner menu adds to your holiday joy. The eight days of Hanukkah are celebrated by lighting candles, which are placed in a special holder called a menorah. One candle is lit on the first evening, two on the second, and so on, until eight candles are lit. It is customary for families to exchange presents on each night of the holiday.

Potato pancakes, or *latkes*, are a traditional Hanukkah food. I serve these crisp pancakes with a vegetarian casserole and a striking blueberry mold. This dairy menu is light but filling, and is prepared in accordance with Jewish dietary restrictions. If you wish to serve a heartier meat meal, substitute the beef brisket in the Passover menu (page 38) for the casserole.

The colorful cookie menorah beautifully accentuates the Hanukkah theme. Arranged on a platter with other holiday cookies, it is guaranteed to light up your party.

This menu serves ten to twelve.

Children will enjoy this *Hanukkah Candle-Lighting Party* with sweet treats, including an edible menorah: Cookie Menorah (page 135), Hanukkah Stars and Cutouts (page 136).

# Herring Salad Spread with Apples

*Herring generously shares the spotlight with crunchy apples, green peppers, and hard-cooked eggs. Bound with sour cream and mayonnaise, it's smooth enough to mold — it looks terrific in a fish shape.*

1 (1-lb.) jar herring fillets
2 green apples, peeled, cored, and coarsely
   chopped
½ cup chopped onion
½ cup chopped green bell pepper
2 hard-cooked eggs, coarsely chopped
½ cup regular or low-fat sour cream
½ cup regular or low-fat mayonnaise
Cocktail rye or pumpernickel breads for serving

**GARNISH (OPTIONAL):**
2 cooked egg yolks, sieved
2 cooked egg whites, sieved
½ cup finely minced parsley

Line a 4-cup mold or bowl with plastic wrap. Drain herring well, reserving onion slices from jar. Place herring, reserved onion slices, and apples in a food processor with the metal blade. Pulse until chopped. Transfer to a medium-size bowl and stir in chopped onion, green pepper, and hard-cooked eggs. Stir in mayonnaise and sour cream. Pour into mold. Cover and refrigerate several hours.

Before serving, invert mold onto a serving plate. Remove plastic wrap. Garnish with rows of egg yolks, whites, and parsley, if using. Serve with bread rounds.

*Makes 4 cups, serves about 12.*

**Make-Ahead Tip** Spread may be refrigerated overnight.

---

# Potato Pancakes (Latkes)

*Every year I am invited to a large Hanukkah party. And every year I hear a friend groaning about the potato pancakes: they taste like soggy brown mashed-potato cakes. No wonder. They are being reheated piled on top of each other, and instead of getting crisp, they are steaming. I am constantly asked if potato pancakes freeze. The answer depends on how you freeze, thaw, and reheat them. Follow my directions (below) for success.*

*I don't advise doubling the recipe, as the last of the raw potato batter gets too starchy and brown when it sits too long. You will probably be surprised by my addition of vitamin C; it helps prevent potatoes and fruits from discoloring.*

1 vitamin C tablet
2½ pounds baking potatoes (about 4 large
   potatoes)
½ onion
2 eggs, lightly beaten
1 teaspoon salt
¼ teaspoon baking powder
2 tablespoons flour or matzo meal
Vegetable oil
Pink Cinnamon Applesauce (page 133) or regular
   applesauce for serving
Sour cream (optional)

Place vitamin C tablet in a small bowl with 2 tablespoons water to dissolve. Shred potatoes, using shredding blade of food processor or hand shredder; place in a bowl. If shreds are large, return to food processor with metal blade and pulse in batches to chop slightly. Remove to bowl and stir in dissolved vitamin C. Shred or finely chop onion. Add to potatoes. Mix in eggs, salt, baking powder, and flour or matzo meal until incorporated.

In a large skillet, heat ½ inch oil over medium-high heat. Using a slotted spoon, place about 2 tablespoons of batter into hot oil for each pancake. Do not crowd pancakes in pan. Flatten slightly with the back of the spoon and fry pancakes until golden on both sides, turning once. As you reach the end of the batter, squeeze it lightly to remove excess liquid. After frying, remove pancakes to paper towels to drain. Pancakes may be kept warm in low oven in single layer.

Serve with applesauce and sour cream, if desired.

*Makes about 24 pancakes.*

**Make-Ahead Tip** Pancakes may be frozen. Freeze on baking sheets in single layers. When solid, layer in airtight container with waxed paper between each layer. Before reheating, place frozen pancakes on baking sheets in a single layer. Bake in a preheated 450F (230C) oven 5 to 10 minutes or until crisp and bubbling.

## Ratatouille Cheese Casserole

*Here's a meatless lasagna, but it isn't layered like traditional ones. In this version, ricotta cheese and eggs are mixed into a robust tomato sauce redolent with eggplant, zucchini, mushrooms, and herbs. The result is a light, custardlike casserole.*

1 small eggplant (about 1 lb.), peeled
3 tablespoons olive oil
1 pound fresh mushrooms, sliced
12 ounces zucchini (about 2 medium), sliced into thin rounds
2 onions, chopped
4 garlic cloves, crushed
2 (28-oz.) cans Italian tomatoes, drained and chopped
1½ teaspoons dried leaf basil
1½ teaspoons dried leaf oregano
1 teaspoon salt
¼ teaspoon freshly ground pepper
1 cup whole- or skim-milk ricotta cheese
6 egg whites or 4 whole eggs
¼ cup all-purpose flour
½ cup grated Parmesan cheese (about 1½ oz.)
8 ounces mozzarella cheese, shredded (about 2 cups)
Paprika

**Grease** a 13" × 9" baking dish. Slice eggplant ½ inch thick and cut into ½-inch cubes. In a large nonstick skillet, heat 1 tablespoon oil. Add eggplant and mushrooms and sauté over medium heat, stirring occasionally, until mixture is very dry, about 10 minutes. Transfer to a large bowl. Add 1 tablespoon oil to skillet. Add zucchini and sauté 3 to 4 minutes until softened slightly; transfer to bowl with eggplant. Add remaining 1 tablespoon oil to skillet. Add onion and garlic, and sauté until softened. Stir in tomatoes, basil, oregano, salt, and pepper. Cook, stirring occasionally, until liquid evaporates, about 30 minutes. Stir into vegetables.

In separate bowl, beat ricotta cheese, egg whites or eggs, flour, and Parmesan cheese until blended. Stir into vegetables. Pour half the mixture into a greased baking dish. Sprinkle with half the mozzarella cheese. Top with remaining vegetables, spreading evenly. Sprinkle top with remaining mozzarella cheese. Lightly sprinkle with paprika.

Preheat oven to 400F (205C). Bake 25 to 30 minutes or until puffed and golden.

*Makes 10 to 12 servings.*

**Make-Ahead Tip** Casserole may be refrigerated, covered with plastic wrap, overnight. Bake chilled casserole 45 minutes.

# Blueberry Star Mold

*Everyone who celebrates Hanukkah knows how difficult it is to decorate food for this holiday — there is not much blue food around. When I created this mold with six-pointed white stars set in shimmering blueberry gelatin, I was very excited. A friend stopped over and I proudly showed her the mold. "What holiday is it for?" I asked her. "That's obvious," she answered confidently, "Fourth of July."*

**SOUR CREAM LAYER:**

1 envelope unflavored gelatin
¼ cup water
1 cup regular, low-fat, or nonfat milk
½ cup sugar
1 cup regular or light sour cream
1 teaspoon vanilla extract

**BLUEBERRY MOLD:**

1 (6-oz.) package lemon-flavored gelatin
1 (15-oz.) can blueberries
2 cups pineapple juice
1 tablespoon sugar
½ cup water

**Make cream layer:**   Grease a 9-inch square or round baking dish or cake pan. Place unflavored gelatin and water in a measuring cup; set aside 5 minutes to soften. In a small saucepan over medium heat, heat milk until small bubbles appear around the edges. Stir in sugar and softened gelatin mixture and cook, stirring, until gelatin is dissolved. Remove from heat and refrigerate until cooled completely. In a medium-size bowl, stir sour cream to soften. Stir in cooled gelatin and vanilla. Pour into prepared pan. Refrigerate until set.

**Make blueberry mold:**   Place lemon gelatin in a large bowl. Drain blueberries, reserving the juice. In a small saucepan, heat pineapple juice, 1 cup blueberry juice, sugar, and water until boiling. Pour over gelatin; stir until gelatin is dissolved. Refrigerate or place bowl in a large bowl of ice water, stirring occasionally, until mixture thickens and is almost set. Fold in blueberries.

Using a cookie cutter, cut stars out of firm cream layer in pan. Place as many stars as desired on the bottom of a 5-cup mold. Carefully spoon thickened blueberry mold over stars. Refrigerate until firm.

Before serving, go around inside edge of mold with the tip of a knife. Dip mold in warm water several times and invert onto a serving platter.

*Makes 8 to 10 servings.*

**Variation**   Omit sour cream layer. Make blueberry mold as directed, leaving out the ½ cup water and stirring in 1 cup sour cream and 1 mashed ripe banana.

**Make-Ahead Tip**   Mold may be refrigerated, covered with plastic wrap, overnight.

# Cookie Menorah

*I'm partial to recipes that play double duty. This clever centerpiece is also the dessert. The recipe makes two menorahs, or you can make one menorah and use the remaining dough for Hanukkah Stars or Cutouts.*

½ recipe prepared spice cookie dough (Spice Cookie Goblins, page 105)
1 egg white, lightly beaten
¼ cup powdered sugar
1 to 2 teaspoons regular or low-fat milk
Yellow and orange food coloring for flames
Multicolored candy decors

Preheat oven to 350F (175C). Divide cookie dough in half. Refrigerate half. Line a baking sheet with parchment paper or foil. Draw a diagram of a menorah about 12 inches long on the paper. Break off one piece of dough and roll with hands into a base for the menorah. Place on paper on baking sheet. For the stand, roll a piece of dough with hands to form a thick triangle. Attach to base. Break off small balls of dough and roll them into 9 pencil-thin candles. Place on menorah; pinch top ends into shape of flames. Make one longer candle for the center. Brush menorah part only with lightly beaten egg white. (Unnecessary to brush the candles as they will be frosted.)

Bake menorah 12 to 18 minutes or until bottom is lightly browned. Cool completely before removing from paper. Repeat with remaining dough for second menorah.

Place menorah on a cake rack over a baking sheet. (Don't be concerned if it breaks; it can be patched together on serving platter.) In a small bowl, mix powdered sugar with enough milk to make a thick frosting. Remove a small amount to a bowl and tint yellow-orange for flames. Thin remaining frosting by adding a few drops of milk and spread frosting on candles. It does not have to be thick or spread smoothly as it will be covered. Sprinkle candles with multicolored candy decors. Spread yellow frosting on flames. Carefully transfer to serving platter.

*Makes 2 menorahs.*

**Make-Ahead Tip** Menorah may be stored, covered with heavy foil, up to 1 week or frozen up to 1 month.

# Hanukkah Cookies

*To make Hanukkah Stars you will need either blue candy chips or white chocolate tinted with blue food coloring and a plastic mold with Jewish stars, available in many candymaking or cake-decorating stores. The Hanukkah Cutouts are decorated with a simple powdered sugar frosting.*

## HANUKKAH STARS

½ recipe Almond Cookie Dough (page 147)
Blue candy chips or white chocolate and blue food coloring, melted

Preheat oven to 325F (165C). Grease, line with parchment paper, or spray baking sheets with non-stick cooking spray. Make ½ recipe dough as directed and divide in half. On a floured board, roll half the dough out ⅛ inch thick. Using star cookie cutters, cut out shapes. Place on baking sheets. Repeat with remaining dough, rerolling and cutting scraps. Bake 12 to 18 minutes, or until edges begin to turn golden. If baking 2 cookie sheets in one oven, rotate their positions halfway through the baking time. Cool slightly and remove to racks to cool. Decorate using blue chocolate and Jewish star molds.

*Makes about 30 cookies.*

## HANUKKAH CUTOUTS

½ recipe Almond Cookie Dough (see page 147)
½ cup powdered sugar
Milk
Blue food coloring

Preheat oven to 325F (165C). Grease, line with parchment paper, or spray baking sheets with non-stick cooking spray. Make ½ recipe dough as directed and divide in half. On a floured board, roll half the dough out ⅛ inch thick. Using Hanukkah cookie cutters, cut out shapes. Place on baking sheets. Repeat with remaining dough, rerolling and cutting scraps. Bake 12 to 18 minutes, or until edges begin to turn golden. If baking 2 cookie sheets in one oven, rotate their positions halfway through the baking time. Cool slightly and remove to racks to cool.

Make frosting by placing powdered sugar in a small bowl. Stir in milk, a few drops at a time, until a thick spreading consistency is obtained. Remove a small amount to another bowl and tint blue. Frost and decorate cookies as desired.

*Makes about 30 cookies.*

# A Christmas Banquet

A holiday as significant and important as Christmas deserves a real banquet. Though duck, goose, and turkey may be traditional Christmas fare, I offer an American bird of a different feather — the Rock Cornish game hen. More exotic than turkey, which has become commonplace on our dinner table, game hens are impressive without being mundane. And talk about easy: Hens roast to golden goodness in about an hour; the last-minute hassle of carving them is eliminated by each guest carving his or her own bird; and there will never be any fighting over parts, since each impressive serving has two legs, two wings, and white meat.

If you wish to bone the hens, but don't feel confident enough to tackle the task, check with the meat department in your market. Many butchers will bone them for a small fee. Instruct them to remove the breast, back, and thigh bones, keeping the drumstick and wings intact.

Stuff the hens with cinnamon-scented rice speckled with bits of dried apricots and accompany them with a glamorous, multicolored vegetable mold and a Christmas red and green salad. To finish, present a Yule Log.

This banquet serves eight and can be planned as either a sit-down dinner or a buffet.

# Cheese Trees

*Have fun cutting a rich cheese dough into Christmas trees or other holiday shapes. The flaky cut-outs freeze beautifully and are a perfect accompaniment to soup or salad, or as an hors d'oeuvre with drinks. Vary the topping: instead of sesame seeds, use poppy or caraway seeds.*

10 tablespoons (1¼ sticks) unsalted butter, at room temperature
1⅔ cups shredded Gruyère or Emmenthal cheese
2 cups all-purpose flour
1 heaping teaspoon salt
1 teaspoon paprika
½ teaspoon baking powder
½ cup whipping cream
1 egg yolk mixed with 2 teaspoons water for glaze
Sesame seeds

In a large bowl with electric mixer or food processor with the metal blade, mix or process butter and cheese until blended. Add flour, salt, paprika, and baking powder, and mix or pulse until incorporated. Add cream and mix or pulse until blended. Divide dough in half. Shape into two flat balls; flatten and wrap in plastic wrap. Refrigerate for several hours or overnight.

Preheat oven to 375F (190C). Grease or line baking sheets with parchment. On a lightly floured surface, roll out 1 ball of dough ¼ inch thick. With a Christmas tree cookie cutter, cut out trees. Reroll and cut scraps. Place cutouts on baking sheets. Repeat with remaining dough. Brush tops lightly with egg yolk mixture. Sprinkle with sesame seeds. Bake 10 to 12 minutes or until lightly browned. Rotate baking sheets halfway through the baking time.

*Makes 60 (2-inch) or 30 (4-inch) trees.*

**Make-Ahead Tips**  Dough may be refrigerated up to 3 days or frozen.

Trees may be stored airtight for 1 week or frozen up to 1 month. Before serving, reheat at 375F (190C) 5 minutes.

---

# Cornish Game Hens with Apricot Rice Stuffing

*This entree works equally well if the hens are not deboned, but it's very elegant when they are (many butchers will bone them for you). They are marinated in a mixture of orange and lemon juice, which makes them extra tender and flavorful. Be sure to begin a day ahead, because they should marinate for 24 hours.*

**HENS:**
8 Cornish game hens (about 1 to 1¼ pounds each)
Seasoned salt
6 tablespoons olive oil
Watercress, parsley, or other greens for garnish

**ORANGE-GINGER MARINADE:**
2 cups orange juice
1 cup lemon juice
2 teaspoons salt
4 teaspoons powdered ginger
1 large bay leaf, crumbled
1 large onion, thinly sliced
2 large cloves garlic, thinly sliced

**APRICOT RICE STUFFING:**
2 ounces dried apricots, chopped (about ⅓ cup)
3 tablespoons currants or chopped raisins
2 tablespoons Grand Marnier
1 (5-oz.) box brown and wild rice mix
¼ teaspoon ground cinnamon
Salt and pepper to taste

**SAUCE BIGARADE:**
¼ cup sugar
2 tablespoons red wine vinegar
2 cups beef broth
2 tablespoons cornstarch or arrowroot
1 beef bouillon cube, crumbled

¼ cup cold water
1¼ cups reserved marinade
3 to 4 tablespoons Grand Marnier
1 tablespoon orange marmalade or apricot
    preserves
Salt and pepper to taste

**Prepare hens:**   Remove giblets from cavities. Dry hens well with paper towels. If boning, place breast side down on work surface. Make a cut down each side of the center of the backbone. Scrape meat away from bone with the edge of a sharp knife. Continue to pull meat away from bone with fingers, pulling it away from bone on each side. Cut joint at wing tips and legs, leaving wings and drumsticks attached to meat. Turn over and carefully cut flesh away from breast bone. Lay boned hens opened out, skin side down. Sprinkle lightly with seasoned salt.

**Make marinade:**   In a medium bowl stir together orange and lemon juices, salt, ginger, bay leaf, onion, and garlic. Place hens in a shallow glass dish into which they fit snugly. Pour marinade over and turn to coat all sides. Refrigerate covered for 24 hours, turning once.

**Make stuffing:**   Soak apricots and currants or raisins in Grand Marnier for several hours; or heat in a microwave oven, covered, on HIGH (100 percent) until boiling and cool to room temperature. Prepare rice according to package directions. Stir in dried fruit, cinnamon, salt and pepper. Cool completely before using.

**Stuff hens:**  Divide cooled stuffing equally among the hens, mounding in the center. Fold each side of hen over stuffing, overlapping slightly. Pat into original shape. Skewer or truss closed. Tie legs together with string. Place a metal skewer through wings to hold them in place. If not boning hens, stuff cavities and skewer or truss closed.

**Make sauce:**   In a medium saucepan, stir together sugar and vinegar. Bring to a boil over medium heat. Cook until sugar dissolves and caramelizes into a thick brown syrup, about 3 minutes. Watch carefully so it doesn't burn. Immediately pour in the broth. Bring to a boil and simmer slowly, stirring occasionally, until caramel dissolves.

Remove hens from marinade and strain 1¼ cups marinade into sauce. Bring to a boil, reduce heat, and simmer 10 minutes. Remove from heat. Mix cornstarch or arrowroot, beef bouillon cube, and water in a small bowl until dissolved. Stir into sauce. Return to heat and bring to a boil, stirring constantly, until mixture comes to a boil and thickens. Stir in Grand Marnier and preserves. Season with salt and pepper. Refrigerate sauce.

**To roast hens:**   If boned, preheat oven to 375F (190C). With bones, preheat to 400F (205C). Brush hens with olive oil and sprinkle with seasoned salt. Place breast side down on rack in shallow roasting or broiler pan. Bake boned hens 20 minutes. Turn and roast breast side up 20 to 25 minutes more, basting occasionally. For hens with bones, roast 30 minutes on each side. Hens are done when drumsticks move easily in their sockets and juices run clear when thighs are pierced. If not golden brown at the end of baking time, broil for several minutes. Remove skewers and string and arrange hens on serving platter. Garnish with greens. Reheat sauce and serve hens with warm sauce.

*Makes 8 servings.*

**Make-Ahead Tips**  Stuffing may be refrigerated up to 2 days or frozen up to 1 month. Thaw frozen dressing in refrigerator overnight.

Sauce may be refrigerated overnight. If too thick, thin with additional Grand Marnier or broth.

# Vegetable Chartreuse

*In the early 1900s the great chef Antonin Carême created a spectacular dish by arranging cut vegetables, cabbage, and boned partridge in a mold. When unmolded, it looked like a magnificent still life. He called this mosaic Chartreuse of Partridge. Here is my version, with thanks to Carême.*

2 (1-lb.) cans yams, drained, or 2 pounds fresh yams
   or sweet potatoes
⅓ cup regular, low-fat, or nonfat milk
½ teaspoon salt or to taste
Freshly ground pepper
1 pound green beans, ends trimmed
2 large carrots, peeled
2 small zucchini, thinly sliced
1 cup fresh broccoli flowerets
1 cup fresh cauliflower flowerets
¼ cup fresh or frozen green peas
6 tablespoons butter or margarine
2 garlic cloves, crushed
2 teaspoons dried basil
1½ cups shredded Swiss cheese (about 6 oz.)

Grease a 2-quart (8-cup) charlotte mold or soufflé dish. Line the bottom with a round of parchment or waxed paper; grease the paper and set aside.

If using fresh yams or sweet potatoes, bake at 400F (205C) 30 to 40 minutes or until tender when pierced with a fork. Cool and peel. Place potatoes in a bowl with electric mixer or in a food processor with the metal blade. Mix or pulse until smooth. Mix in milk and salt and pepper to taste. Set aside.

Trim the beans to the height of the mold. Cut the carrots the same length as the beans, and then cut them into ¼-inch strips, so they are the same width as the beans. Slice any short pieces into thin rounds.

Fill a medium-size saucepan half full of salted water. Bring to a boil and cook beans, carrots, zucchini, broccoli, and cauliflower separately until crisp-tender. Remove with a slotted spoon to a bowl of ice water to stop the cooking. Remove to paper towels and dry, keeping each type of vegetable separate. Season with salt and pepper. Peas do not need cooking.

Melt the butter in the microwave oven or over low heat. Stir in garlic and basil. Arrange a layer of vegetables in an attractive pattern on the bottom of the mold. Spread one-fourth of the yams over the vegetables. Arrange beans and carrot sticks upright around the side of the mold, using some of the yam mixture around the bottom to help hold them in place. Drizzle garlic butter over the yams and sprinkle with ¼ cup Swiss cheese. Continue to fill the mold, alternating layers of vegetables, cheese, yams, and garlic butter. You should have 2 thin layers of yams. Spread the remaining quarter of yams on top, and sprinkle with the remaining garlic butter and cheese.

Preheat oven to 350F (175C). Bake, uncovered, 40 to 45 minutes or until heated through. Run a knife around the inside edge of the mold and invert onto a serving plate. Serve with a spatula and large spoon, cutting and scooping out portions.

*Make 8 servings.*

**Make-Ahead Tip** Mold may be refrigerated, covered with plastic wrap and foil, overnight. Before baking, bring to room temperature.

# Tomato-Cheese Platter with Emerald Dressing

*A wreath of sliced red ripe tomatoes, red onions, and cheese, drizzled with a vibrant green spinach dressing, adds to the Christmas spirit. The dressing is also delicious with cold meats and fish.*

**EMERALD DRESSING:**

¼ cup walnuts, toasted
¼ cup olive oil
3 garlic cloves, minced
⅓ cup dried basil or 1 cup fresh chopped basil leaves
1 green onion, cut in thirds
1 cup packed spinach leaves (large stems removed)
2 tablespoons Parmesan cheese
3 tablespoons white wine vinegar
¾ teaspoon salt or to taste
Freshly ground pepper

**SALAD:**

8 firm, ripe tomatoes
Lettuce leaves for platter
2 small red onions (same size as tomatoes, if possible), peeled and thinly sliced
1 pound regular or low-fat provolone or mozzarella cheese, sliced

**Make dressing:** In a food processor with the metal blade or in blender, process all ingredients until blended. Season to taste with salt, pepper, and additional vinegar or oil, if needed. Makes 1 cup.

**Make salad:** Peel tomatoes by plunging them into a pot of boiling water for 10 seconds. Drain and run under cold water to stop the cooking. Peel and slice into ¼-inch-thick slices. Cover a round platter with lettuce leaves. Overlap alternating slices of tomatoes, onions, and cheese.

Before serving, drizzle some spinach dressing over salad. Pass remaining dressing.

*Makes 8 to 10 servings.*

**Variation** Substitute sliced cucumbers for onions.

**Make-Ahead Tips** Dressing may be covered and refrigerated overnight.

Salad may be refrigerated, covered with plastic wrap, for several hours.

# Yule Log

*My Christmas present to you is a Bûche de Noël, or Yule Log, made easy. Many time-consuming steps are eliminated by using a creamy chocolate buttercream as the filling, the frosting, and even the base for the decorations.*

### CAKE:
6 egg yolks
1 cup powdered sugar
½ cup unsweetened cocoa powder
6 egg whites, at room temperature
Dash salt

### BUTTERCREAM:
3 egg whites, at room temperature
Dash salt
1⅓ cups sugar
⅓ cup water
1 cup (2 sticks) unsalted butter, at room temperature, cut into small pieces
1 tablespoon vanilla extract
8 (1-oz.) squares semisweet chocolate, melted
2 tablespoons rum or strong coffee
Green food coloring for garnish (optional)
Red food coloring (optional)

**Make cake:** Preheat oven to 350F (175C). Grease a 15″ × 10″ baking pan. Line bottom with parchment or waxed paper, letting at least 1 inch overlap short ends for handles. Grease or spray the paper with nonstick cooking spray; set aside. In a large bowl with electric mixer, beat egg yolks until very thick and light. Sift powdered sugar and cocoa into a bowl; gradually add to egg yolks, beating constantly. In a clean bowl, beat egg whites until frothy; add salt and beat until stiff peaks form. Fold whites into chocolate mixture. Spread evenly into prepared pan. Bake in center of oven 12 to 15 minutes or until top springs back when lightly pressed with fingertips.

While cake bakes, place a clean dish towel on work surface. Sprinkle powdered sugar through a strainer or sifter onto towel. Remove cake from oven and immediately invert onto sugared towel. Remove cake pan and pull off paper. Beginning at one long end, roll cake and towel together tightly. Set aside, seam side down, until cool.

**Make buttercream:** In a large bowl with electric mixer, beat egg whites until frothy. Add salt and beat until stiff. Meanwhile, stir sugar and water in a medium-size saucepan over medium-high heat until sugar dissolves. Cook, without stirring, until sugar reaches the soft ball stage, 236 to 238F

(115C) on a candy thermometer. Mixing constantly, slowly pour sugar syrup into whites. Do not be concerned with the syrup that splatters onto the side of the bowl. Continue beating until mixture feels cool to the touch, about 10 minutes. When cool, beat in the butter a small piece at a time. Add vanilla. Remove ¾ cup buttercream to a small bowl. Mix melted chocolate and rum or coffee into remaining buttercream.

**To fill:** Unroll cool cake. Spread cake with half the chocolate buttercream. Reroll as tightly as possible. Roll cake onto a sheet of heavy foil. Wrap in the foil and refrigerate or freeze until chilled; it is easier to frost when it's cold. Refrigerate remaining chocolate and plain buttercream.

**To frost:** Bring chocolate buttercream to room temperature. Place chilled cake on a serving platter lined with strips of waxed paper to catch the drippings. Cut a small diagonal piece off each end of the cake. Place these pieces on top of log for stumps. Frost entire cake, except ends of logs and stumps, with chocolate buttercream. Run tines of fork along the frosting to resemble bark. Spread a layer of plain cream on ends of log and stumps.

**To decorate:** Place remaining chocolate buttercream in a small heavy plastic bag or pastry bag fitted with a small writing tip. If using plastic bag, cut a tiny hole in one corner to pipe cream through. Pipe concentric circles on ends of log and stumps to resemble age rings. Blur slightly with wooden picks.

Divide plain buttercream into two bowls. Stir a few drops of green food coloring into one for leaves and vine. Place in pastry bag fitted with a small writing tip. Pipe vines onto log. Change to leaf tip and pipe leaves on vine.

Tint remaining buttercream with a few drops of red food coloring. Use plastic bag or small writing tip to pipe berries around leaves. Refrigerate until firm. Carefully remove strips of waxed paper.

*Makes 12 servings.*

**Make-Ahead Tip** Log may be refrigerated overnight. Bring to room temperature 1 hour before serving.

# Cookies for Carolers

---

**M E N U**

*Marshmallow Turtle Cookies*
*Wreath Cookies*
*Linzer Cookies*
*Jam Logs & Thumbprints*
*English Currant Tarts*
*Orange Date-Nut Bars*


*Candy Cane Punch*

---

Cookies are an ever-popular dessert, but never as much in demand as they are during the Christmas season. They're terrific for gifts, wonderful to have on hand for company, and deliciously rewarding for neighborhood carolers.

I offer three basic doughs to make a variety of different cookies. To simplify the job, line your baking sheets with parchment. It ensures that the cookies brown evenly, are easy to remove, and eliminates washing the pan. For cutout cookies, roll the dough between sheets of waxed paper and freeze. They are much easier to cut from frozen sheets of dough and are ready to bake as needed. While your cookie sheets are in the oven, prepare the cookies on a sheet of parchment or foil. They are then ready to slide onto cooled baking sheets.

For a tree-trimming party or get-together after a chilly night of caroling, offer a steaming cup of Candy Cane Punch. Or, make up a batch of Cappuccino Mocha Mix (page 153).

# Marshmallow Turtle Cookies

*Pecan legs, a cookie body, and a melted marshmallow back topped with dark chocolate make a deliciously edible turtle. Real turtles move slowly, but these will disappear quickly.*

1 recipe Brown Sugar Cookie Dough (see below)
2½ cups pecan halves
20 marshmallows, cut in half horizontally
6 ounces semisweet chocolate, chopped and melted

**P**reheat oven to 350F (175C). Grease, line with parchment paper, or spray baking sheets with non-stick cooking spray. Make Brown Sugar Cookie Dough. Place 4 pecan halves in clusters on parchment-lined or greased baking sheets. Break off small pieces of dough and roll into 1-inch balls. Place a ball in the center of each of the 4 pecans, lightly pressing dough into pecans. Bake 10 to 15 minutes or until bottoms are lightly browned. Remove from oven. Top each cookie with a marshmallow half, cut side down. Return to oven for 1 minute. Immediately press marshmallow down lightly. Remove to racks to cool.

Dip cookies into the chocolate to cover the marshmallow. Place on waxed paper and cool until chocolate is set.

*Makes 36 to 40 cookies.*

**Make-Ahead Tip** Cookies may be refrigerated or stored airtight for several weeks in a cool place. They may be frozen. Thaw in a single layer.

# Brown Sugar Cookie Dough

*This buttery dough is not overly sweet, so it's particularly suited to cookies that will be frosted or decorated. It is easy to shape with your hands and is used for Marshmallow Turtle Cookies and Wreath Cookies, neither of which require rolling.*

½ cup plus 2 tablespoons (1¼ sticks) butter or margarine, at room temperature
⅔ cup packed golden brown sugar
1 large egg
1 teaspoon vanilla extract
1¾ cups all-purpose flour
¼ teaspoon salt
½ teaspoon baking powder
½ teaspoon baking soda

**I**n a bowl with electric mixer or food processor with the metal blade, mix or process butter and sugar until light and fluffy. Mix in egg and vanilla. Add flour, salt, baking powder, and baking soda. Mix or pulse until blended. Use as directed in Marshmallow Turtle Cookies or Wreath Cookies.

**Make-Ahead Tip** Dough may be wrapped in a plastic freezer bag and refrigerated up to 3 days or frozen up to 1 month.

# Wreath Cookies

*Each wreath is made by arranging twelve balls of dough together in a circle. When they bake, they spread into a lovely fluted wreath. For gifts, cut cardboard rounds a little smaller than the wreaths, cover them with doilies, top with wreaths, and wrap in plastic wrap and cellophane. They can then be frozen, ready to be given to someone at a moment's notice.*

1 recipe Brown Sugar Cookie Dough (opposite)
6 ounces semisweet or white chocolate, chopped and melted (optional)
1½ cups powdered sugar (optional)
3 to 4 teaspoons milk (optional)
Pecan halves, silver ball decorations, sliced almonds, and/or glacéed cherries

**Preheat** oven to 325F (165C). Grease, line with parchment paper, or spray baking sheets with non-stick cooking spray. Make Brown Sugar Cookie Dough. Divide into 3 equal parts. Working with one-third of the dough at a time, divide it into 12 pieces of dough and roll them into 12 (1-inch) balls. Place balls ½ inch apart on a baking sheet, forming a 6-inch circle. Flatten slightly. Repeat with remaining dough, making 2 more circles.

Bake 15 minutes or until bottoms are lightly browned. If baking 2 baking sheets in one oven, rotate their positions halfway through the baking time. Cool 15 minutes and remove from baking sheet. Do not be concerned if they break. The frosting will cover any cracks. Wreaths may be frosted with melted chocolate or powdered sugar mixed with just enough milk to attain a spreading consistency. Before frosting sets, decorate with nuts, silver balls, and/or glacéed cherries.

*Makes 3 wreaths.*

**Note:** To tie a bow through the top, using handle of wooden spoon, make a hole in the center of two of the balls of dough. Bake 10 minutes; press the holes again. When cool, tie colored ribbon through holes.

**Make-Ahead Tip** Wreaths may be stored airtight for several weeks in a cool place or frozen up to 1 month. Thaw in a single layer.

# Linzer Cookies

*A variation of the Linzer torte in the Christmas spirit. Two cookies are sandwiched together with jam and topped with a flurry of powdered sugar.*

1 recipe spice cookie dough (Spice Cookie Goblins, page 105)
¾ cup seedless red raspberry jam or currant jelly
Powdered sugar

**Preheat** oven to 350F (175C). Grease, line with parchment paper, or spray baking sheets with non-stick cooking spray. Make and roll spice cookie dough as directed. Using a 2-inch round cookie cutter, cut out circles. Place on baking sheets. Using an aspic cutter—tree, bell, circle, or other shape—cut out a design from the center of half the cookies. Repeat with remaining dough, rerolling and cutting scraps.

Bake 8 to 10 minutes or until lightly browned. If baking 2 cookie sheets in one oven, rotate positions halfway through the baking time. Cool slightly and remove from pan to racks and cool completely.

Place uncut cookies on work surface; spread with a layer of jam. Place cutout cookies on racks set over baking sheets. Place powdered sugar in a fine strainer and sprinkle over cookies. Gently press powdered sugar cookies onto jam cookies.

*Makes 36 cookies.*

**Make-Ahead Tip** Cookies may be stored in airtight containers up to 2 weeks or frozen up to 1 month. Layer carefully with waxed paper between layers.

# Jam Logs & Thumbprints

*If you've ever baked cookies with jam in them, you most likely ended up with more jam on the baking sheet than in the cookies. These are filled with jam after they're baked, but while they're still warm, so the jam sets exactly where you put it.*

1 recipe Almond Cookie Dough (opposite)
1 egg white, lightly beaten
1 to 1½ cups finely chopped almonds
½ to 1 cup seedless raspberry or apricot jam or preserves

**Preheat** oven to 325F (165C). Grease, line with parchment paper, or spray baking sheets with non-stick cooking spray. Divide dough into 1-inch pieces. Dip into egg white and roll in chopped almonds. Place on baking sheets. Using the handle of a wooden spoon, press an indentation across the center of each cookie to form a log, or in the center to form a thumbprint. Bake 5 minutes; remove from oven and repress indentation. Bake 12 to 15 minutes more or until lightly golden. Remove to racks and while cookies are still warm, spoon preserves into indentations.

*Makes 36 cookies.*

**Make-Ahead Tip**    Cookies may be stored airtight at room temperature up to 2 weeks or frozen up to 1 month.

---

# English Currant Tarts

*The English are known for high tea, and these fruit-filled, bite-size pastries will elevate anyone's tea (or coffee).*

⅓ recipe prepared Almond Cookie Dough (opposite)
1 large egg
⅛ teaspoon salt
2 tablespoons unsalted butter or margarine
¼ cup finely chopped dates (about 8)
½ cup currants or chopped raisins
¼ cup diced pecans
½ cup sugar
½ teaspoon vanilla extract
Glacéed cherries, cut in halves, for garnish

**Make** dough and divide into 16 pieces. Press into bottom and up sides of greased 1½-inch miniature muffin cups. Set aside.

Preheat oven to 325F (165C). In a food processor with the metal blade or in a bowl, pulse or mix remaining ingredients except cherries until well blended. Spoon into tart shells. Top each with half a cherry. Bake 25 minutes. Cool completely in pans. Insert tip of a knife into an edge of each tart and lift from pan.

*Makes 16 tarts.*

**Make-Ahead Tip**    Tarts may be stored airtight at room temperature or refrigerated up to 2 weeks. They may be frozen up to 1 month.

It's *A Christmas Banquet* that's both elegant and delicious: Cornish Game Hens with Apricot Rice Stuffing (page 138), Vegetable Chartreuse (page 140), and Tomato-Cheese Platter with Emerald Dressing (page 141).

# Almond Cookie Dough

*This is a sweet, rich dough that will make Jam Logs & Thumbprints and English Currant Tarts.*

1 cup (2 sticks) unsalted butter, at room temperature
½ cup powdered sugar
½ teaspoon vanilla extract
½ teaspoon almond extract
2 cups all-purpose flour
¼ teaspoon salt
½ cup finely chopped almonds

In bowl with electric mixer or a food processor with the metal blade, mix or process butter and sugar until light and fluffy. Add vanilla and almond extracts, beating well. Mix or pulse in flour, salt, and almonds. Divide dough into thirds. Wrap in plastic wrap and refrigerate until chilled. Use as directed in recipes.

**Make-Ahead Tips**   Dough may be refrigerated up to 5 days. May be frozen.

---

# Orange Date-Nut Bars

*The orange marmalade contributes to the wonderful flavor and moist texture of these fruit-filled bars. One recipe goes a long way — it fills a jellyroll pan and makes forty-eight bars.*

¾ cup good-quality orange marmalade
2 teaspoons grated orange peel
½ cup chopped dates
½ cup raisins
1 cup chopped walnuts
1 cup packed dark brown sugar
½ cup (1 stick) unsalted butter or margarine, at room temperature
1 teaspoon vanilla extract
2 large eggs
1¾ cups all-purpose flour
1 teaspoon baking soda
½ teaspoon salt
1½ cups powdered sugar for glaze
3 to 4 teaspoons milk for glaze

Preheat oven to 350F (175C). Grease and flour a 15″ × 10″ jellyroll pan. In a medium-size bowl, stir together marmalade, orange peel, dates, raisins, and walnuts; set aside. In bowl with electric mixer or in food processor with the metal blade, mix or process brown sugar, butter, and vanilla until fluffy. Add eggs; mix or process well. Add flour, baking soda, and salt; mix or pulse until incorporated. Mix or pulse in marmalade mixture. Spread into prepared baking pan.

Bake 25 to 30 minutes or until top is set and golden. Cool in pan. Cut into 2½″ × 1¼″ bars. Remove to wire racks set over baking pans. Mix powdered sugar with enough milk to make a thick glaze; drizzle over bars.

*Makes 48 bars.*

**Make-Ahead Tip**   Bars may be stored airtight or refrigerated for several days. They may be frozen.

Desserts for very special occasions: 1) Wreath Cookies (page 145), 2) Baby Carriage Apricot Cake (page 82), 3) Yule Log (page 141), and 4) Stars & Stripes Cake (page 98).

# Candy Cane Punch

*Hang a candy cane over the rim of punch cups or mugs and fill with this vivid red punch. It can be served hot or cold topped with a scoop of ice cream.*

2 (10-oz.) packages frozen raspberries in syrup
1 quart cranberry-apple drink
3 tablespoons lemon juice
1 quart peppermint stick or burgundy cherry ice cream
Candy canes for stirrers

In a medium-size saucepan over medium-high heat, combine berries, cranberry-apple drink, and lemon juice. Bring to a boil, reduce heat, and simmer 10 minutes, stirring often. Pour through a strainer set over a bowl, pressing on fruit to release as much of the juice as possible. Serve hot or cold in punch cups or mugs, topped with a scoop of ice cream and a candy cane stirrer.

*Makes 9 cups, 10 to 12 servings.*

# Gifts from the Kitchen

*Vegetable Jardinière*
*Greatest Granola*
*An-Apple-for-the-Teacher Bread*
*Dried Fruit Fruitcake*
*Chocolate Spice Candle Cake*
*Cappuccino Mocha Mix*

At holiday time, stores are brimming with their annual array of gourmet food gifts. Everything from baskets of fruit to exotic ethnic delicacies to chocoholic extravaganzas is wrapped, tagged, and ready to go. But as a recipient I feel these prepackaged, assembly-line holiday edibles are overpriced and impersonal. If you agree, then look no further than the bounty of gourmet goodies no one else can give and everyone will be thrilled to receive — gifts from your own kitchen with an extra ingredient the pros can't match — the heartfelt personal touch.

The recipes included here are inexpensive to make and can be stored for several weeks. There's a pretty arrangement of colorful pickled vegetables layered in a glass jar; a moist and luscious fruit cake made without a morsel of controversial glacéed fruits; a cappuccino mix for a fast and exotic cup of coffee; a mixture of oats, nuts, and seeds baked into a crisp granola; and a low-fat cocoa spice cake decorated like a candle.

Let your imagination fly with out-of-the-ordinary wrappings and containers, such as paper bags, boxes, baskets, planters, tins, cloth napkins, and dish towels. Tie them with oversized bows and whimsical tie-ons. When the package is glorious to behold, the contents become even more delicious. Best of all, when the gift is from your kitchen, the recipient will know it is truly from your heart.

# Vegetable Jardinière

*Layers of lightly pickled vegetables make a bouquet of colors and tastes that are both sweet and tangy.*

2½ cups water
2½ cups distilled white vinegar
1½ cups sugar
1½ teaspoons salt
1 garlic clove, peeled and cut in half
1 bay leaf
¼ cup mixed pickling spices
1 teaspoon dried tarragon
2 bunches broccoli (about 3 lbs.)
2 heads cauliflower (about 4 lbs.)
10 stalks celery, sliced into 1-inch diagonal pieces
6 large carrots, peeled and sliced into ¼-inch diagonal pieces or rounds
3 to 4 red bell peppers, seeded and cut into quarters

**Make pickling solution:**  In a large heavy pot, not aluminum or iron, combine water, vinegar, sugar, salt, garlic, bay leaf, pickling spices, and tarragon. Bring to a boil, reduce heat, cover, and simmer 5 minutes.

Cut stems off broccoli and cauliflower. Cut into flowerets. Add half of the vegetables to the pickling solution. Cover pot, bring to a boil, and cook 15 minutes, stirring once or twice. Using slotted spoon, remove vegetables to a rimmed baking sheet; cool. Repeat with second half of vegetables. Strain liquid into a pitcher or bowl.

Layer alternating rows of vegetables into glass jars. Place the most attractive pieces against the sides of the jar. Fill the center with the less attractive or broken pieces. Pour enough pickling solution into the jar to cover the vegetables completely. If you need more liquid, make more solution, omitting the bay leaf, pickling spices, and tarragon. Cool and add to jars. Cover jars and refrigerate.

*Makes 4 quarts.*

**Make-Ahead Tip**   Jardinière may be refrigerated up to 2 months.

---

# Greatest Granola

*This may be the greatest gift you can give yourself or your family. You won't find anything like it at the supermarket. It's terrific as a snack, in milk, baked in cookies, and sprinkled on ice cream or yogurt.*

2½ cups regular rolled oats
½ cup sliced almonds
½ cup sunflower kernels
½ cup sesame seeds
½ cup shredded coconut
¼ cup wheat germ
½ cup maple syrup
3 tablespoons orange juice
½ teaspoon ground cinnamon
½ teaspoon salt
½ cup raisins

Preheat oven to 300F (150C). Line a baking sheet with heavy-duty foil and grease or spray with non-stick cooking spray. Stir oats, almonds, sunflower kernels, sesame seeds, coconut, and wheat germ together on the baking sheet. In a small bowl, stir together maple syrup, orange juice, cinnamon, and salt. Pour over oat mixture and stir until well coated. Spread out evenly in pan.

Bake 25 minutes. Stir in raisins, tossing the mixture well. Bake 5 minutes more or until golden brown. It will be slightly soft, but will firm up as it cools. Remove from oven, cool, and store in an airtight container.

*Makes 5 cups.*

**Make-Ahead Tip**   Granola may be stored in an airtight container for several weeks, or refrigerated for several months.

# An-Apple-for-the-Teacher Bread

*The moist texture and sweet flavor in this bread come from applesauce. The batter bakes in custard cups and is topped with a cinnamon stick and leaf to resemble an apple.*

1 cup sugar
⅓ cup vegetable oil
2 large eggs or 4 egg whites
1½ cups applesauce
2 cups all-purpose flour
½ teaspoon baking powder
1 teaspoon baking soda
½ teaspoon ground cinnamon
¼ teaspoon salt
¼ teaspoon ground nutmeg
¼ teaspoon ground allspice
½ cup raisins
Red-colored sugar for garnish (optional)
Cinnamon stick for garnish
4 small candied mint leaves or edible fresh leaves
   for garnish

**Preheat** oven to 350F (175C). Grease 4 (10-oz.) custard cups. In a large bowl or food processor fitted with the metal blade, stir or pulse sugar, oil, eggs, and applesauce until blended. Add flour, baking powder, baking soda, spices, and raisins and stir or process until incorporated. Spoon the batter into the prepared cups, filling them three-fourths full. If desired, sprinkle the top with red sugar. Bake 40 to 45 minutes or until a cake tester or wooden pick inserted in the center comes out clean. Cool 10 minutes. Invert onto racks, turn right side up, and cool completely.

Before giving as a gift, insert a ½-inch-long cinnamon stick into top for apple's stem. Insert candied or real leaf next to stem.

*Makes 4 loaves.*

**Variation** Bread may be baked in a greased 9″ × 5″ loaf pan. Bake 50 to 60 minutes or until it tests done.

**Make-Ahead Tip** Breads may be refrigerated up to 1 week or frozen up to 1 month.

# Dried Fruit Fruitcake

*Fruitcakes may be traditional holiday gifts, but most of them are never eaten. This one is the exception. Incredibly moist and permeated with sugar and spice and everything nice, it's chock-full of dried apricots, raisins, dates, and nuts. If you bake these in small aluminum loaf pans and tie the bows on the sides, you can stack them in the refrigerator or freezer, all wrapped, and ready to go.*

1 cup (2 sticks) unsalted butter or margarine, at room temperature
1 cup packed golden brown sugar
½ cup honey
5 large eggs
½ cup apricot nectar
¼ cup half-and-half or whipping cream
2 cups all-purpose flour
1 teaspoon baking powder
½ teaspoon salt
1¼ teaspoons ground cinnamon
½ teaspoon ground allspice
¾ pound dried apricots, coarsely chopped
½ pound golden raisins
1 pound coarsely chopped walnuts or pecans
¼ cup brandy
¼ cup Grand Marnier or other orange liqueur

Preheat oven to 300F (150C). Grease and flour 6 (5″ × 3″ × 2″) aluminum loaf pans. In a large bowl with electric mixer, cream butter or margarine, brown sugar, and honey until light and fluffy. Beat in eggs, 1 at a time. Add apricot nectar and half-and-half. Mix in flour, baking powder, salt, cinnamon, and allspice. Blend well. Transfer to a large bowl and stir in dried fruit and nuts.

Bake 1 hour and 15 minutes or until cake tester or wooden pick inserted in center comes out clean. Remove to wire racks and cool in pans.

In a small bowl, combine the brandy and Grand Marnier. Sprinkle tops of each cake with liqueur and let stand 1 hour. Remove cakes from pans.

*Makes 6 loaves.*

**Variation**   Cakes may be baked in 2 (9″ × 5″) loaf pans.

**Make-Ahead Tips**   Cakes may be refrigerated up to 2 weeks. For longer storage, wrap in cheesecloth soaked with brandy and then in foil and refrigerate up to 6 months. Resoak cheesecloth once a month. Cakes may also be frozen.

---

# Chocolate Spice Candle Cake

*Light up someone's holiday with this candle cake baked in a coffee can and dripped with thick white frosting.*

**SPICE CAKE:**
Unsweetened cocoa powder for dusting
1 cup raisins
2 cups all-purpose flour
1¼ cups sugar
2 teaspoons baking soda
Pinch salt
½ teaspoon ground nutmeg
1 teaspoon ground cinnamon
½ teaspoon ground allspice
¼ cup unsweetened cocoa powder
1½ cups applesauce
½ cup regular, low-fat, or nonfat milk
¼ cup vegetable oil
2 tablespoons dark rum
1 cup chopped pecans

**POWDERED SUGAR GLAZE:**
2 cups powdered sugar
2 tablespoons milk or cream
1 pecan half, split lengthwise, for wick

**Make cake:**   Preheat oven to 350F (175C). Grease 2 (1-lb.) coffee cans and dust with cocoa. Shake out excess. In a food processor with the metal blade, pulse raisins until chopped. Remove to a bowl. Add flour, sugar, baking soda, salt, nutmeg, cinnamon, allspice, and ¼ cup cocoa to food processor and pulse until blended. Add applesauce, milk, oil, and rum. Pulse until incorporated. Pulse in raisins and pecans. Divide batter between the prepared cans. Bake in center of oven

50 to 55 minutes or until a cake tester inserted in center comes out clean and top springs back when pressed with fingertips. Cool in cans 30 minutes. Invert onto cake racks, turn right side up, and cool completely.

**Make glaze:** In a small bowl, stir together powdered sugar and milk. If too thick, stir in more milk, a drop at a time, until glaze thickly drops from a spoon. Drizzle it over top of cake, letting it drip over the sides like melted wax on a candle. Insert split pecan into the top for a wick. Refrigerate until set. Wrap in plastic wrap before wrapping as a gift.

*Makes 2 cakes.*

**Variation** Recipe may be doubled and baked in a 13" × 9" baking pan.

**Make-Ahead Tip** Frosted cakes may be refrigerated up to 1 week or frozen up to 1 month.

# Cappuccino Mocha Mix

*For an easy-to-assemble gift that won't make a big dent in your wallet, fill a coffee mug to the brim with this chocolate-scented mix and wrap it up in cellophane. Write directions for preparation on a small paper scroll and tie it to the handle with several cinnamon sticks.*

**FOR 10 SERVINGS:**
6 tablespoons plus 2 teaspoons instant espresso coffee powder
3 tablespoons plus 1 teaspoon unsweetened cocoa powder
1¼ cups coffee whitener, plain or Irish cream
½ cup plus 2 tablespoons sugar
2 teaspoons ground cinnamon

*Makes about 2½ cups mix.*

**FOR 1 SERVING:**
2 teaspoons instant espresso coffee powder
1 teaspoon unsweetened cocoa powder
2 tablespoons coffee whitener
1 tablespoon sugar
Dash of cinnamon

Stir all ingredients together in a medium-size bowl. Store tightly covered.

**Label:** For each cup of cappuccino, measure 4 tablespoons mix into a coffee mug and stir in 6 ounces of boiling water.

# METRIC CONVERSION CHART

## Comparison to Metric Measure

| When You Know | Symbol | Multiply By | To Find | Symbol |
|---|---|---|---|---|
| teaspoons | tsp | 5.0 | milliliters | ml |
| tablespoons | tbsp | 15.0 | milliliters | ml |
| fluid ounces | fl. oz. | 30.0 | milliliters | ml |
| cups | c. | 0.24 | liters | l |
| pints | pt. | 0.47 | liters | l |
| quarts | qt. | 0.95 | liters | l |
| ounces | oz. | 28.0 | grams | g |
| pounds | lb. | 0.45 | kilograms | kg |
| Fahrenheit | F | 5/9 (after subtracting 32) | Celsius | C |

## Liquid Measure to Milliliters

| | | |
|---|---|---|
| 1/4 teaspoon | = | 1.25 milliliters |
| 1/2 teaspoon | = | 2.5 milliliters |
| 3/4 teaspoon | = | 3.75 milliliters |
| 1 teaspoon | = | 5.0 milliliters |
| 1-1/4 teaspoons | = | 6.25 milliliters |
| 1-1/2 teaspoons | = | 7.5 milliliters |
| 1-3/4 teaspoons | = | 8.75 milliliters |
| 2 teaspoons | = | 10.0 milliliters |
| 1 teaspoon | = | 15.0 milliliters |
| 2 teaspoons | = | 30.0 milliliters |

## Fahrenheit to Celsius

| F | C |
|---|---|
| 200-205 | 95 |
| 220-225 | 105 |
| 245-250 | 120 |
| 275 | 135 |
| 300-305 | 150 |
| 325-330 | 165 |
| 345-350 | 175 |
| 370-375 | 190 |
| 400-405 | 205 |
| 425-530 | 220 |
| 445-450 | 230 |
| 470-475 | 245 |
| 500 | 260 |

## Liquid Measure to Liters

| | | |
|---|---|---|
| 1/4 cup | = | 0.06 liters |
| 1/2 cup | = | 0.12 liters |
| 3/4 cup | = | 0.18 liters |
| 1 cup | = | 0.24 liters |
| 1-1/4 cups | = | 0.3 liters |
| 1-1/2 cups | = | 0.36 liters |
| 2 cups | = | 0.48 liters |
| 2-1/2 cups | = | 0.6 liters |
| 3 cups | = | 0.72 liters |
| 3-1/2 cups | = | 0.84 liters |
| 4 cups | = | 0.96 liters |
| 4-1/2 cups | = | 1.08 liters |
| 5 cups | = | 1.2 liters |
| 5-1/2 cups | = | 1.32 liters |

# INDEX